PORSCHE *Sixty Years*

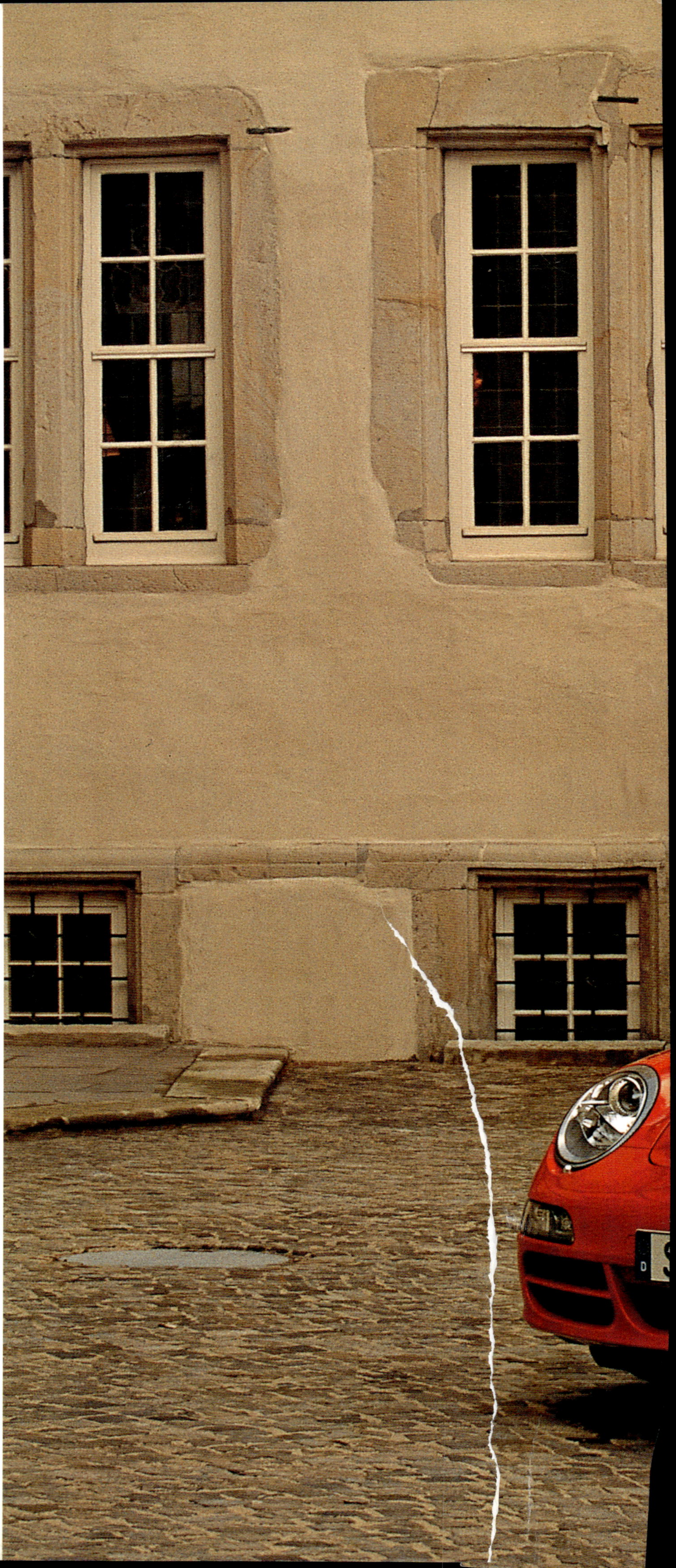

RANDY LEFFINGWELL

Dedication: For Bob Carlson

Disseminating and conserving the information—current and past—about any company's products and business are challenging and fascinating tasks. In twenty years of authoring books, I have never worked with a better group of individuals than those at Porsche AG and at PCNA. But in particular, Bob Carlson has become a friend and a colleague whom I deeply respect. He has supported, encouraged, and aided my book efforts immeasurably for two decades. Bob is a devoted student of history of all kinds (especially American Civil War). He loves books as much as I do. Our conversations nearly always begin with, "What have you read lately." I am profoundly grateful for his help, friendship, and support. Bob, this history is for you. I can never thank you enough.

Randy Leffingwell, Santa Barbara, CA

First published in 2008 by Motorbooks, an imprint of MBI Publishing Company, 400 First Avenue North, Suite 300, Minneapolis, MN 55401 USA

Copyright © 2008 by Randy Leffingwell

All rights reserved. With the exception of quoting brief passages for the purposes of review, no part of this publication may be reproduced without prior written permission from the Publisher.

The information in this book is true and complete to the best of our knowledge. All recommendations are made without any guarantee on the part of the author or Publisher, who also disclaim any liability incurred in connection with the use of this data or specific details.

This publication has not been prepared, approved, or licensed by Porsche.

We recognize, further, that some words, model names, and designations mentioned herein are the property of the trademark holder. We use them for identification purposes only. This is not an official publication.

Motorbooks titles are also available at discounts in bulk quantity for industrial or sales-promotional use. For details write to Special Sales Manager at MBI Publishing Company, 400 First Avenue North, Suite 300, Minneapolis, MN 55401 USA.

To find out more about our books, join us online at www.motorbooks.com.

ISBN-13: 978-0-7603-3483-6

On the cover: Porsche 356

On the endpapers: 1978 Typ 935/78 "Moby Dick"

On the frontispiece: 1938 Typ 60K 10 Berlin-to-Rome Racer

On the title pages: 2005 997

On the back cover: Geneva, Switzerland, Auto Show 1964, 1970 914/6 R, 1972 911 Carrera RS, 1974 Carrera 2.7, 953, 959, 961, 1988 928 S4, 1993 968 Cabriolet, 1993 Boxster Concept Car, 1997 911 GT1, 2006 911 Typ 997 GT3RS, 2007 Cayenne Turbo S, 2005 Carrera GT, 2006 Cayman S

Editors: Darwin Holmstrom, Tim Parker
Designer: Mandy Iverson
Jacket Design: John Barnett/4 Eyes Design

Printed in China

CONTENTS

		ACKNOWLEDGMENTS	6
CHAPTER ONE	1938–1958	FROM **VOLKSWAGEN** ROOTS TO **PORSCHE** PRODUCTION	8
CHAPTER TWO	1952–1961	**RACING** IMPROVES THE BREED	28
CHAPTER THREE	1959–1965	THE NEXT GENERATION	46
CHAPTER FOUR	1962–1965	**RACING** IMPROVES THE BREED *MORE*	60
CHAPTER FIVE	1964–1972	THE **NEW** BREED	80
CHAPTER SIX	1965–1970	**RACING** TAKES ON ITS *OWN* **DESTINY**	100
CHAPTER SEVEN	1970–1976	**INVITING** THE **NEXT** GENERATION	116
CHAPTER EIGHT	1969–1975	THE **WIDOW MAKER** BECOMES A ***LEGEND***	128
CHAPTER NINE	1973–1979	**NECESSITY** IS THE MOTHER OF **INVENTION**	144
CHAPTER TEN	1973–1981	**NECESSITY** IS ***STILL*** THE MOTHER OF **INVENTION**	166
CHAPTER ELEVEN	1981–1985	RACING TO **NEW** HORIZONS	182
CHAPTER TWELVE	1982–1989	FROM **OBLIVION** TO THE **ULTIMATE** DRIVING MACHINE	198
CHAPTER THIRTEEN	1989–1995	**EXTENDING** LINES ON THE **WALL**	218
CHAPTER FOURTEEN	1995–1998	THE **END** OF **AIR-COOLING** ON **ROAD** AND **TRACK**	236
CHAPTER FIFTEEN	1997–2005	***TWO*** CARS **ONE** FACE	250
CHAPTER SIXTEEN	1994–2007	REMINDING *LE MANS* OF **PORSCHE'S CAPABILITY**	272
CHAPTER SEVENTEEN	2003–2008	**CHANGING** PERCEPTIONS AND THE *BOTTOM LINE*	284
CHAPTER EIGHTEEN	2004–2005	HEARING A *NEW* **DRUMBEAT**	300
CHAPTER NINETEEN	2005–2008	*BACK* TO THE **FUTURE**	320
CHAPTER TWENTY	2005–2008	**THREATENING TRADITION**	336
		INDEX	346

ACKNOWLEDGMENTS

Foremost I must thank Dieter Landenberger, Manager Historical Archives; and Jens Torner, the man responsible for photographs at Historical Archives. Next I must express deep gratitude to Michael Baumann, General Manager International Press, Zuffenhausen; Porsche Presse. These three individuals provided exceptional help in producing this book. Mr. Landenberger and Mr. Baumann opened doors that I only had hoped to peek through. Then Dieter spent two weeks *ensuring* that I got stories that very few others outside of Porsche ever had heard before. Jens Torner patiently directed me—and ultimately redirected the visual approach of this book—through more than 10,000 images in pursuit of the hundreds of photos previously unpublished in the U.S., and nearly as many previously unseen in Europe. Jens has a photographic memory—an incredible gift for a visual archivist—and he continually found images that fit my wishes. If you like what you see in this book, thank Mr. Torner. His archival discoveries influenced every photograph that I shot myself. Furthermore, without the tireless assistance of Yvonne Notuck, Historical Archives, my ambitious and complicated schedule of 15 interviews in nine days never would have happened. In addition I must also single out Dieter Gross, Media Archives & Documentation, Chief Technical Officer, Historic Archives, for his work in organizing dozens of design and concept sketches. Aside from dedicating this book to Bob Carlson, I wish to express my appreciation to him, as Manager, Automotive and Motorsport Press; and to Bernd Harling, General Manager, Public Relations; and to Gary Fong, Press Fleet Management; and Robin Baker, Administrative Assistant, Public Relations; at Porsche Cars North American, Atlanta, Georgia, for their support. Their support of my projects for many years now has encouraged me to raise the bar for each successive book. Their role in the Rennsport Reunion events ensures than an increasing number of enthusiasts can meet and mingle with living history.

Porsche's history is the story of thousands of individuals who have worked to make the series production and race cars into the legendary vehicles they have been. I wish to thank the following individuals for sharing their thoughts, ideas, stories, and histories with me: Dipl.-Ing. August Achleitner, Director Product Line Management, Carrera; Herbert Ampferer, Director Environment & Energy; Jürgen Barth, Customer Motorsports Coordinator, retired; Derek Bell; Nuccio Bertone, Carrozzeria Bertone; the late Bernhard Blank; the late Helmuth Bott; Tilman Brodbeck, Director, Exclusive Program; Wolfgang Dürheimer, Executive Vice President of Research and Development; Vic Elford; Ted Field; George Follmer; the late Ernst Fuhrmann; Dan and Evi Gurney; Anthony R. Hatter, Manager of Design, Sports Cars, Style Porsche; Michael Hölscher; Jo Hoppen, Motorports Director, retired, Porsche-Audi Division, Volkswagen of America; John Horsman; the late Ghislane Kaes; Bernd Kahnau, Project Manager Complete Vehicle, Product Line Carrera; Jürgen Kapfer, Project Manager, Powertrain, Product Line Boxster and Member of the Supervisory Board; Dipl.-Ing. Stefan Knirsch, General-Manager Base Engine Development Department; Roland Kussmaul, Manager Motorsports Development, Performance; Harm Lagaaij, Director, Style Porsche, retired; Pinky Lai, General Manager, Design, Global Customer and Special Project, Style Porsche; Tony Lapine, Director of Design, retired; Grant Larson, General Manager, Advanced Design, Exterior, Style Porsche; Katja Leinweber-Schafer, International Press; Herbert Linge, retired; Jack McAfee; Stirling Moss; Stephen Murkett, General Manager, Design, Sports Multipurpose Vehicles, Style Porsche; the late Johnny von Neumann; Dr.-Ing. Heinz-Jakob Nüsser, Director, Powertrain Development; Malcolm Page; the late Vasek Polak; Ferdinand Alexander Porsche, director of design, retired; Dipl.-Ing. Andreas Prüninger, Project Manager, High Performance Cars; Peter W. Schutz, Chairman, Porsche AG, retired; Norbert Singer, Manager, Motorsports, retired; Franz-Josef Siegert, General Manager Interior Design, Style Porsche; Rico Steinemann; Jörg Thilow, Public Relations, Porsche Museum; Carl Thompson; Dipl.-Ing. Georg Wahl, General Manager, Chassis Development, Axles; and Dipl.-Ing. Klaus-Gerhardt Wölpert, Director, Cayenne Operations.

I am deeply indebted to Jerry Reilly, Hardwick, MA, for his perspective, wisdom, wise counsel, and invaluable function as "co-brain" throughout the European research and interview phases of this book. I am equally grateful to David Stone, Camarillo, CA, for serving as West Coast "co-brain," through research and production stages of this book. If I am fortunate enough to have a "third" brain, it is Pete Stout, editor of *Excellence* magazine, who served as the soft voice whispering in my sub-conscious mind throughout the production of this book.

Owners throughout Europe and the U.S. have opened their garage doors to me and allowed me to include their vehicles in this book. I want to express my gratitude to Ernst Freiberger, EFA-Automobil Museum, Amerang, Germany; Bob Garretson, High Bentham; Thomas Gruber; Fred Hampton; Dr. George Konradsheim; Jack Logan; Marco Marinello; Jakob Meier, General Manager, EFA-Automobil Museum; David Mills; Helmut Pfeifhofer; Alois Ruf; Jacky Setton; Mike Smith; Alfredo Stola, StudioTorino, Torino, Italy; Paul Ernst Strähle; and Heini Walter, Curator, Collier Historics, Naples FL; Dick Barbour; Jerrod Bradley; Rob and Molly Brenner; Bob Cagle; Tony Callas, Callas Rennsport, Torrance, CA; Dr. Joe Carrastro IV; Christian Clarke, Blackhawk Collections, Danbury, CA; Linda and John Clinard; Tom Dalton; Wayne Dempsey, Pelican Parts, El Segundo, CA; Douglas Dodge; Matthew Drendel; Michael Duffey; Warren and Cheri Eads; Roger and Kathy Forse; Tom Gaither; Frank Gallogly; Bart Galloway; Paula Golus; Wayne and Houri Greko; Eugenio Gutierrez; Marty Harris; Henry Hinck, Schneider Autohaus, Santa Barbara, CA; Mike Hodson; Victor Ingram; Dr. Dan Jacobs; William Jackson; Ray Jordan; Prescott Kelly; Carla Korda; Steve Krein; Dirk Layer; George and Roberta Lehtinen; Jeff Lewis; Nick Liakis; Dan Lindsay; Robert Linton; Ken Lubell; Patrick Martin, Market Scan Racing, Newbury Park, CA; Doug and Jacob Meier; Steve Michaelson; Jim Middlebrook; Wesley Minear; Kent Morgan; Dave Morse; Dave Mosesson; Richard Newton; Josh Ofstein; George Olson; Brent Overacker; Malcolm Page; Bill Peters; Linda and Rich Peters; Loren Peters; Chris Roman; Eddie Sakamoto; Tony Samojen; Jon and Kelly Samuels; Joe Schneider, Schneider Autohaus, Santa Barbara, CA; John and Daryl Stegall; Kevin Stensrud; Dave Stone; Gary Swauger; Steve Talbott; Carl Thompson; Bruce Trenery; Allen Trowbridge; George Vorgitch, Roy Walzer; Ranson Webster; Devin, Anita and Eugene Wolver; Chet and Joan Yabitsu; and Greg Young.

I am a fortunate man to have met all of these people, heard their stories, and photographed their cars. What makes me all the more fortunate is a loving partner, my wife Carolyn, who encourages me and puts up with the passions, the time, and the energy it takes to do books like these. I hope you all enjoy this. I am deeply grateful to all of you,

Randy Leffingwell, Santa Barbara, CA

Photo Credits:
Cover, 9, 10, 13, 14 both, 15, 16–17, 18 both, 19, 25 left, 27, 29, 31,32, 33, 35, 36–37, 37 right, 39, 40 left, 42, 47, 48, 49, 50, 54, 55, 57 top left, 59, 62, 63 lower, 64, 65, 66, 67, 68, 69, 70, 71, 72, 73, 75 both, 76, 77, 81, 82, 83, 84, 85, 88–89, 90, 91, 101, 102, 103, 105, 109, 110 both, 111, 112 both, 113, 114, 115, 117, 118, 119, 120, 121, 125–126, 129, 131, 132, 133 both, 134, 135 both, 138 lower, 140, 142, 143, 145, 148, 149, 151, 152, 153 both, 154, 160, 161, 162, 164, 172, 173, 174, 175, 176, 177, 188, 189, 190, 192, 194, 195, 196, 197, 199, 201, 204, 205, 206, 207, 208, 209, 210, 212 lower, 213, 217, 219, 224–225, 228, 237, 243, 245 both, 248, 249, 251, 253, 254, 255, 256 both, 257, 261, 262–263, 267, 268 upper, 273, 275 both, 278–279, 280, 281, 285, 287 both, 288, 289 both, 290, 291, 293, 294, 295, 296–297, 298, 299, 301, 302, 303, 304–305, 306, 310 both, 328, 329, 337, 339 both, 346 courtesy *Porsche Archiv*. All others by Randy Leffingwell.

CHAPTER ONE

FROM **VOLKSWAGEN** ROOTS TO **PORSCHE** PRODUCTION

1938 Typ 60K 10 Berlin-to-Rome Racer
In 1939 Dr. Ferdinand Porsche had his staff assemble three Typ 60K 10 cars to compete in a road race planned from Berlin to Rome using German autobahns. Porsche's head of body engineering Erwin Komenda created the shapes, and chief engineer Karl Rabe married the lightened VW platform to Komenda's aluminum body and made it work.

Professor Dr. Ferdinand Porsche was growing impatient. Clients with financial resources and governments with demands repeatedly pushed aside his dream. Germany's Chancellor Adolf Hitler became a fan of Porsche in 1933 during a 35 minute meeting with him, racing driver Hans Stuck, and Auto Union Executive Director Klaus-Detlov von Oertzen. Stuck had argued that Germany needed "a second first-rate racing car" to run with Mercedes-Benz in international competitions, and he asked Porsche to design it. Hitler granted Porsche half of the 500,000 reichmarks he had earlier granted Mercedes to develop both Grand Prix and hillclimb race cars for Mercedes.

A decade earlier in 1923, Mercedes' parent Daimler-Benz had hired Porsche, and by the end of the decade, he had developed their unbeatable SSK and SSKL supercharged racers. But Daimler's board of directors dismissed Porsche in 1930, according to a postwar British Intelligence report, because effects of the U.S. stock market crash reached Europe.

"Porsche's designs were of too expensive a nature," the report stated, "and he was consequently removed from the firm. About this time the management of Daimler-Benz, Stuttgart, ostracized Porsche, forbidding any of their employees to have any dealings with him. This attitude is not understood," the report continued, "unless it was caused by a very healthy respect for his designing capabilities."

Ferdinand Porsche started designing motorized vehicles before the turn of the twentieth century. In 1899 at age 24 he developed a

This was the second Typ 60K 10 Porsche mechanics built. After the German government cancelled the Berlin-to-Rome race, Porsche put the car to use as an experimental vehicle, developing and testing parts for the Volkswagen Beetle. A mechanic named Schlichter posed beside the car for this photo made in the factory's central courtyard.

CHAPTER ONE

town car for Jakob Lohner in Vienna. Porsche used electric motors that directly drove the front wheels at each hub. The Lohner-Porsche won a grand prize at the 1900 World Fair in Paris. Later work for Austro-Daimler and others brought him international attention and earned him two honorary doctorates in engineering. He launched his own company, Porsche Konstrucktionen Ges.m.b.H, in December 1930, backed by steel and iron merchant, friend and racer Alfred Rosenberger.

With Rosenberger's resources, Porsche began in 1931 to design a six-cylinder mid-size (Typ 7) sedan for German carmaker Wanderer. Then in 1932 he developed a compact car (Typ 12) with a water-cooled radial engine in the rear. It used a torsion bar suspension. Motorcycle maker Zündapp in Nuremberg took on the project as a way to introduce itself to the automobile industry. Before leaving Zündapp, Porsche also developed an *Auto für Jedermann*, a car for everyone, using a flat four-cylinder air-cooled engine.

During the mid-1930s, before twice visiting the United States to study mass-production car manufacturing techniques, Porsche designed the *Volkswagen*, or another "People's Car," for the German government. Hitler's ambitious goal for his "VW" pegged inaugural production at 150,000 units; he imagined output growing to 500,000 cars annually. Porsche conceived several variations, including a convertible, a panel van, a coupe with right-hand drive, another for invalid drivers, and a high-clearance utility-type vehicle.

A large-capacity 50-liter fuel tank intruded into the passenger footwell, forcing Porsche to design the car with staggered seating, placing the passenger slightly behind the driver. On a bright day, the interior is airy, but the space is cramped and crude.

As head of the Third Reich's Tank Commission, Porsche Ges.m.b.H designed tanks and armored weapons carriers and their engines, transmissions, final drives, and suspensions, as well as some aero engines. Government work continued, as the British Intelligence report stated, "until a difference of opinion between him and the new Minister of War Production [Albert] Speer" cost him his job. Work on the VW, or Typ 60 as those inside Porsche knew it, and on other wartime projects enabled Porsche to buy out Rosenberger in 1937 and reorganize his company as a *Kommanditgesellschaft*, a KG or limited partnership.

The start of World War II killed Porsche's plan for this car. The German National Labor Front, *Deutsche Arbeitfront*, DAF, operated a subsidiary known as "Strength through Joy," *Kraft durch Freude*—KdF, to manufacture the VW. KdF could not sell parts to a private company even if that company, Porsche in this case, had designed them. What's more, a sports car was not the vehicle KdF officials deemed suitable for the masses.

In September 1938, with income from other wartime projects in their hands, Dr. Porsche and his son, Ferdinand Anton Ernst, known as Ferry, assigned several engineers working under Karl Fröhlich to re-energize the sports car project. Now they could design, pay for, fabricate, and assemble something like this on their own. They designated this new vehicle Typ 114 and nicknamed it the *F-Wagen* for Ferdinand and Ferry. In this car, they placed the engine between the occupants and the rear axle. This was a configuration Dr. Porsche already had proved successful with his Auto Union efforts and its Grand Prix cars and hillclimb racers. A complex aluminum 1.5 liter V-10 engine would drive the Typ 114's rear wheels through a five-speed ZF transaxle. Despite the DAF and KdF, Ferdinand still dreamt of his sports car as a Volkswagen "performance" project.

Germany's Third Reich managed motorsports as it did everything else in the 1930s. In mid-1938, Major Adolph Hühnlein, the *Korpsführer* of the National Socialist Motors Corps (NSKK), met with Ferdinand Porsche. In Chris Barber's authoritative book *Birth of the Beetle*, he theorizes that Porsche lamented to Hühnlein the lack of promotion for the VW and "the vehicle's sporting potential." Hühnlein was a personal friend of Hitler, and he had colleagues in Mussolini's government in Italy. He soon organized a 938-mile (1,500-kilometer) race from Berlin to Rome to run in September 1939. The course would incorporate the new autobahn to Munich, through Austria, over the Brenner Pass, and south into Italy. For Germany and Volkswagen, this race would show off the capabilities of the new road and the new People's Car that Ferdinand Porsche had designed and built.

Ferdinand Porsche originally conceived the Typ 60K 10 car to run an intricate air-cooled V-10, but instead he used this basic 985cc VW engine that developed 32 brake horsepower. Later experiments conducted after the race was cancelled increased output to around 40 brake horsepower, but records are vague and incomplete.

Porsche assembled three cars under the Typ 64 designation for this event. Porsche loosely based these on Volkswagen platforms, but engineers added rectangular-section tube aluminum structures extending out from the center backbone that combined strength with light weight. Body engineer Erwin Komenda's streamlined Typ 114 *F-Wagen* body inspired these cars, but Komenda covered the front and rear wheelwells with removable spats. He kept the cockpit and roofline narrow and accommodated an oversize fuel tank for the long-distance race by staggering seating. This set the driver ahead and the passenger to the side and slightly aft.

Reutter manufactured the bodies. Franz Xaver Reimspiess' engineers bored out the VW engine he had designed from 985cc to 1,131cc, and reports suggest they obtained more than 40 horsepower. According to historian Hans-Karl Lange, Dr. Porsche hoped to convince the German government not only to build his sports car, but also to pay for production versions of it. He renamed it the Typ 60K10; Typ 60 was the designation for the KdF Volkswagen, and "10" represented the tenth car assembled.

Porsche completed the first car. With two weeks until the race, the staff had begun on numbers two and three. Then in early September, German troops invaded Poland.

This triggered an international chain reaction leading England and France to declare war. Harsh reality rendered the race too frivolous, and Major Hühnlein cancelled it, consigning Porsche's dream again to his imagination.

Hoping to evade the chaos of World War II, Dr. Porsche divided his operations into three parts. He kept the headquarters in Zuffenhausen, outside Stuttgart, Germany. He moved VW production to Fellersleben and transferred design and testing to Gmünd, Austria.

Ferry, who had just turned 30, recommended the company complete the other two Typ 64 cars as development vehicles. Porsche craftsmen finished the second riveted body in December 1939 and the final one in June 1940. The company provided them for Porsche and Volkswagen management. A DAF labor union boss, Bodo Lafferentz, destroyed the first car in a crash in 1941. The second survived the war only to fall victim to joyriding American soldiers who cut off its roof in the summer for a cooler ride and to open space for more passengers. They drove it till the engine seized.

Car number three was Ferdinand Porsche's personal vehicle, which his friend and chauffeur Josef Goldinger drove most often while Porsche read the many documents he got each day from VW, the Tank Commission, or his own factory. On one run, Goldinger averaged 83 miles per hour (133 kilometers per hour). Ferdinand continued to use the car in Gmünd after the war. He replaced the cable-activated brakes with hydraulics. Italian

In mid-1949, Austrian racer Otto Mathé purchased this Typ 60K 10 from Porsche and registered it in his home district of Tyrol. Here he competed in the *Coppa D'Oro Delle Dolomiti* in July 1952. He had lost his right arm in a motorcycle accident before the war, so he had mechanics convert the car to right-hand drive so he could steer and shift with his left arm.

1947 356/1 roadster

Body engineer Erwin Komenda teamed up again with Karl Rabe, who created an all new hand-welded full-girder frame for the 356. But where the Typ 60/64 had been a competition vehicle, Porsche wanted this new car to be a road car providing comfortable room for driver and passenger.

coachmaker Battista "Pinin" Farina repaired its bodywork in 1947. After Pinin Farina's work, Ferry attached a name badge to the front of the car, the first time the name "Porsche" appeared on any car. In 1949, he sold the car to Austria's legendary one-armed racer Otto Mathé, who campaigned it successfully with the license registration T2.222 (for Tyrol) through 1950. He converted it to right-hand drive so he could shift gears more easily and installed a 1.3-liter 60-horsepower engine. Mathé kept the car, which he called "the ancestor," *die Ahnherr*, of all Porsches until he died in 1994.

Because, as historian Lange suggested, the Typ 64/Typ 60K10 cars represented a project

Ferdinand's son Ferry based his 356/1 roadster loosely on the VW that had inspired Ferdinand's Typ 60, 64, and 114 variations. This car set the direction for the car manufacturing company. Like a compass, it has influenced the direction of design, philosophy, engineering, and marketing.

At some point during the time Swiss architect Bernhard Blank supported Porsche, he obtained the first roadster. No one knows whether he or Porsche painted the car. The paint scheme had appeared on racers a few years earlier. Here he starts a mountain tour with a friend in 1957.

"born under the patronage of the National Socialist regime to serve as a propaganda tool . . . , Ferry was desperate to cut all links with the regime." The factory generally refers to 356-001 as the first Porsche. The 356, Lange surmised, was a new vehicle born from Ferry Porsche's determination, not that of a national government.

Porsche's Zuffenhausen plant had manufactured armored military vehicles. Allied bombing smashed through the works building into the basement in April 1944. Fires destroyed sets of drawings stored there. The German military command would not ensure safety to Porsche's facilities or its workers, so the family relocated operations to Austria. They set up storage in a former flying school in their hometown of Zell am See. Production, design, and engineering—some 250 managers, technicians, craftsmen, and fabricators in all—moved into a sawmill outside of Gmünd, 50 miles (80 kilometers) southwest of Zell. When the war ended, Gmünd fell under British supervision, while Zell went to the Americans. Ferry moved to Gmünd.

Ferdinand's hard times were not over. The work his firm did for the German government haunted him. British officers arrested all the Porsche men in July 1945. Photos showed Porsche with Hitler. Ferdinand appeared sober, but Hitler was smiling, not unreasonable from a happy client meeting the brilliant engineer who had made *his* dreams come true. After three months of interrogation and production of a lengthy report on his wartime activities, the British concluded that Porsche was a shrewd engineer and practical businessman doing what he could to stay in business and out of a wartime prison.

Less than a month later, French officials arrested the men, accusing them of sabotaging Peugeot works and using

948 356/2 Gmünd Coupe
The family's work showed well against the family villa in Zell am See. The Volkswagens towered over the streamlined 356 coupe bodies from Gmünd and cabriolet bodies that Beutler in Switzerland produced for the company.

French workers as forced laborers. Fifteen months passed before the French released Ferdinand Porsche and his brother-in-law Anton Piëch, demanding payment of one million French francs as bail.

Fortunately, an Italian industrialist, Piero Dusio, approached Ferry to design and build the Typ 360 Formula One Grand Prix car for his company, Cisitalia. Dusio's payments transferred through Gmünd to Dijon, France, to free Porsche and Piëch.

In his absence, Ferry's sister, Louise Piëch, ran the firm. Once work began on the Cisitalia racer, Ferry resurrected his father's ambitions for a sports car. Parts were easy to find; there were many VW *Kubelwagen*, the off-road utility vehicles, around Gmünd. Abandoned by retreating soldiers, local farmers had adopted the functional vehicles. Before long Ferry had his first roadworthy Typ 356. Word spread that the family was back in business. Engineers, designers, and others made their way to Gmünd. Body engineer Erwin Komenda, finance officer Hans Kern, engine designer Franz Xaver Reimspiess, chief engineer Karl Rabe, body panel beater Friedrich Weber, aerodynamicist/mathematician Josef Mickl, and Ferdinand's

Ferry Porsche glanced at the camera while his father studied a new Pre-A coupe body at the Zuffenhausen works. In the center, chief engineer Karl Rabe conversed with two other colleagues.

Paris Salon de l'Automobile 1953

(OPPOSITE PAGE): Crowds filled the small Porsche stand at the October 1953 Paris auto show. The cabriolet—a Beutler Brothers creation—won the show's Coupe du Salon, the "best of show," and garnered slightly more interest than the show version of the upcoming 550 Spyder.

personal secretary (and nephew), Ghislane Kaes, rejoined the group.

Rabe and Komenda mounted improved engines in the middle of the 356 similar to the Typ 64 and 114. The car ran its tests reliably. Ferdinand Porsche gave birth at last to his dream. Along with engineer Wilhelm Hild and nearly 200 designers, fabricators, engineers, and laborers, he launched a sports car different from all others at the time. But this new car was a roadster, "only a provisional prototype," as Richard von Frankenberg, factory test driver and racer, described it years later. This open car proved impractical: Its tubular frame configuration limited interior storage; the mid-engine placement held the car to two occupants; it had no top to keep out rain or snow. "It had

Gmünd Body Production

Frederick Weber, left, and a young apprentice fit the rear bodywork onto a 356 at the Gmünd works. Weber and his apprentices hammered each body panel by hand, contouring them on wooden forms such as the one shown at the right.

18

CHAPTER ONE

1938–1958

been planned from the very beginning to fit the type 356 with a fixed head coupe," von Frankenberg wrote in its defense.

For the second-generation 356, Porsche resurrected the VW system using a floorpan and installing the engine behind the rear axle. Freidrich Weber hammered out closed coupes. Porsche's engineers mounted the basic Reimspiess–designed 24-horsepower VW 1,131cc engine and used the VW suspension, gearbox, brakes, and running gear. The first roadster weighed 1,340 pounds (609 kilograms) while the coupes came in at 1,580 pounds (718 kilograms). Road-testing over the *Katschberg Höhe*, a nearby mountain, showed that this new car needed better brakes and more power.

Another outsider stepped in. Bernhard Blank, a hotel owner in Zurich, Switzerland, loaned his architect 50,000 Swiss franks (about $16,000) at the time, unknowingly financing Porsche's growth. The architect, Richard von Senger, had met Dr. Porsche's brother-in-law Anton Piëch, who was seeking investors. Von Senger used Blank's money to order ten Porsche coupes and establish himself as Switzerland's Porsche importer. Von Senger loaned a car to Robert Braunschweig, editor of Switzerland's influential *Automobil-Revue*, who wrote, "We batted this vehicle around the Bremgarten circuit and became very confident with it in a very short time. This is how we imagine modern road motoring to be." Orders began to reach von Senger and Porsche. But late in the summer of 1948, Blank encountered von Senger with Piëch, who quickly surmised who was the real backer. Later that fall, Blank helped Porsche hire Swiss coachbuilders Ernst and Fritz Beutler to develop a prototype cabriolet. They manufactured five production versions before stepping away. As custom body makers, their capacity was limited. They never had sought production work.

Because Swiss citizens traveled freely through postwar Europe, Blank became Porsche's worldwide distributor. He displayed a Gmünd coupe with a sunroof and a Beutler-bodied cabriolet at the Geneva Auto Salon in March 1949. Swiss-educated Egyptian Prince Mohammed Abdel Moneim, a cousin of Egypt's King Farouk, was one of the first buyers.

Blank recalled the early cars. "I didn't like to drive the bloody things," he explained in an interview in early 1991 when he was 89. "But they were interesting, and we could make some money!" He hired a salesman whose most effective technique was to demonstrate the car to his wealthy friends. It was a hard sell. Porsche's first production cars were rough when Blank received them. He had some car bodies completely refinished at Pilatus, an aircraft manufacturer near Lucerne that had experience with aluminum. Much of the raw materials for the cars,

1952 356 1500 America Roadster (Typ 540)

Californian Johnny von Neumann convinced East Coast importer Max Hoffman to order a series of 20 or 21 "America Roadsters" for competition. Von Neumann wanted the last one assembled without interior or extras so he could make a real race car out of it for friend Jack MacAfee to campaign.

instruments, lighting, even the raw aluminum for Weber's hammer, came from Switzerland. Yet because Porsche had so few customers, it had neither adequate cash nor capacity to expand production. Shortly after the Geneva show in March 1949, another door opened, however.

Ferdinand Porsche finally regained his freedom to travel. He recognized that his facilities in Gmünd would limit production. He hoped to return his shops and studios to Zuffenhausen. Childhood friend and former German Foreign Office economist Professor Dr. Albert Prinzing met with Stuttgart's Lord Mayor Arnulf Klett in July 1949. Klett offered to take Porsche's request to the military government. U.S. Army personnel used Porsche's shops as motor pool headquarters. By late 1949, Porsche learned he could move back to Stuttgart. Plans included relocating production as well. Rabe and Komenda visited local manufacturers to take bids. Reutter Karosserie's shops in Zuffenhausen nearly were adjacent to Porsche's. Reutter had manufactured trolley cars and repaired private car bodywork throughout the war to keep its workers employed and its bills paid. They and other companies expressed interest, but Ferdinand made the choice: "Never mind the money," he told von Frankenberg. "Reutter has the best foreman."

Porsche was full of confidence, and with Albert Prinzing now on staff to watch the funds, he ordered 500 car bodies in November 1949. Then Prinzing and another friend left Stuttgart in a Gmünd coupe and

1954 356A 1500 Speedster #200

The last Speedster that Porsche manufactured in 1954 remained true to the first. Porsche was reluctant at first to produce a car at a price—that is, to pull features out of a car in order to sell it at $3,000. First-year cars originally had roll-up windows that Reutter removed and then welded strips over the window openings.

Von Neumann introduced the 1500 Speedster at his own house, gathering racers and journalists around his swimming pool for cocktails. For those who missed that social introduction, he took the car racing the next weekend.

1957 356A Speedster 1600

By 1957, Porsche was installing 1,582cc 60-brake-horsepower engines in Speedsters. Between 1956 and 1958, the company manufactured 2,910 of the cars, selling them for $2,833 (about DM 11,900) at the factory.

a Beutler cabriolet driving to visit potential customers around Germany.

Bernhard Blank committed to the March 1950 Geneva show. But he had little luck and chose not to display in 1951. He cancelled his space in September 1950. In two years, he had sold just 43 coupes and 8 cabriolets. Then two months later, Ferdinand Porsche, weakened from his two prison stays, suffered a stroke. He died on January 30, 1951, at age 75.

Porsche's fortunes swung again. Days before the 1951 Geneva Salon opened in March, French car importer/racer Auguste Veuillet took his own Adriatic blue Gmünd coupe and a second car to Montlhéry circuit south of Paris to demonstrate their capabilities to journalists. He covered several officially timed laps at 89.9 miles per hour (143.89 kilometers per hour).

That kind of speed generated publicity, and Blank leapt to action. He could only get a vacant showroom beside Geneva's exhibition hall. He plastered the area with signs and displayed coupes and cabriolets inside his showroom with drivable demonstrators parked out front.

"Until the record run," he explained, "we didn't have much success and so I didn't think it was worth the time and money to sign up for something in March 1951 way back in September 1950. Now, at least, we had something." For Porsche, this was not enough. Not listed in the official program of the show, Porsche appeared left out.

Months later, on September 29, Porsche returned to Montlhéry with three vehicles and a team of five drivers. They hoped to set records for 500 miles (1,000 kilometers) and six hours in the 1,100cc class. The record for 1,000 kilometers went from 98.16 miles per hour to 101.4 (162.7 kilometers per hour). In a highly dramatic follow-up the next night, von Frankenberg and the others drove a

California was one of Porsche's major sales destinations, and Malibu was one of von Neumann's targets. Hollywood movie stars and producers lived along the ocean, and when they went for dinner, they followed Mulholland Highway inland to Cornell to order steaks at the Old Place.

1,500cc coupe to a new class record for 1,875 miles (3,000 kilometers) at 99.35 miles per hour (158.96 kilometers per hour). Over the longest run, 72 hours, the car and drivers set a new world record at 95.2 miles per hour to cover 6,861.3 miles (152.34 kilometers per hour to cover 10,978 kilometers).

Veuillet, not part of the factory-sponsored run, nevertheless displayed the record car on his firm's stand, Son-Auto, at the 1951 Paris show in October. Dealers or Porsche displayed cars in Brussels and Turin. Max Hoffman, a Viennese citizen living in New York City, loved European cars and recognized America's appetites. He showed Porsches in his Park Avenue showroom beginning in late 1950. His distributor, Johnny von Neumann, covered the West. Charles Meisl, a perceptive sales manager with Connaught Engineering in England, displayed Porsche's inaugural right-hand-drive coupe and cabriolet at Earl's Court, London's auto show. New cars reached South Africa. A solid market grew in U.S. racing, and international rallying had returned to the enthusiast world. Owners and racers spread the word of Porsche's superior—if initially challenging—handling as well as their quality and durability. Ferry listened to his customers, and new customers sought out the firm.

Missing Geneva cost Bernhard Blank his exclusive agreement. He became simply one of many agents throughout the world who received cars from Porsche's new worldwide distributor, *Auto und Motore, AG,* AMAG. It was strictly business, and there was no shortage of people wanting to participate.

Not least among these were Porsche's U.S. distributors Max Hoffman and Johnny von Neumann. By late 1950, Karl Rabe and Erwin Komenda had completed designs for a low windowsill cabriolet designated the Typ 540, which Hoffman and von Neumann had commissioned for the growing audience in America. Komenda's design furthered the stylistic evolution from 356-001 through the six subsequent Beutler cabriolets. With Reutter's capacity strained producing coupes for Porsche, Rabe and Komenda found Heinrich Gläser Karosserie in Dresden as a suitable fabricator. Gläser's grandson-in-law Erich Heuer had inherited the company, and he relocated operations to Nuremberg after the war. Gläser had specialized in cabriolets since the turn of the century when they did their first automobiles. Porsche contracted Heuer to assemble 250 standard cabriolets as well as 16 special roadster bodies.

The work bankrupted Heuer. He bid production time at 500 hours, but his craftsmen needed 640 for each car. Erich delivered cars late, and reportedly he lost 1,600 deutsche marks (about $380) on each roadster. Anxious banks closed his doors in November 1952, halting production on incomplete cars.

Porsche produced three series of the America Roadsters in 1952 and 1953. The first cars had a single air grille on the

1958 356A 1500 GS Carrera GT Speedster

Porsche recognized the competitive nature of the market for the Carrera Speedsters and made the roll bar standard equipment for 1958. These potent cars won races around the world.

CHAPTER ONE

rear deck. Von Neumann was a racer, and he urged Hoffman to deliver the first cars stripped of all luxury as potential racers. Overheating problems kept them from being competitive, so the two entrepreneurs ordered later interiors with upholstery. Second-generation models got a second air intake. Von Neumann ordered a final car, number 17, stripped, with a body from Drauz Karosserie in Heilbronn near Zuffenhausen, which he planned to modify for his racing driver friend Jack McAfee.

"A prototype," von Neumann recalled in 1992, "unpainted, shipped to me. I said, 'Don't paint it. Don't put upholstery in because I'm going to rip it out.'"

McAfee had raced circle track roadsters, and he had techniques to hold speed while sliding. These served him well with the swing-axle America Roadster.

"I adapted to it," McAfee explained, "because I ran the sprinters so long and throwing the car to scrape off the speed." He grinned at the memories. "The thing

The Fuhrmann four-cam Typ 547 engine powered coupes, cabriolets, and Speedsters. With 100 to 110 brake horsepower available, buyers of the GS-GT package paid a premium price to get narrow gear ratios in second, third, and fourth, as well as aluminum doors and front and rear deck lids.

The ticket to win races cost $5,260. That gave buyers two Weber two-barrel carburetors and cold-air boxes to ensure the air that entered the engine was as cool and dense as possible.

1938–1958

Convertible "D" models replaced the Speedsters. Drauz Karosserie in Heilbronn near Zuffenhausen assembled these bodies. Porsche gave them roll-up windows, a larger windscreen, and a larger convertible top rear window.

Porsche fitted its 1,582cc 75-brake-horsepower engines into the Drauz-built convertibles, although buyers could order Carrera engines as well. For 1959 Porsche produced 1,330 of the Convertible "D" models, which sold for $3,290 (DM 13,750) at the factory.

26

CHAPTER ONE

that upset everybody was the swinging axle suspension in the rear. When you came off the gas, the rear just got light in back. It was very scary. Dive into a corner and at the right moment, come off the gas. Just a little flick of the wheel and you set it up so the back end is doing the steering. It takes some courage but you don't even use the brakes.

"Two great things came out of it," McAfee said. "One, they decided they could produce the Speedster with its steel body and windshield wipers. And two: They recognized that winning races was a good way to advertise cars. I think, now, that the America Roadster, this little Johnny von Neumann special, was a prototype really for the Speedster. Von Neumann, through Hoffman, complained that they needed something for a price for the American market." It was difficult for Porsche to accept the concept of an inexpensive car at first. But von Neumann knew his customers.

"They want to go, on a Saturday evening in June," Von Neumann explained, "down Sunset Boulevard with their elbow over the door and the girls can see them in the car. And they can see the girls on the walks. I pushed Maxie. I wanted a roadster and I wanted it for less than three thousand dollars." At the time, Hoffman sold well-equipped Porsches for $4,500. Engine and trim options could take the car above $5,500 in Germany, more in America. Porsche's director of publicity and competition, Huschke von Hanstein, was a baron, and many cars went to his friends. An unspoken rule early on suggested that if you weren't royalty, you needn't inquire. . . .

1955 Typ 356 Speedster 1500
Within days of showing his first Speedster at his home in Los Angeles, West Coast Porsche distributor Johnny von Neumann entered the car in races at Torrey Pines, near San Diego. When the Speedster won its class, he opened his order book.

Yet Ferry Porsche and economist Albert Prinzing knew that Hoffman was selling cars. Reutter simplified and minimized the lines of Komenda's new convertible and gutted the interior. They brought over the frame, suspension, and the 1500cc Normal engine to this new open car. Reutter created a lightweight cloth roof cut low to the sill, which they already had lowered an inch and a half. They created a "chopped-and-channeled" Hollywood hot rod, and Porsche introduced it for 1955.

Buyers could customize their Speedsters. Porsche offered the 1500 Super motor. A tachometer was optional. So was a heater. Padded seats were available. If someone purchased the car as barren as Reutter could ship it, the new Speedster sold for $2,995 in Hoffman's showroom at 59th and Park Avenue. Europeans couldn't even get one for the first nine months. Von Neumann displayed his first one beside his swimming pool at home in Sherman Oaks in suburban Los Angeles for a crowd of invited VIPs. The next weekend, he raced it at Torrey Pines, a road course in a state park near San Diego. He took first place in the 1,500cc class. The second most important race of the weekend was to get in line to order a Speedster from von Neumann. ■

CHAPTER TWO

RACING IMPROVES THE BREED

1951 Glöckler-Porsche

Frankfurt VW dealer Otto Glöckler and his shop chief Hermann Ramelow built their first "special" racer in 1948. This second-generation car reflected their growing relationship with Porsche, from whom they got engines and nameplates.

AFTER THE COMPANY'S STILLBORN EFFORTS WITH ITS TYP 64 BERLIN-TO-ROME STREAMLINER, Ferry Porsche watched outsiders campaign his products in the early 1950s. The strategy benefited the firm and the participants. The Glöcklers of Frankfurt were racers. Otto Glöckler had raced motorcycles before World War II, and before that his family had sold, raced, and rallied Hanomag automobiles during the 1930s. His son Walter, born in 1908, followed his father's footsteps, and at 19 he won a 250cc motorcycle race in 1927 at the Nürburgring.

After the war, Walter acquired an existing VW agency. This advanced the family's ambition of assembling their own racers. After building a Hanomag-powered single seater with their workshops manager Hermann Ramelow for the 1949 Freiberg hillclimb, they started fresh for 1950.

They obtained a 1.1-liter Typ 369 Porsche engine. Settling on an 80.7-inch (2050mm) wheelbase, they fitted VW running gear and mounted the engine ahead of the transmission and rear suspension similar to 356-001. Ramelow mounted the driver's seat nearly in the middle of the car. They surrounded this with a basic tubular-steel ladder frame that historian Karl Ludvigsen characterized as "underslung, passing below the swing axles at the rear." Their sleek, simple body came from C.H. Wiedenhausen Karosserie, a Frankfurt body builder located nearby.

The car weighed 980 pounds (445 kilograms) and, with its 48-horsepower engine, took Walter to the 1,100cc class championship in 1950. Glöcker named the car *VW Eigenbau*, or "homebuilt," though its success through the year brought favorable attention to Porsche and earned Walter what Ludvigsen called "a mutual assistance pact." Beginning with their 1951 cars, Glöcklers wore Porsche nameplates, and newspaper and racing reports referred to them as Porsches. In exchange, Porsche provided Walter with the latest engines, modifications, and tuning techniques.

The 1951 car used a Typ 527 1.5-liter engine and VW headlights. The body partially enclosed the rear wheels and added a faired-in headrest behind the driver. Porsche developed as much as 85 horsepower for short events with an experimental Typ 502 engine. For longer circuits, Wiedenhausen fabricated a removable hardtop for the car. The car set several distance records including a 625-mile (1,000-kilometer) run at 114.4 miles per hour (185.6 kilometers per hour).

Walter's relationship with Porsche made his third car even more Porsche-like. Glöckler and Ramelow shortened a 356 platform to their 80.7-inch (2050mm) wheelbase. Walter's nephew Helm raced the car to the German sports car championship for 1952. For 1952, they produced two cars. The first roadster, finished in a smart two-tone paint scheme, ran the 1951 mid-engine configuration with Porsche's latest 1.5-liter Typ 528 engine. Porsche showed the car at the Geneva and Frankfurt auto shows. Built for a privateer, Hans Stanek, he raced the 1,210-pound (550-kilogram) roadster for two years and sold it back to Walter in 1954.

The second roadster went to Richard Trenkel, who won the 1,100cc championship with it. While Stanek's car resembled a loaf of bread before baking, Trenkel's was more radical, dipping low in front between its

Glöckler and Ramelow created a lightweight 990-pound (450-kilogram) single-seater and used a Porsche 1.5-liter flat-four that they modified to achieve 85 brake horsepower. C. H. Wiedenhausen, a small car-body shop near Glöckler's shops, designed and fabricated the body.

1953 Typ 550-01

In its first race ever, Typ 550-01 ran as a spyder at the Eifelrennen at Nürburgring, May 31, 1953. Porsche asked Otto Glöckler's son Helmut to drive, which proved a wise decision because he won the race, run during a hard rain.

headlights. In 1954, Trenkel upgraded to the 1.5-liter engine.

In Zuffenhausen, Porsche's racing manager Huschke von Hanstein was a Glöckler family friend, having raced with them before the war. He and Ferry watched and read the publicity that Walter's and Helm's exploits brought to the company. With growing competition in Europe from O.S.C.A. in Italy, Gordini in France, Jowett in Britain, and EMW and Borgward from East and West Germany, Ferry recognized that his racing strategy must change. No longer would his company badge be applied to someone else's work. Racing must be homegrown at Porsche.

After Le Mans in 1952, Karl Rabe directed development of a new engine, the Typ 547, and Wilhelm Hild and his crew designed and began to assemble a new car to use it, the Typ 550. Wiedenhausen

1953 Typ 550-02

Porsche used C. H. Wiedenhausen, who had made the bodies for Glöckler's racers, to produce bodies for the 550s. They fitted tapered headlights from a Ford Taunus onto this first-generation model. Before Le Mans, Porsche redesigned the front end and set vertical headlamps much further back into the front fenders.

1953 Typ 550-01

Competition director Huschke von Hanstein and engineer Wilhelm Hild decided to race closed cars at Le Mans only after practice. The coupes reached 124 miles per hour (198.4 kilometers per hour), which was slightly faster than open spyders.

The claustrophobic interior buzzed, rattled, and baked the drivers for 24 hours. Richard von Frankenberg and Paul Frère won the 1,500cc class in 550-02, though "Helm" Glöckler and Hans Hermann were just meters behind in this car.

completed the bodies for these cars as well, including removable fastback tops. Fitted with 1500cc pushrod engines, the Typ 550 weighed 1,200 pounds (545 kilograms).

Walter Glöckler's nephew Helm got the first racing drive. He won at the Nürburgring, first in the 1.5-liter category in the *Eifelrennen*. This lifted Porsche's hopes, and they took the first and second cars to Le Mans two weeks later. Walter entered Helm and Hans Herrmann in Helm's Eifel winner, 550-01, wearing number 44. Factory driver/journalist Richard von Frankenberg joined Belgian driver/journalist Paul Frère in 550-02, number 45. It was Frère's first drive for Porsche and his first Le Mans. He had seen the circuit before but had never driven it.

"The engine was turned one hundred eighty degrees compared with the production car," he recalled. "The suspension arms of the production car were not long enough to clear the engine. So they reversed them to have them behind the gearbox. It made the car oversteer more.

"By the time I had my first drive, it was dark. It's absolutely impossible to learn a circuit in the dark, and to learn in a car I had assumed would handle *better* than a standard Three-Five-Six. I very nearly lost it in the first left-hander after the Dunlop Bridge on the first lap."

Porsche entered Le Mans in 1953 with two goals: win its class and capture the Index of Performance (a measure of running efficiency). With fastback tops, the cars reached 125 miles per hour (200 kilometers per hour) on the long Mulsanne Straight. Yet during practice and in the race, oil temperatures soared. By Sunday morning,

At Johnny von Neumann's Competition Motors on Highland Boulevard in Hollywood, clients' 550 racers littered the back lot before a race weekend. California became prime Porsche territory with plenty of young talented drivers and older wealthy backers.

Hans Herrmann's class-winning 550-4 number 55 sat under protective shade while Ernst-Joachim Hirz's 70th place 356 number 53 and the 12th place 550-06 number 58 of Herbert Linge and Fernando Segura got less respect. Or perhaps this just was a case of who reached the cantina first?

with Frère and von Frankenberg driving fast but carefully, they had averaged 93 miles per hour (148.8 kilometers per hour) for more than 18 hours and led their class by ten laps. Porsche and von Hanstein reduced paces to ensure the class win. It disappointed Frère, he recalled, "to be unlapped by cars they had passed during the night." But when the clock ticked 4:00 p.m. on June 14, car number 45, with co-driver von Frankenberg at the wheel, won the class and established a record.

Porsche "retired" those cars to Central America. Before shipping them to Guatemala, the factory increased their cooling and breathing capabilities. Jaroslav Juhan entered 550-01, sponsored by the Canada Shoe Company of Guadalajara, in the 1953 Carrera Panamericana. But he did not finish. Teammate José Herrarte managed to avoid the boulders and beasts that foiled Juhan's race, and 550-02 won its class.

For 1954, Porsche entered four cars at Le Mans, one a 1,100cc spyder co-driven by Zora Arkus-Duntov, a Russian engineer on vacation from General Motors in Detroit. With only 72 horsepower, his car was not the speediest in his class but after 24 hours,

CHAPTER TWO

Factory racer Richard von Frankenberg steered this 550 into a turn. A journalist and photographer himself, von Frankenberg racked up dozens of European victories in Porsches.

speedier cars had broken. Arkus-Duntov won his class. Following the race, he returned with the cars to Zuffenhausen, where he met Porsche's new chassis engineer Helmuth Bott working for Helmut Rombold in the Experimental Department.

Bott knew of a paper Arkus-Duntov had helped prepare with GM chassis chief Maurice Olley called "Manners of the Modern Car." It dealt with road holding and vehicle handling. Duntov accompanied Bott to Malmsheim airport to show him a dozen tests GM used to evaluate handling.

"With his tests," Bott recalled, "You could get a very good picture of what the car does on the road. You could measure it and write it down. And if you could measure, you could do better." Arkus-Duntov and Bott performed tests on a 356A. They

Drivers and occasional co-drivers or navigators had to make do with padded seats in the 550s. The seat back slots were for cooling, not access for lap or shoulder belts.

Two Solex 40 PII twin-choke downdraft carburetors helped Ernst Fuhrmann's four-cam Typ 547 engine develop 110 brake horsepower. Porsche fitted brushes at the bottom of the torsion bars to resist grit entering the engine compartment.

markedly improved the handling. Ferry Porsche asked Bott to begin the same work on the new race car, the Typ 550.

"And so the Five-Fifty was my first race car project," Bott said. "I did all the road holding things. We picked up thirty seconds on the Nürburgring without changing the power of the engine."

Porsche expanded production in early 1954. Max Hoffman wanted cars to sell in New York but he argued that vehicles designated by a number didn't excite buyers; they needed a name. The "Spyder" name had an exotic appeal. Wendler Karosserie in Reutlingen took on aluminum body production for "customer" cars. With a spring-loaded trip door, remotely operated from the dashboard to control

1954 Mille Miglia Sixth Place

Hans Herrmann and Herbert Linge (center in this photo with other mechanics) finished sixth in the Mille Miglia in 1954 in this car. Racing hard to hold their place, Hermann drove under lowered train-crossing gates, holding Linge's head down with his hand. They barely missed getting hit by the express train to Rome.

airflow to the oil cooler, the cars weighed about 1,298 pounds (590 kilograms), not quite 132 pounds (60 kilograms) more than factory racers. Erwin Komenda slightly restyled the 1955 Le Mans cars and subsequent customer cars, which got lower fenders and 356A-production-style headlights. Karl Rabe and Wilhelm Hild made significant changes on this version designated the 550A. They found they could handle the power from the new Typ 547 engine by replacing the old ladder frame with a tubular space frame, suspending the rear axle beneath it. With the new engine, the 550A, named the 1500RS for *Rennsport* at Ferry's request, gained 40 horsepower to 135.

"The main question," engine designer Ernst Fuhrmann recalled in describing his radical new engine, "was the movement of the valves. The second question was the movement of the pistons. This was the decision for the movement of the camshafts, the shaft through the middle. So the engine could become shorter."

Fuhrmann's assignment, to design a new racing engine, came with few restrictions. Nowhere in his brief did he find a limitation on its size.

"I designed the engine so it fit into the normal Porsche Three-Five-Six. My interest was always to have that engine in my personal car!" On March 2, 1953, Fuhrmann ran his first engine on a test stand. He had designed hemispherically domed cylinder heads. He used dual spark plugs, dual-overhead camshafts, twin ignition, a pair of dual-barrel carburetors, and a roller-bearing crankshaft. His big-bore/short-stroke engine— 3.35x2.6 inches (85x66mm)—developed 112 horsepower the first time they ran it. His boss, Franz Reimspiess, designed a new fan that pulled

1958 Typ 718 RSK Center Seat Formula Two
The 718 succeeded the 550 and 550A models with a revised suspension. Through 1958 and 1959 the modified center-seat cars proved indomitable with class wins at Buenos Aires, Sebring, the Targa, Le Mans, and Great Britain in 1958, and Sebring to start 1959. Carel Godin de Beaufort drove this center-seater 718 during the 1959 Grand Prix of Holland.

Porsche's racing customers bought the 718 RSK for $8,000, which included the hardware to convert the car from left steering to center seating. The Fuhrmann motors developed 148 brake horsepower after switching over to Weber 46IDM carburetors.

Wendler produced the sleek aluminum bodies for the RSKs. Conversion from left side to center steering took about four hours.

in cooling air from both sides of its shroud. While that was innovative, Fuhrmann's decision to drive the cams by shafts and bevel gears off the main crankshaft was more significant. Porsche had done it before on the final Auto Union Grand Prix and the postwar flat-12 cylinder Cisitalia Grand Prix car for Piero Dusio. They would do it again decades later with their large racing flat-12s.

The engines first appeared in Typ 550 race prototypes in 1953. They were strong, but their repair costs kept them from introduction in 356 series models for two more years. Racing applications, especially the first factory efforts, always came attended by trained mechanics. Yet good customers lobbied hard with von Hanstein and Ferry

While California was a long way from Zuffenhausen, that distance did not mean that racers were any less competitive, even if taking a tighter line through a turn meant the hay bales bent a fender. Available with as little as 55 horsepower in 1955, by mid-1957, 356A buyers could get 110-brake-horsepower GS Carrera GT packages.

1960 Typ RS61LM

Porsche evolved the RS60 from its RSK in 1960 and upgraded the car slightly for 1961 when the racing season seemed to belong to Zuffenhausen. Driving RS61s, Bob Holbert won his class at Sebring, and Jo Bonnier and Dan Gurney won theirs at Targa.

Porsche. So, late in 1955 Porsche announced its new model 1500GS as part of the new 356A series. The company christened it the Carrera in honor of its participation in the 1953, 1954, and 1955 Mexican road races.

Over the next two years, factory improvements in tuning saw 130–135-horsepower power at 7500 rpm from the 90-cubic-inch engine.

If racers hoped to win in 1.5-liter classes, they drove spyders. At some events, most of the starting field ran 550A/1500RS models. At an early 1955 race at Hockenheim, 21 spyders roared away at the start. At the Öst Curve, the East Turn, a huge crash involved 15 of them and took out 6 completely.

CHAPTER TWO

Stirling Moss and Graham Hill had led the 1961 Targa Florio for nine of its ten laps and set new records nearly every time around, but this strained the bolts that held the transmission case together. Fluid leaked out, the transmission seized, and Moss walked back to the pits.

In the United States, racers up and down the length of California campaigned 550A models. Jean-Pierre Kunstle, a Swiss businessman who worked in the United States at the time, raced through city streets and along airfield runways bordered with haybales. Distributor Johnny von Neumann sold cars to Kunstle and other racers and offered technical support.

"I bought that spyder in fifty-five," Jean-Pierre explained. "I was pretty well-known by that time. Richie Ginther and I were going to race one weekend up in Salinas. Rolf Wütherich always took care of our cars.

"Rolf called up and said Johnny von Neumann had just sold one of the five new spyders and that he was going to ride up with the owner Friday afternoon. The fellow had raced a Speedster before, but would Richie and I show the guy how to drive a spyder?

"I said I didn't mind, so long as he could take care of all our cars.

"'Fine, sure,' Wütherich said. 'We'll be arriving late at night. You know the guy. He's an actor. James Dean.'"

CHAPTER THREE

THE NEXT GENERATION

Zuffenhausen 356 Assembly

Hand-built cars were a collaborative effort. Porsche technicians turned out 30 cars a day in 1960 and 1961 over their 253-day production year.

PORSCHE ADVANCED ITS TECHNOLOGY CONSIDERABLY when it introduced the 356A models at Frankfurt in September 1955. Engines grew from 1.5 liters to 1.6, and the company offered two levels of output, the Normal and 1600 Super. These resulted from racing regulations allowing engine displacement increases of 100 cubic centimeters. Solex 32PBIC carburetors fed both the 60-horsepower 1600-series engines and the 44-horsepower 1300 models as well. The 1600 Supers developed 72 horsepower. To improve drivability, engineers increased the mass of the flywheels, and they added a second rubber mount to the nose of the transaxle, which enhanced its durability. A lower floor height and relocated handbrake-and-release made entry and exit easier.

A new instrument panel and a curved windshield, among many other updates, improvements, and evolutionary steps, made the 356A a measurably better car than its predecessors.

To enhance ride and road holding, Helmuth Bott read everything he could find. He had gotten to know Zora Arkus-Duntov. Duntov, a Belgian-born Russian émigré, worked at General Motors in chassis engineering for Maurice Olley, who was GM's chief of research and design. Olley first tried his ideas at Rolls-Royce both in England and then in Springfield,

1960 Typ 356B 1600GS Carrera 90 GT Coupe

Paul Ernst Strähle and Herbert Linge (driving) charged down a mountain pass in their 356B to win the 1960 Tour of Corsica. Porsche produced just 40 of these models, which developed 115 brake horsepower from their Typ 692/3 1,588cc engines.

CHAPTER THREE

Massachusetts, where he developed a series of tests and "exercises" for automobiles to improve their road holding and handling. Working with Olley on Chevrolet's new sports car, the Corvette, Duntov adopted those procedures to performance-oriented vehicles. After Zora wrangled a drive at Le Mans in 1953 in a 1,100cc coupe (entered by Son-Auto in which he and co-driver Gustave Olivier finished 14th overall), Ferry Porsche invited him to Stuttgart to see Porsche's production cars.

"He came to the company for two days," Bott recalled several decades later, "to be with Professor Porsche, with von Hanstein, and so on. I asked him a lot of things, because I wanted to learn. I had this paper from his boss who wrote 'Manners of the Road, Manners of the Modern Car.' That was the most important paper at the time. Then I took his ideas on to the airfield [at Malmsheim]. And I developed ten or fifteen more tests, very simple tests. . . .

"You see, after the war, we had 'dots' in the road so if the driver came too far to the middle or to the edge of the road, the driver would feel *bumpbumpbumpbump*. We had a steering gearbox in our car which was designed for Professor Porsche. It was for a long time the Beetle [steering] box. It was a difficult design because of friction inside. I thought we should have a better steering gearbox. One of the tests was around Stuttgart to drive on these dots. On our [steering] box, you could not get more than five or six *bumpbumpbumps*, then you would be moved off. It couldn't hold against

Porsche introduced the Super 90 line in 1960 and continued production of coupes, cabriolets, hardtop coupes, and hardtop cabriolet models through 1963. The company already had learned the value of good photography that placed its automobiles in luxurious settings.

the vibration. I tried different gearboxes and different systems. With others, you could drive twenty or thirty or forty bumps. It was so simple. It taught us what was wrong and showed us what we needed.

"We did another test to measure what you do on the steering wheel. We could write down in a curve where you could see left and right from the zero point. You have a lot [of play] and you come down to less and less,

1960 356B 1600 Super 90 Coupe

Super tuning the Typ 616/7 engine pushed power output to 90 brake horsepower. Huschke von Hanstein's own coupe suffered a partial covering of spring tree blossoms.

to about three degrees left and right. If you have a good center point with a good gearbox, instead of [turning wildly], it looks like this, [turning tightly]. We did this test on a bumpy road, a good straight with woods on both sides so you have no influence from the wind. A third test [measured] the speed on different diameters at different speeds on the airfield. And braking in the corner, driving around the corners like everybody does today!

"With about ten tests you could get a very good picture of what the car does on the road. You could measure it and write it down. If you can measure, you can do better; if you have ten or fifteen little steps together, then you get an improvement that everybody realizes."

For drivers wanting not only better handling but crisper acceleration and higher speed, Porsche introduced the already legendary Typ 547 racing engine in 1955. Ernst Fuhrmann's dual-overhead camshaft dual-distributor powerplant was conceived as a racing engine with street capabilities; it won its earliest races handily including one that gave it a name that Porsche has used for decades since: Carrera, so named for Porsche's class victory in the 1954 Carrera Panamericana in Mexico.

The Typ 547 was a radical improvement over the engines that came before. To achieve such a performance increase required an equally radical design change from the engines for earlier 356s.

"The problem was that we had an engine that was too slow." Fuhrmann spoke about the engine in 1990, five years before his death. "This was because of the camshafts in their position. The design of the [new] engine improved that situation." In one engine concept, Fuhrmann overturned decades of prior thinking. His ideas set in place precedents that later Porsche engine designers called on for racing and high performance engines.

"Look," he said, "that was the first engine I ever designed. I had no other experience at all! That was the reason that some things were new, because I didn't know what was done before! So, if you go fresh into a situation, I had no teacher, no adviser. I made it myself."

When the Typ 547 engine first ran, Fuhrmann and his fellow engineers encountered few problems. So few, in fact, that nothing required him to change his design.

Racers and wealthy production customers began pestering Porsche to offer the engine in series production cars. Fuhrmann and his bosses resisted, knowing the performance capabilities of the engine demanded careful use and even more careful service and maintenance. But Fuhrmann had one installed in his personal car—to test its reliability, he insisted. Word got out, and customer requests became irresistible.

"Since I was the development engineer of this car and this engine, I had the first engine in my own car. This was a normal [coupe], you know, every test engineer had a car, so it was nothing special looking, not built for beauty or comfort. But of course it was a good car because it had this engine. It was fast!

"There was a fair in Paris and Mr. von Hanstein gave me a telephone call and told me I should send my car. He had to show it to some important customers.

"I simply refused. Not possible. I won't give it away. Then von Hanstein called on Dr. Porsche and complained. Dr. Porsche then called and said that he would like it if I would rethink my refusal. He was very friendly. But he would like me to send the car.

"So it was driven to Paris. One day later von Hanstein called me. The car was completely destroyed by a customer. Dr. Porsche was really fair. He said that in Paris, on the Porsche stand was the first Carrera car. This was the nicest one. It had leather seats, I remember, red leather seats, and gold letters outside, 'Special Carrera.' Everything was special. So Dr. Porsche said, 'Okay, this car now goes to Dr. Fuhrmann.' So I had, even before Dr. Porsche, the finest Carrera in the company!"

Carreras, with Fuhrmann's 1.5-liter four-cam, eight-spark-plug, 100-net-horsepower engines, appeared in Carrera de Luxe, or GS—Grand Sport for road and racing purposes using Solex 40 PII-4 carburetors—and GT configurations. This gave them 110 net horsepower and offered optional Webers. GTs also got the brakes from the racing 550s.

An improvement that every Porsche customer recognized arrived in 1958 with the new body and engine series designated T-2. While the 356 had appeared radically modern when automotive journalists and enthusiasts first saw it in 1949, the T-2 series was a significant evolutionary step. It offered buyers opening front quarter windows and exhaust pipes integrated into rear bumper uprights to accommodate steeper ramps. Cast-iron cylinders replaced the aluminum ones on the 44-horsepower 1600 Normal engines, and their noise dampening made up for their slight additional weight. Hirth crankshafts appeared in the 1600S series, but Porsche took this opportunity to end production of its 1300 series engines. Solex carburetors disappeared as well because Porsche switched to Zenith 32 NDIX models for the 1,582cc 1.6-liter engines. Inside the car, a front-mounted gasoline heater kept driver and passengers warm in winter.

Carreras also got T-2 upgrades and the GT model's fitted aluminum deck lids and doors as well as aluminum bucket seats. Carrera engines also grew to 1.6 liters with output reaching 125 net horsepower.

Helmuth Bott's work on steering came to fruition on the T-2 models. The factory fitted the 16.75-inch-diameter steering wheel from the Carrera models onto all 1600s and coupled it to Bott's more responsive and sensitive ZF unit and a hydraulic steering damper. Further improving handling, cornering, and ride comfort, the T-2s rode on radial-ply tires. The factory offered an optional hardtop not only for the Speedster models but now also for 1600 Normal and Super cabriolets.

Throughout the T-2 line, from 1958 through 1960, customers could order Carrera 1600GS or GT packages on any of Porsche's body styles. Speedsters, cabriolets, and coupes all existed in quick Carrera form. But

1962 356B 1600 D'Ieteren Roadster

In February 1961, Porsche ended Roadster production with Drauz Karosserie at nearby Heilbronn. D'Ieteren Frères, in Brussels, Belgium, automobile body makers since 1900, assumed the task.

Porsche introduced the Roadster in 1960. However, the D'Ieteren 1962 models were the least common, with around 249 produced. Woven floor mats were $7.12 Porsche options some dealers promoted as "floor soundproofing."

the car, many of whose improvements Porsche designers and engineers targeted to a growing and influential American market, was an acquired taste. Its finicky four-cylinder engine was prone to foul its eight spark plugs if driven for long below 2,500 rpm, and its price

1962 356B 1600 Cabriolet

Reutter made Porsche's most common open cars, the cabriolets. The 356B model line introduced higher headlights, part of a series of improvements known as Technical Program 5, or T-5 among enthusiasts, while T-6 models arrived in 1962.

premium—it added at least $1,100 to the cost of the car—consigned it to a diminishing market. Porsche decided to offer only the GT variation with its lightweight race-ready coupe body for 1960. By the end of 1961, they had sold just 40 of these at, according to historian Karl Ludvigsen, $5,551 each.

Those who had loved the T-2 weren't so sure about its replacement, the 356B, shown first at Frankfurt in September 1959. Yes, it was still a 356, with its rounded organic forms readily identifiable from some distance away. But a new nose held a heftier front bumper. Fenders that had arced gently forward to meet low-set headlights now swept horizontally backward from more prominent headlights, still mounted above air-cooling vents and front marker turn signal lenses. Porsche slipped additional cooling grilles in below the bumper to bring air to the front brakes.

CHAPTER THREE

1960 356B 1600 Karmann Hardtop Coupe
The 1960 356B 1600 Karmann hardtop coupe models started life as cabriolets that Porsche transported to Karmann G.m.b.H in Osnabrück. Karmann technicians welded hardtop roofs onto the bodies.

Erwin Komenda's new body, designated the T-5, saw equally significant changes to its rear end, again aiming toward impact safety and damage resistance. Rear-end mechanical changes enabled the body engineers to increase rear headroom, and a new split rear seat allowed a passenger in back to share space with luggage. Drauz Karosserie continued to produce the convertible D body, although in its 356B designation the car was renamed the Roadster.

New larger brake drums of aluminum also brought to production cars the lateral cooling fins of the current Typ 550A and Typ 718 RSK racers rather than the circumferential rings of the 356A models. And a new transaxle, the Typ 741, provided improved synchronizers and easier shifting for Leopold Schmid's four-speed that dated back to tests in 1952.

To excite American buyers, Porsche introduced a new engine, the Typ 616/7, 1600S-90, or Super 90. Unmuffled in racing trim the engine developed a conservative 90 horsepower, but with factory silencing, output was closer to 86. As exciting as its engine was Porsche's introduction of new "air" shock absorbers, manufactured by Koni of the Netherlands. The Super 90s also got a compensating spring, mounted transversely beneath the transaxle. This was Porsche's first effort at more equitably distributing high-speed cornering loads between the rear wheels and the front. Effectively, this reiterated the Olley-Duntov-Bott thinking that installed anti-roll bars on the front.

Softening—slightly—the rear suspension forced the front to work harder.

Porsche's continuing success with the 356 model expanded the line. The T-5 series through 1962 represented the most extensive array ever offered for one chassis line. Reutter produced standard and GT lightweight coupes as well as the cabriolet with its optional removable hardtop. Drauz continued its Roadster (though that ended in late 1962), and the Belgian firm, D'Ieteren Frères in Brussels, produced their own roadsters briefly in 1961. What's more, the Beutler brothers of Thun, Switzerland, who had produced Porsche's first cabriolets, reappeared as custom body makers and turned out a number of two-door four-seat variations of greater and lesser appeal. As if that were not enough,

1962 356B 1600 Karmann Hardtop Coupe

Porsche's T-6 improvements for 1962 squared off the lower lip of the front trunk for easier loading. Karmann hardtops were available with nearly all engine choices: the 60-horsepower 1600 Normal, the 75-horsepower 1600 Super, and the 90-horsepower Super 90.

Porsche manufactured only 699 Karmann hardtop coupes over three years. The cars provoked strong reactions: Some purists disliked the notchback, while others enjoyed the brighter, more spacious interior.

Wilhelm Karmann in Osnabrück produced a number of hardtop coupes through 1961. These resembled the body of the removable hardtop on cabriolet bodies, but these were permanently attached roof structures. Karmann discontinued the model for 1962 but continued manufacturing regular coupes until the 356s ended production in 1965.

Porsche introduced the next generation 356C in 1963, commencing production in July. Body changes had appeared in late 1961, known internally as the T-6, offering larger windows on the coupe bodies and a reconfigured front storage "trunk" that provided more capacity. To help accomplish this, the characteristic rounded lower edge of the front trunk flattened out further down on the body. It eliminated the long-lived "smile" from the front of Porsche's cars. Interior mirrors and variable-speed wipers joined the list of standard equipment as did an anti-theft lock on the gearshift lever.

Months after the T-6 arrived, performance followed with Porsche's introduction of the Carrera 2, a 2-liter variation on a 1,996cc expansion of Ernst Fuhrmann's original 1,498cc four-cam. Racing efforts already had proved this engine reliable, and Porsche eventually sold 436 of these cars,

Manual sunroofs were options with T-5 1960–1961 coupes. Porsche introduced an optional electric sunroof with the T-6 cars in 1962.

For a collector, well-equipped coupes like this 1965 356C are the cars to look for. Interior options on the build card included seat belts, a right-seat headrest, clock, interior and exterior temperature dials, multiband pushbutton radio tuner, and the pushbutton shortwave band receiver below the radio.

126 of them on the final 356C chassis. As the 356B/2000GS, fitted with Solex 40 PII-4 carburetors, the big Carrera engine developed 130 net horsepower.

The only thing lacking from this kind of high performance was equal capability in braking. Porsche had long clung to drum brake technology, developing it to nearly the equal of others' discs. Engineers steadfastly worked to develop a disc that would function with their wheels, the design of which it had inherited from Volkswagen mounting them directly onto the large drums. Ironically, Porsche's development efforts yielded some of the largest disc diameters of any sports car at the time and allowed parking brake shoes to fit inside the 11.8-inch rotors (299mm), using the inner diameter as the brake drum. What's more, according to Ludvigsen, the Porsche system only cost the car two-thirds of a pound more than the original drums, where competing Girling and Lucas systems penalized the car from 8 to 15 pounds (3.6

1965 356C 1600 Coupe (T-6)

With the final-generation 356, Porsche dropped the previous 60-horsepower Normal engine and offered only the 75-horsepower C version and a 95-brake-horsepower SC version.

to 6.8 kilograms) of unsprung weight, which would hurt ride and handling. This system, designated Typ 695, appeared first on the Carrera 2 models.

For Porsche, 1963 marked a pivotal year. Prototypes of the 356 replacement already were on the road testing every system, and the new ones were numerous. The 356 had become a venerable presence in the automobile world. In production without interruption and with regular updates, upgrades, and improvements, for 15 years by then, the 356 had two final bursts to deliver, the 356C and the SC. Still

1965 356SC 1600 Cabriolet

After 17 years of production, Porsche had greatly civilized its final 356 model, the SC. Four-wheel disc brakes, manufactured by ATE, were standard, as was the 95-horsepower Typ 616/16 engine with twin Solex carburetors.

Recaro seats became a key element in Porsche's driver comfort. In March 1964, Porsche acquired Reutter Carosserie, its neighboring coach builder. The firm retained seat production under a newly formed company whose name came from the first letters of each word, Re and Caro.

a T-6, the C model provided changes mostly in its engine and its brakes. Reutter, fully involved in development and premanufacture work on the next generation car, yielded 356 production to Karmann.

Suspensions continued to evolve. Anti-sway bars at the front grew by 1mm while rear torsion bars shrunk by 1mm. The combination added back a bit of oversteer while improving ride quality.

As frequently was the case with Porsche—and it would remain so for the following half century—"cosmetic" changes often masked significant internal or engineering improvements. To the naked eye, customers saw new wheels and handsome hubcaps. Removing them, they saw four-wheel disc brakes, now manufactured by Alfred Teves, under the ATE brand.

The 60-horsepower Normal engine range disappeared as Porsche concentrated on last

CHAPTER THREE

Geneva, Switzerland, Auto Show 1964
While Porsche introduced its last-generation 356 on its stand, it also tantalized visitors with a prototype 904 racer and a 901 coupe. This 901, painted Quick Blue, became engineer Ferdinand Piëch's personal transportation until regular 911 production began.

improvements to its solid fours and development of its new six. The 1600S, also called the Super 75 in 356B models, now was the 1600C. The Super 90 became the 1600SC. Fuel supply remained the same, with C models using Zenith 32 NDIX carburetors and the SC holding on to the 40 PII-4 models. Porsche's newest engine meister, Hans Mezger, fresh from an ill-fated Formula One effort with complicated 1.5-liter flat-eights, took over management of the 1600C and SC engines. He fitted counterweights to the SC crankshaft, which improved drivability even at 5,800 rpm, the peak for a pushrod flat-four. Mezger achieved 97 net horsepower with the SC engine and 75 from the C motor. The SC's aluminum cylinders, carried over from the Super 90 engines, went away in 1964 when Mezger developed "Biral," in which a finned aluminum cylinder wall was cast in place around a cast-iron sleeve, allowing a very efficient transfer of heat away from the pistons.

Porsche produced its last 356, a C cabriolet, in September 1965. The company continued to sell SC models in the United States through the end of the year, having manufactured 77,766 of the 356s over its life, including a final ten produced for the Royal Dutch Police in May 1966.

Its loyalists numbered at least twice that many, and over the ensuing decades, thousands of additional owners have succumbed to the charms and challenges of Porsche's first road car. But if they had liked—or even loved—the first car, what would they think of its replacement? ∎

CHAPTER FOUR

RACING IMPROVES THE BREED *MORE*

1962 Typ 356B 1600GTL Abarth Carrera Zagato

Porsche records indicate that Carlo Abarth assembled just 21 of these coupes, meant for the FIA Gran Turismo category. Scale is deceiving: the car stands just 52 inches (1320mm) tall and measures just 157 inches (3988mm) long.

From his first version of the 356, the prototype roadster in 1948, Erwin Komenda continually modified the body. These efforts reflected the company's earliest recognition that a car's frontal area affected aerodynamic drag and related to the car's top speed. Komenda's T-2 body represented an advance. But its taller nose and headlights slowed the car slightly in high-speed racing conditions. When the Fédération Internationale de l'Automobile (FIA) set a weight minimum of 1,708 pounds (776.5 kilograms) for the 2-liter category, Porsche recognized that if it hoped to remain competitive, it needed a new car.

The factory went outside for design and construction of its 1960 GT class contender. Von Hanstein queried Wendler Karosserie in Reutlingen about their interest and their ideas. Wendler had done the 550 Spyder bodies and still produced the aluminum RS61 coupes at that time.

Porsche also looked across the border to Carlo Abarth. Von Hanstein and others in the company knew the bodies that Ugo Zagato's design and fabrication firm just outside Milan had done for Abarth, Alfa Romeo, and Lancia, all competitors in racing and sales.

Zagato was interested. His bid was lowest. He put his young stylist Franco Scaglione to work on a new racing coupe based on the 356B.

Scaglione's design trimmed the frontal area 16 percent by shrinking each exterior dimension of Komenda's stock T-2 body by about 4.92 inches (125mm). Porsche shipped bare floorpans to Milan, and Zagato's craftsmen started in early 1960. The bodies, of heavy-gauge aluminum hand hammered over wooden body bucks, were mostly similar. But of course, these were race cars, so each was slightly different.

In Germany, whether at club races or international points events, it seemed the most certain way to win was to drive a Porsche. At least one of the Ferraris wore Modena plates, the home of Ferrari, but did the E-Type Jaguar convertible get lost trying to find the autobahn to Koblenz and Aachen?

CHAPTER FOUR

Porsche was pleased with the car's performance, but less so with Carlo Abarth's performance in finishing the cars. Zuffenhausen mechanics had much work to do plugging leaks from rain and puddles and modifying the interior to fit tall German drivers.

Zagato assembled 21 cars. Cramped interiors, spartan even by contemporary GT standards, were barely large enough for some of Porsche's intended drivers. When the first completed cars reached Stuttgart for detailing, mechanics had to lower seat rails and enlarge front wheelwells. As writer/photographer Jesse Alexander reported in *Sports Cars Illustrated* in late 1960, "The interior had obviously been designed for an Italian as no one at Porsche could sit in it." Zuffenhausen's body engineers fitted standard factory instruments including a 10,000 rpm chronometric tachometer.

Scaglione's efforts had pared 90 pounds (41 kilograms) off lightened Reutter-bodied B-GT models and took nearly three times that off production coupes. He also produced one of Porsche's most sensuous car bodies. His lines covered the headlights under Plexiglas (in most but not all of the cars), extruded the driver's outside mirror from the fender like a piece of molded clay, and flipped air up over the windshield wipers with subtle lips. For reasons attributable only to racing politics or egos, the cars initially wore no Zagato badges, only those of Carlo Abarth's works. Abarth had done only final assembly; his shop, like that of the Beutlers, was too small to accommodate a "series" production of even 21 race cars.

The first Abarth Carrera reached the factory, and racing mechanics prepared it for the 1960 1000-kilometer race at Nürburgring. Abarth had cut five louvers

Porsche fitted its Typ 692/3A engines into the Abarths using either Solex or Weber carburetors. With total displacement of 1,587cc, these twin-cam engines developed 135 brake horsepower and drove their dual distributors off the crankshaft.

Paul Ernst Strähle was one of motor racing's foremost practitioners with the Abarth Carreras. He bought three over a three-year period and painted the noses orange so civilians in small towns and competitors ahead could see him coming.

CHAPTER FOUR

down low on each side of the rounded rear deck lid. Engine cooling problems developed quickly. The car eventually had 43 slots for cooling. An air box operated from inside the car fed the large Weber carburetors cool outside air.

While Zuffenhausen prepared number 1001 for late May in the Nürburgring, local racer Paul Ernst Strähle picked up the second car, number 1002, and took it straight to the Targa Florio. He raced with another familiar talent, Herbert Linge.

"We did one practice session in the Carrera," Strähle recalled in a conversation in the early 1990s. "But we had a very curious problem. The people in traffic didn't see the silver cars. We came around a corner in Cerda in practice. The people

1962 Typ 356B 2000 GS/GT (Also known as the Carrera 2)

Jo Bonnier and Carlo Mario Abate were on their way to overall victory in the 1962 Targa Florio, but not before a two-lap-long downpour humbled their Ferrari challengers. Porsche originally planned to assemble one hundred of these coupes designed by Gerhard Schröder and Butzi Porsche. The nickname *Dreikantschaber,* or three-edge scraper, referred to the radical shapes.

heard the car but just didn't see it. If you had a yellow car, a red car . . . , okay. So we made the front orange and that became the sign of Carrera Sixteen."

Strähle's orange-nosed number 16 was a significant contributor to Porsche racing history. It went straight from Zuffenhausen to Sicily and finished sixth overall, first in class. A month later, he took tenth overall, first in class at Nürburgring. In 1961 with the new Typ 692/3 2-liter Carrera engine and disc brakes at the Targa, he came in sixth overall and first in class again. In 1962, he replaced his original number 1002 with a new car, number 1016, and his ongoing successes earned him a factory drive in 1963 at the Targa in number 1018.

Porsche engineers learned many things from the Abarth Carrera. Even if Porsche could have enforced tighter control over outside assembly, Ferry chose to work closer to home for future projects. Still, a smaller car body with a more slippery shape went faster. Abarth Carreras at Le Mans saw 137 miles per hour (220 kilometers per hour) through timing traps. And as a name, Carrera, originally designated Ernst Fuhrmann's four-cam Typ 547 engine, had come to mean more. Its use had only begun at Porsche.

Von Hanstein sent two Abarth Carreras to Daytona and Sebring in early 1963 to begin the international endurance season. But to him and the factory these already were old cars, and they had new ones back in the Zuffenhausen works. These new racers drifted further away from the production 356 shape and put distance on the Abarths as well. Another young designer took inspiration from the earlier RS60 and RS61 racers and from a different project on which he had been working.

Ferdinand Alexander Porsche III, Ferry's son whose family nickname was "Butzi," had joined the family company in 1957 after brief training at the new cutting-edge design school at Ulm, 90 miles southwest of Stuttgart. But Butzi, who preferred modeling to drawing and was much better at shaping forms than sketching them, left before his first school year ended. His father sent him immediately to work for overall design chief Karl Rabe. Rabe moved him along to Franz Xaver Reimspiess, head of engine design, who assigned him the task of learning the 356 Carrera engine.

"I had the assignment," Butzi Porsche recalled in an interview in 1991, "to memorize every piece of the engine parts list, all the screws, the cylinder heads, the cylinders themselves, crankshaft, camshafts. Then I had to draw the engine

Butzi Porsche always maintained that the nearly horizontal seam through the 904 represented the functional point at which steel changed to fiberglass. He also maintained that he was not good at drawing, but this design became an icon that others mimicked and pirated for another generation.

1964 Typ 904 Carrera GTS

If the 718 *Dreikantschabers* were prototypes, these 904s were Butzi Porsche's working models. Often described as one of racing history's most beautiful automobiles, they also were one of its most successful.

in profile. . . . I 'constructed' the engine by way of the parts list drawings." After nine months with Reimspiess, Butzi moved along to the car body division, working for Erwin Komenda.

"Mr. Komenda was very strict. He naturally had formal views about steering wheels, about everything. He would say to me, 'No, no, it's not done like that. That's not the way to do it.'" Despite Komenda's rigidity, Butzi's

apprenticeship with the older man clarified his goals: "I was already sure what I was going to do one day. It was definitely to work with the car body in relation to the engine, and in connection with that, the design."

Komenda gave Butzi racing car assignments, starting first with a new Formula One body for the Typ 804 to debut in 1962. Working with Wilhelm Hild (who had been with Porsche as a racing engineer since 1951) and Hubert Mimler (a racing mechanic for nearly as long) in the competition department, Butzi created a relatively simple cigar shape in hammered aluminum. He watched Mimler and others lay up seats in fiberglass for the factory drivers and customer racers. Butzi's 804 met Porsche's fabrication deadlines and cost parameters. As a result of the success the department had with the fiberglass seats, they decided to do an entire car in fiberglass. This next-generation endurance racer was designated the Typ 904.

The 904 had to meet specific FIA rules concerning wheelbase, wheel track, length, width, and interior. The body had to accommodate a "suitcase" of prescribed dimensions.

"The most important parameter for us with this car was aerodynamics," Butzi explained. "But the most exciting feature of the Nine-Oh-Four was really that it took only four months from making the plasticine [a kind of car modeler's clay] model to completion of the one-to-one car model that was ready to drive.

"That's the reason the car body remained unchanged, because we were told, 'Nothing can be changed. There is a deadline by which this car must be completed.' Hans Tomala [the engineer who took over Porsche's

From every angle the 1964 Typ 904 Carrera GTS was visually striking. That it also won race after race from its debut onward was testimony to Gerhard Schröder's ladder-frame chassis, Hans Tomala's concept to sheath the car in fiberglass, and the latest versions of Ernst Fuhrmann's Carrera flat-four engine.

technical directorship while both 804 and 904 projects were underway] wanted to lengthen the car body. The aerodynamics would have been slightly better that way. But there simply was no time."

There was no time because, while Porsche hurried to get its Formula One effort working, and planned ahead for 1964's FIA regulations, there still was an endurance season to run for 1963. And that car would be the 356B 2000GS Carrera 2, a project that Butzi hurtled through the design process.

Prototype RS61 models had run as coupes in the 1961 Le Mans race. These doors, like those on the 904 still hidden away in Wilhelm Hild's racing shops, wrapped up into the roof. A truncated roofline trailed back and abruptly descended to the body over the rear tires. Aerodynamic experiments with Typ 550 and 550A coupes with faired in "fastbacks" proved less beneficial in fact than in imaginations. The chopped roof, already in development with the 904 and in wind tunnel tests at Stuttgart University, caused less rear lift. By 1962, versions of these cars ran the Targa Florio with 2-liter flat-eight-cylinder engines developing 210 horsepower.

Butzi applied his new 904 nose to this interim racer. He lengthened the roofline, providing better rear and side visibility by adding side windows. He moved the "back light," or rear glass, to the back of the structure, making it more coupe-like. That was a goal. The FIA had accepted the Abarth Carreras as an "optional body." There were 21 of them, and customers could, if they had $6,000, roughly 25,000DM at the time, order and take delivery of one. These new 2-liter racing coupes were strictly factory entries, and yet, by not giving it a new name, von Hanstein hoped FIA inspectors would accept it as another Carrera 2 coupe. But "just another Carrera 2 coupe," was as cumbersome a reference as its official 356B 2000GS Carrera 2. As often happened with Hubert Mimler and his colleagues, the distinctively shaped car quickly got a nickname, *die Dreikantschaber*, or "three edge scraper," because it resembled an ice scraper. FIA rules ultimately allowed different bodies but no changes to engine or suspension, so the "DKS" ran Ernst Fuhrmann's 1,996cc variation with four overhead cams that developed 155 horsepower. The engine and slippery car body could reach 146 miles per hour (235 kilometers per hour).

Hild, Mimler, and Butzi completed the first one for the Targa Florio in May

Dreikantschaber

Schröder and Porsche began to develop ideas in these racers that led to the 904, including tall doors that opened into the roof. The bulky door sill replaced an X-type reinforcement that blocked the doors, making driver changes slower.

While engineers labored long and hard over a 1.5-liter flat-eight-cylinder Grand Prix engine, they succeeded quickly with this 2.0-liter Typ 771. Displacing 1,982cc and using four 42mm twin-throat Weber carburetors, the engines developed 210 brake horsepower for the Targa in the DKS.

1963. Edgar Barth and Herbert Linge finished third overall and first in class, followed by a fourth-place-overall/first-in-class performance at the 1000-kilometer Nürburgring. Porsche entered two cars running the flat-eights at Le Mans and referred to them as the "Le Mans Coupé." But they failed to finish. Porsche's 2000GS Carrera 2s campaigned for another year, serving as running mates to the company's newest competitor, the 904, which first ran in the Targa in 1964.

This was a time of feverish excitement and anxiety for Ferry Porsche. His son and his engineers had designed and were testing a risky and expensive 356 replacement model designated the 901. Porsche was racing internationally in endurance and rally events and supporting hundreds of privateers around the world. All this cost money. Yet so long as customers bought road or racing cars from the company, its efforts in those series made sense. There was one series, however, where Porsche understood that precious few privateers could afford to compete. Winning here was more about publicity and image than selling similar cars to faithful fans.

Ferdinand Porsche had anchored his reputation for brilliant engineering with his 16-cylinder Auto Union Grand Prix cars from 1934 through 1937. The cars defined performance for the era and bestowed as much prestige on Auto Union as they did on the designer. The long view of history makes it fair to question if Ferry's entry into Formula One in 1962 meant to reclaim a historical significance that eluded the racing operations up till then. Contemporary journalists illuminated the other side of that historical burden. Harry Mundy, technical editor of England's *The Motor*, summed it up concisely:

"Many people, especially those from Germany, expected this small firm to take over the mantle of Daimler-Benz and sweep [away] all before them as the sole German firm participating in modern racing."

Whatever the motivation, Porsche's Formula One efforts were frustrating and painful. It began in the winter of 1958–1959 with Wilhelm Hild enlisting skill and knowledge from Helmuth Bott and the other recent arrival, Hans Mezger. Knowing that the FIA regulations for Formula One would require 1.5-liter engines starting with the 1961 racing season, Mezger shrewdly started his work with Ernst Fuhrmann's Carrera four-cam. With costs of developing the 356 replacement escalating and the need to build additional manufacturing facilities for the new series car looming, Ferry Porsche began the 1961 season using the 1960 Formula Two cars, the 718/2 versions, knowing that Cooper and Lotus were doing the same.

Huschke von Hanstein and Helmuth Bott sent Herbert Linge out to test the 804 at Malmsheim airport. The car handled well, although the engine developed only 195 of the 210 horsepower they needed to beat the competition (but still enough for Linge to slide it).

This decision bought Mezger time to improve the complicated 1,494cc flat-eight-cylinder Typ 753 engine he had developed. He elaborated on Fuhrmann's dual-overhead cam and valve configurations. Neither engineer relied on gears or chains to drive overhead cams but instead used perpendicular shafts linked by bevel gears to operate one another. Fuhrmann used one such configuration for both intake and exhaust cams and valves. Mezger chose to duplicate systems, one for intake cams and valves, and the other to handle exhaust. He incorporated still another vertical shaft to drive the horizontally mounted cooling fan.

Its first tests inspired no one. On dynamometer runs in December 1960, it produced only 120 horsepower. By spring, Mezger and colleague Hans Hönick routinely saw 160 horsepower. It was a big improvement, but they wanted 180 for their first race. They believed they would need 210–220 horsepower to win the championship.

Overall success eluded them. However, Dan Gurney won both the Grand Prix of France at Rouen and the Formula One race at Solitude in Stuttgart before a home crowd of 350,000. His victory parade lap was pure pandemonium.

"It was a very special moment," he explained almost 30 years later, "something I'll never forget. When they took me around that [victory] lap in the convertible, at least one hundred thousand of them were throwing their hats in the air when we went by."

Typical of the time, drivers Dan Gurney and Jo Bonnier sat cradled between fuel tanks on the 1,001-pound (455-kilogram) car. The complicated 1.5-liter Typ 753 flat-eight-cylinder never achieved the power the drivers needed nor that designer Hans Mezger believed it could.

CHAPTER FOUR

Dan Gurney recalled his first impression of the car: "I couldn't fit in it. I looked like a giraffe driving around in the thing." Here was Gurney on the way to his first victory at the French Grand Prix at Rouen.

1962 Typ 804 Formula One

For Porsche and driver Dan Gurney, the high point of a frustrating year came at Solitude circuit on the east side of Stuttgart. Gurney raced his car past these pit boxes and the control tower at left to win before a hometown crowd of 350,000.

For Ferry Porsche, two victories were too little, too late, and far too costly. He needed his resources for the new car, new building, new staff, and new racing season with cars he knew would win more than twice.

One of those was the 904 Carrera GTS, the latest of the successful designs from his son Butzi. Technical director Hans Tomala conceived the car for the FIA's 2.0-liter Group 3 Grand Touring category.

These were the last of the cars from the era when racers drove their cars to the tracks, raced them, and then drove the cars back home. Porsche engineers gave the car a heater and an adjustable steering wheel. Regulations called for a passenger seat and luggage compartment, but both spaces were cramped. GT rules also required the manufacturer to produce one hundred identical models, and from the start Ferry

Porsche planned to sell 90 of them to his customer racers. The factory price was set at 29,700DM, about $7,425 at the time.

Constrained by time and budget, Porsche's body engineer Gerhard Schröder stepped away from a traditional space frame and adopted a quick and simple steel ladder arrangement. Tomala specified glass-reinforced plastic for the body. He had specified fiberglass for some body panels on the F1 Typ 804 late in the

1962 season and for doors and lids on the 718 W-RS *Grossmütter* Spyder at the same time. Heinkel-Flugzeugwerke, an aircraft manufacturer near Hockenheim, assembled the 904's resin bodies made of 50 separate pieces. Heinkel finished two a day while Porsche assembled one frame each day. Technicians in Zuffenhausen bonded the fiberglass body to the steel chassis. This yielded a race car much stiffer than Porsche's space-frame cars had been. Schröder carried over brake and wheel assemblies from the production T-6 356C. He used the 15-inch-diameter 5-inch-wide wheels and even adopted the rear parking brake system inside the 11.2-inch (284mm) diameter rear rotors. He placed the 2-liter Typ 587/3 Carrera engine ahead of the transaxle. The factory quoted 180 net horsepower and ran it through a new five-speed gearbox. Porsche listed weight at 1,540 pounds (700 kilograms). Fiberglass supplier BASF in nearby Ludwigshafen had trouble initially controlling wall thickness, and early cars came in heavy, some racers weighing more than 1,710 pounds (775 kilograms) in a class where the legal minimum was 1,260 pounds (618 kilograms). Weights dropped and wall-thicknesses became consistent as technicians grew accustomed to working with the material.

The factory introduced the 904s at the Daytona Continental in 1964, alongside the soon-to-be discontinued *Dreikantschabers*. Each car ran the 2-liter four-cylinder engines in competitions through the Targa

After debuting with a class win at Sebring and then first and second overall at the Targa Florio in 1964, the 904 remained indomitable through the season. For spectators, watching the 904 race was most enjoyable over portions of the Nürburgring where flight was assured.

1963 Typ 718 W-RS *Grossmutter*

Wendler Karosserie built just three of these 718 RS models (hence the W-RS designation) and only this one spyder for 1961. Porsche cycled it through flat-four- and then flat-eight-cylinder engines, campaigning the car for four years, prompting the mechanics to nickname it "Grandmother."

At age 28, Butzi Porsche already was the company's chief of styling, though he still had to contend with Erwin Komenda's body-engineering philosophies. Doors opened high into the roof to ease racer's access, but the doors opened below the doorsill despite its high inner structure to satisfy Komenda's conventions.

1965 Typ 904/8 Bergspyder *Kanguruh*
Jo Bonnier disliked the handling of the 1965 Typ 904/8 Bergspyder *Kanguruh* so much he handed it off to Gerhard Mitter and Colin Davis who, running with the Typ 771 flat-eight engine, fought it around Sicily during the Targa Florio and finished second. Here, Mitter started the Rossfeld hillclimb, which he won outright in June 1965.

Florio early that summer. After that, the factory, which had been developing a racing version of the flat-six for the Typ 901-356 replacement, began installing them in von Hanstein's factory entry 904s. Ferry was adamant that none of the initial 90 customer cars would be available with these engines.

The first customer cars went to the United States, two of them destined for the Daytona Challenge Cup on February 15, 1964, where they finished third and fifth. Fifth-place finisher Chuck Cassell teamed with Augie Pabst the next day for the Daytona Continental, a 1,250-mile (2,000-kilometer) endurance event.

They finished fifth but took first in the prototype class. Five 904s started the Sebring 12 Hours on March 21. Briggs Cunningham and Lake Underwood finished ninth overall and won the under-3-liter prototype class.

Then on April 26, Porsche scored its biggest win yet when the new 904s took

The Typ 904/8 Bergspyder has been called the ugliest Porsche, and it certainly was a dramatic change from the full-bodied 904GTS models. Without driver but including fuel, the 130-inch-long (3,300mm) car weighed 1,245 pounds (566 kilograms), and with 240 brake horsepower on hand, it was a handful to drive.

1965 Typ 904/6 Carrera GTS6

"We were told," Butzi Porsche recalled, "nothing can be changed. This car was four months, working days and nights, from the first Plasticine model to completion of the driving prototype."

first and second at the Targa Florio and beat more-powerful Ferraris and Cobras. That same day Porsche got confirmation of its potential. Tomala and Gerhard Schröder had fitted one of the Typ 771 flat-eights from the *Dreikantschabers* and the *Grossmütter* into the engine bay of Butzi's 904. It was an easy installation. The 904/8 lead the first half of the race until the rear suspension failed from Sicily's unforgiving roads and the eight-cylinder's high torque.

The next iteration of the 904, running the flat-eight, debuted at a 1000-kilometer race at Monthléry on October 11, 1964, and finished third. For 1965, Porsche developed still another car using a race-prepared version of the Typ 901 flat-six. This combination was Hans Tomala's vision of the car from the moment Ferry Porsche

Hans Tomala conceived the Typ 904/6 Carrera GTS6 to use Porsche's new Typ 901 flat-six engine. But after manufacturing something like 110 cars plus prototypes using four- or eight-cylinder engines, mechanics assembled another six cars that used the 901/20 racing version of the engine.

approved the project. This 1,991cc engine was another Hans Mezger project. Several 904/8 and 904/6 factory cars competed through 1965, including the Targa Florio, in which the prototype 906-001 finished third, Nürburgring where it came fifth, and in the 24 Hours of Le Mans where the same car finished fourth overall. It won the Index of Performance for most efficient running and took first in the under-2-liter prototype category.

Students of the 904 tend to agree that Porsche manufactured about 120 of these cars, including those with the different serial number. This was not a typographical error but a new designation. The racing department produced about a dozen of the six-cylinder models. Racing engineer Ferdinand Piëch, Butzi Porsche's cousin, referred to it as the GTS6 in at least one memo outlining updates and improvements for the 1965 version. Some documents suggest Porsche considered producing and selling as many as 100 customer versions of the GTS6. Instead, they continued the 906 serial number series with an entirely new car. ■

CHAPTER FIVE

THE NEW BREED

1964–1972

1964 901 Geneva Auto Show

Initiated in the late 1950s, the 901 car was Ferry Porsche's big gamble. His company needed a replacement for the 356, and after a sizable investment in time and money (including acquiring Reutter body works next door), Porsche launched this car at Frankfurt in October 1963 and at Geneva in March 1964.

PORSCHE'S FIRST DECADE MANUFACTURING AND RACING ITS OWN CARS HAD PUT IT ON SOLID FINANCIAL FOOTING. Creating a new model, while always risky, seemed to Ferry Porsche and the family as a fair gamble to undertake. The Gmünd coupes had provided customers with an intimately proportioned automobile that fit within the reticent nature of postwar Germany. Over the decade Erwin Komenda's body design evolved and Franz Xaver Reimspiess' engines and Leopold Schmid's chassis gave buyers increasing power and pleasure in driving.

Customers, however, had begun to communicate with the factory. They asked for more luggage capacity, larger rear seats, less noise inside the car, and more power. The B-series had addressed these issues.

But everyone inside the company recognized they needed to go much further. Sales watched 356 production quantities rise and fall, and Wolfgang Raether, Porsche's sales chief, told Ferry he feared the worldwide market for expensive two-seat sports cars might be reaching saturation.

In Werke I, Wilhelm Hild, Leopold Schmid, and Karl Rabe had installed a Mercedes-Benz-derived front suspension on a customer's badly damaged 356. This became a rolling test bed. In Rabe's and Komenda's design department Butzi had completed his first scale model designated the Typ 754 T-7. He based his concept on a 94.5-inch (2400mm) wheelbase that Komenda used on a four-seat prototype known as the Typ 530. But Ferry hoped to maintain a sporty nature for the car. He shortened the wheelbase by roughly 7.9 inches (200mm) to 86.6 inches (2200mm). Butzi told his father that a full four-seater would require a longer flatter roofline. Still favoring the fastback shape, Ferry agreed that rear seats in the new car would be used only occasionally. The roofline would remain more sporting.

Preproduction 901s had not yet received the rocker-panel rubber strip. This prototype also showed an early dual exhaust configuration.

CHAPTER FIVE

1964 901 Coupe

Ferry Porsche had told his staff, "Interior room should be greater and trunk room as well," when he described the proportions of the car to replace the 356. While his son Butzi designed this car, Erwin Komenda supervised the body engineering.

Ferry based this decision on Germany's car history and a hierarchy that acknowledged that some companies produced economy and compact cars, others manufactured family cars, still others assembled luxury models, and his own company did the two-seat sports cars. A year later, in 1960 the prototype Typ 644 T-8 took shape as a pure two-seat model on an 82.7-inch (2100mm) wheelbase. Its complicated front suspension left too little room for a fuel tank, so that ended up in the rear. In October 1961, Ferry set production start for the two-seater for July 1963. This target quickly became unrealistic as he understood how many problems and considerations would not be resolved in time.

Working for Leopold Schmid, chassis engineer Helmuth Bott's efforts with Porsche's new MacPherson strut front suspension concept were more space efficient than what they originally had planned to carry over from the 356. This additional space allowed a safer, larger fuel tank up front as well as more storage capacity. Ferry returned the car to a 2200mm wheelbase. Now it was a 2+2 seater in its final form. Aerodynamicist Josef Mickl worked with Butzi on the front end to fair-in the bumper, smooth shapes, and finish the elegant sweep of the roof angle. Tests in Stuttgart University's wind tunnel with Butzi's latest version as a 1-to-7.5 scale model were encouraging.

"I just think," Butzi Porsche said in an interview 30 years after he designed the car, "that you start creating edges when the body of the car is bad. This is true, too, for protective stripes, or styling stripes.

83

1964–1972

They are lines that support something that ties the designer down." For his inspiration he attended motor shows in Frankfurt, Geneva, Turin, and Paris. "When you go to automobile shows," he continued, "you subconsciously do things that you had seen there." He explained that his inspiration for the 901's inset rear window came from Pinin Farina's prototype for the Lancia Flavia 2+2 that he saw at a show in 1957. Butzi conceived it as an opening hatchback.

Inside Porsche, the transfer of design influence from Professor Porsche's trusted colleague Erwin Komenda to Butzi was not always smooth. Ferry eventually learned that in the process of advancing his son's work, Komenda changed lines and overruled concepts. As a body engineer, Komenda was not exactly a stylist. Yet Butzi had the advantage of being the son of the man who made the decisions, whose name was on the buildings and on the cars.

"People would pay more attention to what I said," Butzi said, "due to the fact that I was the son and had a direct line to the boss. I would be able to work out a proposition, put it in front of him, and say, 'See! That's it!'"

Ferry finally took the proposition around Komenda to his neighbor, Reutter Karrosserie. Walter Beierbach, Reutter's managing director, assigned his own design department to complete the engineering drawings for Butzi's designs. Komenda eventually accepted the new hierarchy, but he conspired with Beierbach to dissuade

Houndstooth upholstery defined the classic interior of the 901. Writer Bernard Cahier tested one of the cars and described the interior unflatteringly as "rather sad looking, Teutonic."

Ferry from adopting Butzi's opening hatchback rear window. This caused Butzi to redesign the coupe's B-pillar, angling it rearward from the door frame for easier rear passenger and luggage access.

An unwanted expense arose to complicate Ferry's planning. The Reutter family, having collaborated with Porsche production since 1951, balked at the size of investment they calculated to manufacture the 901. Beierbach recommended they sell the business. Porsche was the logical buyer. However, to Ferry this was a huge expense that changed nothing for Porsche other than who paid one thousand employees and taxes. Porsche went ahead and acquired its neighbor, adding substantially to its own estimated start-up costs.

The Typ 901 engine displaced 1,991cc, based on bore and stroke of 80mm and 60mm. The flat six-cylinder configuration developed 130 brake horsepower with fuel fed through two triple-throat Solex overflow carburetors.

Between late June and Christmas 1963, Butzi designed a full line of models. This included a sunroof coupe, a model with a removable roof panel, and a full cabriolet. Packaging problems put the cabrio on hold even as Butzi finished it, however. His side views did not allow enough space for the new 2-liter six-cylinder engine. But with 15 million DM committed (about $3.75 million), the additional work this change required was a luxury the company could not manage.

The new car offered advances in every area. Not only was Hans Mezger's 2-liter engine a significant step forward in smooth power and reliability, but Ferry and Hans Tomala recognized that Helmuth Bott's new MacPherson strut front suspension was as important to the company as the engine and Butzi's lean car body. Helmut Rombold, Porsche's chief of testing, and Bott introduced rack-and-pinion steering for testing. This fulfilled Ferry's desire to deliver right-hand steering for customers in the United Kingdom and provide a collapsible steering column for front-crash safety. Porsche had committed to show the car at the 1963 International Automobile Association Frankfurt Show, opening September 12, 1963.

Ferry Porsche's goal for the car was 130 net horsepower, the same as he had with the 2-liter Typ 587/1 Carrera 2 twin-cam model. But he wanted this performance capability without the Carrera's complex engine or its noise. Reimspiess test-mounted Kugelfischer fuel injection onto the reliable old Typ 616 four-cylinder pushrod engine. But this failed to meet Ferry's performance and noise targets. Franz's next engine was the 1,991cc flat-six Typ 745. But its overhead cams and side-draft carburetors made the engine too bulky, and with 120 horsepower, it still fell below Ferry's horsepower target.

Reimspiess enlarged bore to 84mm from 80mm while holding stroke at 66mm. This created a 2,195cc engine. It developed 130 net horsepower at 6500 rpm. But it was nearly as complicated as the Typ 753 flat-eight Formula One engine, whose valve gear Hans Mezger had developed. Mezger had established Porsche's computer program to design camshafts. After working on the

1965 911 2.0

Porsche used sheet steel for its unitized body structure. While Butzi Porsche originally designed a coupe, a cabriolet, and other body configurations, only the coupe appeared at first without even an optional sunroof.

intricate Typ 753, it was a much easier task to create the intake system and valve gear for a 2-liter production car engine.

Mezger's first attempt, the Typ 821, used dual overhead camshafts and a wet sump lubrication system. So-called air-cooled engines are really oil-cooled, but sump requirements for this car were too large. The engine stood too tall for Butzi's body. Mezger's next engine, the Typ 901, used a dry sump. Body and chassis engineers agreed they could lower the engine in the car closer to the ground. This would improve balance and road holding as well. It made Butzi's roofline a sure thing. Ferdinand Piëch, Butzi's cousin, supervised 901 engine development and got it production-ready in time for late 1963 testing and the 1964 manufacturing start-up. With one three-choke Solex carburetor for each cylinder bank, the engine developed 130 DIN net (also called brake) horsepower at

CHAPTER FIVE

6100 rpm. In the United States, the Society of Automotive Engineers (SAE) measured gross horsepower, and using their SAE standard, the engine developed 148 horsepower.

Two final decisions set the character of the car: Ferry authorized a new five-speed transmission and the latest rear suspension for production. This system reoriented the trailing arms and the transverse torsion bars, but Bott's new configuration used open half-shafts connected to two universal joints per side, one at each end, from the transaxle instead of an axle tube as the primary means to contain rear-wheel movement. While it cost more, it was necessary. The 901, at 405 pounds (184 kilograms) was the heaviest car engine Porsche ever had produced. Nobody was sure how customers of average driving skill would do with so much weight so far back.

When the Frankfurt show closed, Porsche had booked sales, even though everyone in the company made it clear that delivery was months away. Journalists loved its looks and specifications, as well, even if they had to wait till year's end to get hands on one for a test.

Meanwhile, Porsche prepared for its one show car (a yellow Karmann-produced coupe for Frankfurt) for the next display at the Paris Salon in October. There it caught the attention not only of enthusiastic French drivers, but also of Automobiles Peugeot, who disputed model nomenclature with Porsche despite the vast differences between their products. In 1921, Peugeot had introduced a Model 201.

The shape that Erwin Komenda first gave the 356s with broad shoulders—that is, a wider body over the wheel housing and mechanical features and a narrow cockpit above—carried over into Butzi Porsche's 911. The 130-brake-horsepower cars could reach 130 miles per hour (210 kilometers per hour).

The company registered with the French government's office of copyrights and patents to use three-digit model designations using a zero in the middle. The 201 was the second chassis series with a 1.1-liter engine. By 1963, Peugeot's numbers had passed through 301s, 401s, and 601s to 203s, 403s, and 404s. After Paris closed, Peugeot notified Porsche it could not use the 901 designation in France.

France was a large market for Porsche. Ferry chose not to antagonize the other carmaker. He didn't remind anyone that 904 GTS Carreras already had raced in France and his 804 Formula One car had won at Rouen Circuit without comment from Peugeot. Porsche renumbered the new car as the 911. Parts numbers and internal designations at the factory and in design and engineering shops remained 901 because Porsche and Volkswagen had jointly developed a part-numbering system with that prefix available.

After a brief wait, Huschke von Hanstein appealed to the FIA. He explained that

Porsche's racing models, rarely available to traditional customers, should be able to retain the 804- and 904-middle-zero designations. The FIA agreed. Von Hanstein then announced the 904 successor known as the 906 Carrera 6. Peugeot said nothing.

Reutter, Karmann, and Weinsberg body works hurried to get production up to Porsche's goal. With demand higher than Porsche hoped, Karmann assumed a larger role in assembling and trimming completed 911 car bodies. Production of both 356C and SC coupes and cabriolets continued in the shadow of journalistic praise and customer enthusiasm for the new model. Ferry chose to discontinue the older models by the end of the 1965 model year.

Butzi had designed a full car line back in late 1963. His father and sales director Wolfgang Raether had conceived the 911 in as complete a range as the 356s had been. They planned a deluxe model, to be shown at Frankfurt and fitted with a leather interior. A Sport, or "S," model with 150 horsepower would crown the lineup. An entry-level standard version utilizing remaining 102-horsepower four-cylinder 356-1600SC engines would be their third model. Originally designated the 902, this became the 912 after Peugeot's complaint.

By the end of 1965, Porsche had produced 3,390 of the 911s and 6,401 of the 912s. Raether and Harald Wagner trimmed frills from the 912 to keep its price close to the 356C coupe. Many Frankfurt show customers enticed by the 911 learned they could have

Early production ran fairly smoothly, but Zuffenhausen assembly staff sometimes worked ahead of available parts. New cars, complete and ready to go, and those awaiting only headlights, filled the production parking lot.

911 looks and handling for about DM 4,000 less, about $1,000, if they could do without the 911's engine. To care for loyal customers in Europe, Porsche limited 912 availability to the Continent until 356 production ended in September 1965.

Ferry wanted an open version of the 911. The company's first prototype automobile had been the Roadster. Then soon after it introduced the Gmünd coupes, it introduced open cars, first from Beutler and then done internally. Finding room for a collapsible top above the 911 engine was a challenge. What's more, although Bott had diminished the new car's handling peculiarities, removing the steel roof would harm the 911's chassis stiffness and thus its handling characteristics. Still, in late 1961, Ferry asked Reutter's Walter Beierbach to consider how to develop a cabriolet out of Butzi's Typ 745 T-7 proposal. That request got lost, so a year later Ferry forwarded scale drawings and a model to Karmann to determine the feasibility of manufacturing an open car. Butzi's first variation, done with Gerhard Schröder's input on convertible bows and folding systems, showed a car with a collapsible padded top that stored below a boot to provide a low silhouette. A

1965 911 and 912 Coupe and Targa
Porsche's 1965 display stand at Frankfurt already showed Porsche's Targa at far left, its answer to the question of open cars. Butzi originally designed a cabriolet, but the engine occupied space needed to store a top, so he conceived a reinforced open car and finished the rollover bar in brushed stainless steel to emphasize its role.

second version used a removable top that owners stretched over bows they stored in the boot. One final option offered a removable two-piece roof that consisted of one panel over the driver and passenger and a second for the rear window. These pieces attached either to a fixed-in-place roof bow or to something that could collapse in order to present a cleaner profile.

Butzi preferred the true cabriolet. "Open cars at Porsche," he said, "always had been roadsters or speedsters. These have followed a distinctive shape for the roof that is not the same fastback as our coupes. I wanted a clear break in the roofline to the rear of the car so as to reemphasize that roadster character."

But his roof silhouette did not follow the clean sweep of the coupe. This line required new body panels for the rear end of the car, something his father found too costly.

Worse, making the roof bow collapsible, whether one stout piece or several slender ones, required body changes Butzi had not foreseen and Komenda had not suggested as engineering drawings of the car developed. The only alternative was to use a broad center bow that remained rigidly in place to support removable panels. This also offered additional stiffness to the open car body.

One other consideration influenced Porsche's direction with its open car. The U.S. government was increasing its role in what Americans could choose to drive. Consumer activist Ralph Nader's assault on General Motors blamed those who refused to install an inexpensive rear anti-sway bar on the Chevrolet Corvair with its rear-mounted air-cooled six-cylinder engine and independent swing axles. Engineers argued vigorously for it, but the board of directors refused the added cost. Bad crashes brought disastrous publicity. GM attempted to smear Nader. The effort backfired, embarrassing the U.S. auto industry and inciting Congress to begin questioning public safety. Porsche worried that Congress might legislate against convertibles or even its 911. Bott and others advocated the strong bow as an

1967 911S Targa
Herbert Linge looked for a spot to park his 911S Targa for journalist days at Hockenheimring. In 1967 Porsche introduced both the high-performance S package with 160 brake horsepower and the open-topped Targa with its zip-out plastic rear window.

integral rollbar that made the 911 stiffer and safer.

Harald Wagner christened it the "Targa" during a conversation with other sales executives. They had discussed how many automakers used race event names for their models. Porsche had used "Carrera." Targa was a word pronounced easily in any language. When Wagner learned its translation meant "shield," it resonated well with Butzi's insistence that the central bar form remain highly visible. He highlighted its function with its brushed stainless steel finish. Targa manufacture began around September 1966 as a 1967 model though the company started cautiously. Out of 55 cars Porsche assembled each day, just seven were Targas, each equipped with a zip-in rear window to enhance the open car feeling.

The Targa wasn't open enough for Porsche's opinionated southern California distributor, Johnny von Neumann. Von Neumann and Max Hoffman had pressured the factory to develop the America Roadster and the Speedster primarily for the California market. Now Johnny had another idea. With Hoffman dead, he bypassed Porsche and approached Nuccio Bertone with his idea to do a series of at least one hundred roadsters. Bertone made sketches and von Neumann went to Zuffenhausen to talk about buying complete platforms for delivery to Bertone to fit his body and interior. The amount of refinishing the Abarth racers had required made Ferry Porsche and Harald Wagner wary. "It has our name on it," Ferry told von Neumann, "so we are concerned to be sure it is going to be right."

Bertone's striking body, more Italian than Porsche-like, debuted in March 1966

1966 911 Bertone Roadster

Johnny von Neumann and Italian designer Nuccio Bertone teamed up to produce a prototype roadster on the 911 chassis, but von Neumann forgot an open car needed reinforcing.

at the Geneva International Auto Show, close to Porsche's new Targa. Bertone got inquiries but not a single order.

"The thing that killed it," von Neumann explained, "was something they already knew. . . . When you make a convertible out of a coupe, there's some chassis movement, flexing."

While Helmuth Bott reinforced the Targa's chassis, he engineered another highly anticipated project, the 911S "Sport" model. Engineer Paul Hensler made small but significant changes to Hans Mezger's engine yielding 160 net horsepower at 6600 rpm. Hensler enlarged valve diameters and altered valve timing to get more fuel in and exhaust out of the cylinders.

Weber carburetors accounted for another improvement in performance, starting in March 1966. The throttle bodies of the Solexes proved to be too soft. Porsche mechanics experienced difficulty keeping them in tune. Base 911s appeared with Weber 40IDA3C carburetors and the S got 40IDS3Cs.

New forged aluminum wheels from Fuchs let more cooling air reach brake rotors and saved nearly 5 pounds (2.25 kilograms) of weight on each corner. To improve road holding, Bott fitted a larger front and a new rear anti-sway bar along with adjustable Koni shock absorbers from Holland. Interiors got vinyl seats with corduroy or houndstooth cloth inserts with optional full leather. Leather wrapped the steering wheel, and the dash lost its wood trim, replaced in the S with an embossed padded vinyl.

For 1966, Porsche produced a record 12,820 cars, of which nearly three-fourths, 9,090, were affordable 912s. More than half of Porsche production came to the United States. In 1967, production slipped slightly to 11,011 cars. More than half, 6,472, were 912s, and the United States took 5,400 of the total.

United States emissions laws began affecting all makers for 1968. Porsche's new research facility at Weissach had opened Europe's first U.S. Environmental Protection Agency (EPA)–approved test operation. But Porsche could not get its 1968 911S certified for U.S. import as part of its A-series cars. It developed a new model, the 911L, for *luxus*, or luxury. It used the 130 horsepower base engine, but with 911S level interior trim and features including ventilated disc brakes. The base 911 came with solid brake rotors. In Europe the new 911L fit between the 911S and another new issue, the 911T.

Harald Wagner's sales force had conceived the T as a six-cylinder model to sell in Germany at less than DM 20,000, about $5,000. It had a four-speed transmission, solid disc rotors, and no anti-sway bar. Its engine developed 110 net horsepower. Devoid of the trim and luxuries standard even on the base 911, this car provided the competition department with a production model about 77 pounds (35 kilograms) lighter than the base 911. This weight saving gave the entry car performance matching the base model, with 0-to-100-kilometer-per-hour times of 8.1 seconds and a top speed of 129 miles per hour (206 kilometers per hour).

For the high-performance "Super," or S model, Porsche abandoned Solex carburetors for Weber downdraft models. The S also got ventilated disc brakes and anti-sway bars at both the front and rear to improve handling to match the power.

Porsche expanded and relabeled its 911 line for 1968, renaming the base 911 as the 911L (for Luxury) and introducing a 911T (for Touring) in Europe. For the United States, Porsche did not export the 911S, so American customers got a base 911, and the 911L featured S interior trim.

Porsche introduced its Sportomatic transmission in 1968. This was a semiautomatic gear-shifting system aimed primarily as U.S. buyers who had, it seemed, forsaken shifting gears as something they had done "before" but did not need to do now. Yet Ferry was aware that enthusiasts perceived that sports cars with automatic transmissions weren't true sports cars. Corvettes first appeared in 1953 with two-speed automatics. Chevrolet called the car a sports car, but sales stalled. Ford introduced its more powerful Thunderbird in 1955, calling the car "a personal luxury car," and buyers viewed the automatic as a necessity.

Porsche's transmission blended a hydraulic torque-converter with its own four-speed transmission through a clutch that disengaged automatically whenever the driver touched the gear lever. Ironically, it was more successful in Europe than the United States. Buyers paid about $235, DM 990, for something European magazine reviewers generally liked and American journalists lambasted.

Production reached 14,300 cars in 1968, a new record. The six-cylinder 911s took the lead from the 912s for the first time by a slim margin. But big changes were due for B-series cars to appear for the 1969 model year, including Ferry's decision to move the rear wheels back 2.25 inches (57mm) on the platform. Lengthening the wheelbase to 89.3 inches (2,268mm) without changing the platform delivered the effect of moving some weight off the rear wheels and onto the front. This changed weight distribution and further stabilized handling. It required longer suspension trailing arms and new half-shaft universal joints to accommodate the greater angle coming from the engine to the driving wheels.

For 1969, Porsche introduced a self-adjusting hydropneumatic front suspension system on its new 911E models. Manufactured by Boge, this system automatically accommodated front-end load changes ranging from additional fuel in the tank to luggage for a week-long trip. Porsche switched from a single 12-volt battery up front to two 6-volt cells, one located below each headlamp housing, which improved weight distribution.

Bosch mechanical fuel injection brought the S model into U.S. emissions compliance and returned the car to anxious American buyers. Paul Hensler tested both Bosch's new electronic system that Volkswagen had selected and its mechanical system. The diesel-type mechanical operation worked better with Porsche's high-speed engines to provide even distribution among each of the cylinders. What's more, this closed system eliminated the fuel evaporation problems that carburetors suffered and against which states such as California had begun to mandate. The 1969 version of the 911S engine developed 170 brake horsepower. The new E boasted 140. All of Porsche's crankcases were cast in aluminum rather than magnesium as they had been before.

Porsche brought in a new styling director, Tony Lapine, a Latvian-born designer, in 1969 to assist Butzi in managing Porsche's many projects. He had worked at Chevrolet on Corvettes for both Harley Earl and Bill Mitchell. Then he went to GM's European counterpart, Opel in Russelsheim, as head of design. Several assignments greeted him when he arrived in Zuffenhausen. Porsche's decades-long research and development relationship with Volkswagen led to the creation of a jointly produced mid-engine two-seater, the Typ 914. Racing projects that followed the successful 904 and 906, designed by Butzi and his colleagues, kept Lapine and his own staff busy.

The 1970 C-series cars brought Porsche buyers 2.2-liter engines in the 911. As part of their solutions to controlling evaporation of hydrocarbons, Paul Hensler's engineers enlarged engine bore to 84mm from 80, among many other changes. This increased displacement to 2,195cc. Horsepower from the 911T engine reached 125 brake horsepower, 155 for the 911E, and the S hit 180 horsepower. Just before production started on the 1970 models, Porsche opened its new 160,000-square-foot (14,864-square-meter) assembly plant, paint shop, and interior trim facility.

Through 1970, while Porsche battled for world supremacy on racetracks, a fight went on inside the extended family of Porsches and

"Time capsule" cars such as this U.S. specification 911L still exist. Discovered in a barn in southern California, still owned by its original owner, it hadn't been driven in more than 20 years.

1969 Typ 912 Targa

This was the last year of 912 production, and all Targas, both 912 and 911, could be ordered with fixed heated safety-glass rear windows or removable plastic. Porsche extended the wheelbase of both 911 and 912 models by 2.24 inches (57mm) to 89.3 inches (2268mm) to improve handling. Slightly flared fenders on both 911 and 912 models handled 6-inch wheels.

Piëchs who controlled its destiny and reaped its profits. Ferry Porsche had done a stringent job of controlling costs on the production cars. Price increases that American buyers experienced largely were the result of currency fluctuations. But where Ferry had been frugal, his nephew, development chief Ferdinand "Bürly" Piëch, had run the racing department as if he had endless reserves. Piëch held out for the highest-quality pieces and workmanship. He assembled new race cars from one event to the next.

What's more, Butzi's and Bürly's brothers and sisters regularly arrived at the factory doors seeking their role in managing their family's company. These concerns put Ferry Porsche and his sister Louise Piëch (Bürly's mother) at increasing odds. Following a weekend-long retreat at the family home in Austria in the fall of 1970, both families agreed to vacate their jobs. They would hire qualified professionals to perform them instead. This changed the company from a family-led organization into a corporation with limited liability.

In a decision that would have profound effects for nearly two decades, the board hired Ernst Fuhrmann to come back. Passed over for a promotion he believed he deserved in 1958, Fuhrmann had left Porsche. He returned in September 1971 to fill the roles of purchasing and production chief.

Although Porsche and Piëch family members departed, Ferry stayed on as managing director and the voice and identity of the company. Around all this family and corporate drama, 1972 production began. It was not easy, and morale slipped. The 1970 Clean Air Act in the United States required cars that would be sold in the United States in 1976 to emit 90 percent fewer hydrocarbons than 1971 levels. Manufacturers concluded it was impossible to achieve these targets without catalytic converters to superheat the already hot engine exhaust. These would bake out remaining unburned vapors and particles before they reached the atmosphere. Tetraethyl lead, the additive in gasoline that increased its octane rating to give it higher performance, destroyed the heating pellets within the converter. By the early 1970s, automakers throughout the world were redesigning engines to operate on lead-free gasoline. Engineers at Porsche understood that its high-rpm, short-stroke, big-bore engines produced great horsepower with dirty exhaust. Smaller bores coupled to longer strokes offered a double benefit in a changing world. Their longer burn cycle combusted fuels more fully, meeting emissions standards more easily. This configuration also developed greater torque at lower engine speeds, a characteristic urban Porsche drivers needed to survive stop-and-go traffic.

Porsche kept cylinder bore at 84mm but increased stroke 4.4mm to 70.4mm from 66 for the D-series. This enlarged total displacement to 2,341cc. Porsche rounded this figure upward to 2.4 liters for marketing and labeling purposes. To simplify an otherwise complex process, Hensler's engineers designed a common aluminum cylinder head with a single camshaft for use on the T, E, and S engines. To meet ever-tightening U.S. emission standards, Hensler fuel-injected the T engine for American markets, as well as the E and S. (Other countries still got the Solex or Zenith carburetors introduced on the T.) With a view toward cost-effectiveness, Porsche chose to carry the same engines over into 1973. The 911T now rated 140 DIN horsepower. Hensler coaxed 165 DIN horsepower out of the E, and the S still remained the racer's favorite with 190 DIN horsepower. The torque figures represented an average 10 percent increase over what was available

Air conditioning, an option on 911s since 1969, hugged the bottom of the dashboard. The optional Recaro sport seats hugged the driver and passenger.

1971 911E Coupe

In 1969, Porsche replaced the 911L with a new series 911E model. Both it and the 911S received Bosch mechanical fuel injection. T, E, and S engines grew to 2.2 liters displacement in 1970. For 1971, E and S engines changed over to Biral cylinders and got larger intake and exhaust valves as well as Bosch capacitive discharge ignition systems.

to 2.2-liter owners, making a noticeable difference to city traffic drivers.

This 2.4-liter engine represented one of Ferdinand Piëch's three final production car influences before he left Porsche. The second was a new transaxle targeted at better acceleration. Piëch's new gear ratios sacrificed top speed and increased fuel consumption but made the cars easier to drive in cities and therefore more enjoyable for many buyers.

This kind of development was additional evidence of Piëch's character and his near obsession with extraordinarily high standards. Karl Ludvigsen, who has thoroughly chronicled the history of nearly every one of Porsche's cars, put it best. This new transaxle, he wrote, "reflected an almost reckless drive for perfection in Porsche cars, for only two years earlier the change had been made to a magnesium die-casting for the housing of the earlier transaxle." Worse, the new one added 20 pounds of weight to the car. It epitomized the classic Porsche conundrum: save weight or update technology. But Piëch had not finished in his pursuit of perfection. Always concerned by weight at the car's corners, for the 1972 model he relocated the dry sump oil reservoir behind the right door ahead of the rear wheel. Body engineers cut a filler cap and lid into the rear fender behind the B-pillar. It represented a year of work for an engineer and a stylist. But achieving this target caused not one, but two problems. It had the unfortunate effect of confusing some innocent gas station attendants who, unaware that Porsche's fuel filler was on the left front fender, pumped gasoline into the side oil reservoir. For the following year, recognizing that problem and suspecting that side-impact safety regulations in the U.S. might affect the placement—its second problem—Porsche moved the tank back in the rear fender behind the engine.

For 1972, Porsche shifted the Boge hydropneumatic struts from standard equipment on the 911E models to optional. The struts leaked, and owners found them more expensive than Konis to replace. Despite its lower top speed, the 911S still was a potent automobile. Capable of reaching 100 miles per hour (160 kilometers per hour) from a standstill in just 15 seconds according to *Car and Driver* magazine, the car easily would run on another 40 miles per hour (64 kilometers per hour) from there. At those speeds, with its wider tires and fenders increasing frontal area to 18.4 square feet from the original 17.4 and raising the coefficient of drag to 0.41 from 0.38, the 911 had a noticeable tendency to lift at the front. A young engineer in the racing department, Tilman Brodbeck, who had joined Porsche in October 1970 with a technical education in mechanical engineering and aerodynamics, got the assignment early in 1971 to work on the 911S in Stuttgart University's wind tunnel. Design chief Tony Lapine assigned

To address growing concerns over noxious emissions, especially for U.S. customers, Porsche introduced a new engine with 2.4 liters displacement, slightly lengthening the stroke (to 70.4mm) while retaining the bore at 84mm. The resulting S engine developed 190 brake horsepower, an increase of 10.

1972 911S Targa

Aiming for better weight balance, Ferdinand Piëch urged engineering to relocate the dry sump oil tank to the middle of the car behind the passenger door, with a filler opening there as well. Governmental assessment of side-impact spillage risks—and the odd service station attendant who filled the oil tank with gasoline—forced a return to its original site.

one of his modelers to join Brodbeck in case the engineer came up with something.

A wind tunnel technician moved the oil vaporizer wand up and down over the nose of the car. Brodbeck noticed the tendency for this stream to disappear directly under the front valance below the bumper. He wondered if there wasn't some way to stop the air, to redirect it. He held a finger in the path of the oil stream at the base of the valence and watched the stream detour around it. He and the modeler looked around for other things that might work, a pencil, a business card. By the end of the first day, Brodbeck had taped a piece of rope across the bottom lip. The oil stream caught the rope and shifted right or left. Technicians in the control room read the results. At the end of the third day, Brodbeck and the modeler had roughed out with fiberglass a piece that provided the same results but with smoother edges and greater effect. It reduced lift by nearly half, to 102 pounds from 183 (46.3 kilograms from 83.2), and it dropped the drag coefficient (Cd) from 0.41 to 0.40.

Just before leaving Porsche, Piëch put Brodbeck and one of Lapine's stylists on a crash program to produce this front spoiler in fiberglass as a production part and as an accessory piece that owners could buy for their earlier cars. "There were some who wanted this piece made in steel," Tillman Brodbeck recalled recently. "That would have taken a year. They worried that in a crash, pieces of the fiberglass might hurt someone else. Mr. Piëch said it was too important to wait. It improved safety and handling so much."

These E-series bodies were ready to yield to 1973 F-series cars that would wrap up Porsche's first generation of its 911. The company had taken in slightly more than 300 million deutsche marks in 1972 (about $94 million) under the cost-conscious Ferry Porsche. However, its motorsports programs had spent more than $30 million under the quality conscious Ferdinand Piëch. In 1972, as Porsche prepared this next series for production, status quo seemed a thing of the past. ■

1964–1972

CHAPTER SIX

RACING TAKES ON ITS *OWN* DESTINY

1965 Typ 911 Monte Carlo

Peter Falk, left, and Herbert Linge prepare to start the 1965 Monte Carlo Rally with a slightly modified 911. Little did they know this eleven-stage, 2,000-mile event would prove to be one of the coldest and snowiest ever, yet they still finished fifth, three spots behind Eugen Böhringer and Rolf Wütherich in a 904.

PORSCHE CREATED AN EIGHT-CYLINDER SPYDER, the Typ 906-8, nicknamed Kanguruh (kangaroo!) for its inelegant lines and clumsy shape, for the 1965 European Hill Climb Championship. Based on the 904GTS, the car also ran in the Targa Florio where Gerhard Mitter and Colin Davis drove it to second place. But it was a challenge to handle because the short stubby spyder evolved from a fiberglass coupe—missing its roof. Helmuth Bott had made 29-year-old Ferdinand Piëch responsible for racing and competition design. Hans Mezger, who had proven himself with the Typ 901 engine for the production 911 and the competition version for the 904GTS6, took over the newly established Konstruction Rennfahrzeuge, racing vehicle design department,

working directly for Piëch. Their racing engineers embarked on a hastily developed program and produced two stiffer spyders. But they could do no better than third and fourth in the next hillclimb championship meet at Trento-Bondone in Italy.

With only three events to go in the series, Piëch abandoned the 904 platform and launched a new car with a tubular space frame. He conceived an entirely new suspension as well. Demanding 13-inch wheels for this car but finding none in house, or through normal suppliers, Piëch went to Colin Chapman and purchased a set of wheels from Lotus. Engineers worked feverishly on this new car, nicknamed the Lotus-Porsche, to prepare it for the Ollon-Villars hillclimb in France. But employee unions refused to let the mechanics work over a weekend, and the car went to the race assembled but untested.

Mitter came second to a Ferrari, giving the championship to Ferrari but convincing

1965 Typ 906 Carrera 6

Porsche's new Typ 906 Carrera 6 racer earned class wins throughout the 1965 season at Daytona and Monza, and first overall at the Targa, Nürburgring, and Le Mans to claim the 2-liter prototype championship. Here Helmut Leuze races his number 25 at Innsbruck in 1967.

It was the 1960s, after all, but photos such as this one inspire questions about what inspired this photo. The fashions came from French designer André Courrèges.

Piëch and his engineers that this new car had potential. Its eight-cylinder engine developed 250 net horsepower, yet the racer had a dry weight of only 1,076 pounds (488 kilograms).

The FIA established a new racing category for 1966, the Sports Car class. Rules called for 50 identical cars completed before the season began. Piëch wanted to utilize the smaller 13-inch wheels such as those he had obtained from Lotus because it would have given the car lower fenders, but Ferry Porsche overruled him. The racing department had dozens of surplus 904GTS suspension parts in stock from its anticipated second production run, and Porsche insisted they use these and their 15-inch wheels to lower costs. Piëch was able to develop a new tubular space frame for this car, which created a car that still was less than 1 meter tall—38.6 inches, (980mm). Engineers pulled 200 horsepower out of the car's 2-liter six-cylinder engine, and with this power and its sleek body, the car reached 175 miles per hour (280 kilometers per hour), depending on course gearing.

Porsche set a customer price of DM 45,000 on these cars known as the 906 Carrera 6, roughly $11,250, and all 50 cars sold quickly. Mezger's engineers hurriedly assembled 15 more. Weinsberg Karosserie produced all the fiberglass bodies. Of the total 65, 9 cars were fitted with fuel injection six-cylinder engines (with 215 horsepower) and another 4 of them used 2-liter flat-eights. Porsche also had run a single Typ 771 bored out to 80mm from 76 for total displacement of 2,195cc and developing 250 horsepower to run like a rabbit during the 1966 Targa.

Herbert Linge and Hans Herrmann took a prototype to Daytona and won the 2-liter class. For the Targa's fiftieth running, Porsche entered five cars, but it was a privately entered carbureted 906 that won. Porsche sent five cars to Le Mans, two carbureted and three "prototypes" with fuel injection tweaked to develop 220 horsepower. Two of these ran with design engineer Eugen Kolb's new long-tail (*langheck*) bodies. The cars weighed more, 1,562 pounds (710 kilograms) versus 1,485 pounds (675 kilograms) for the short tails. However the more aerodynamic long tail allowed top speeds almost 10 miles per hour (15 kilometers per hour) higher, 185 miles per hour versus 175 (295 kilometers per hour versus 280). The Carrera 6s finished fourth, fifth, sixth, and seventh overall, and they won their class and the Index of Performance.

While the 906 coupes grew longer (and won outright at the season closer at Hockenheim), Piëch's engineers continued work on hillclimbers. Rules required a higher windshield, but the car ran a 90.6-inch (2300mm) wheelbase. Piëch prevailed on his wheel and tire preference this time,

1966 Typ 906 Carrera 6 Le Mans-Wagen

For Le Mans, Piëch suspected longer bodies might offer an advantage. Former Reutter body designer Eugen Kolb, who had joined Piëch's experimental department in 1963, extended the sub frame and added 15.75 inches (400mm) along with a longer, slightly lower nose. Co-drivers Jo Siffert and Colin Davis brought this car home fourth overall to win their class at Le Mans.

1967 Typ 910-8

Chassis number 3 first ran at Daytona in 1967. Starting 17th on the grid, Hans Herrmann and Jo Siffert completed 618 laps to finish fourth overall and first among 2-liter prototypes in this car.

CHAPTER SIX

1967 Typ 907/8 Coupe

The new 907s won outright at Daytona and the Targa Florio and took class victories at Sebring, Monza, Spa, and Le Mans. At Brands Hatch, Gerhard Mitter and Ludovico Scarfiotti shared driving duties in this car, winning their class and finishing second overall.

1967 911R Prototype Number 3

Ferdinand Piëch imagined these "R" models would be cars that would win events no one had yet conceived. Huschke von Hanstein hoped Porsche would manufacture 500 to homologate them as Grand Touring Cars and win events everyone else wanted to claim. Porsche records indicate they produced 20, plus 4 prototypes.

and the new car, known as the Typ 910, ran on 13-inch wheels. Rules allowed a minimum weight of 1,268 pounds (575 kilograms), and that is how the first 910 entered its debut on the Trento-Bondone climb, using the Typ 711 2-liter flat-eight.

Racing department designers conceived the car as both a spyder for short races and a coupe for longer runs. For these events, such as Daytona, Sebring, Le Mans, and others in Europe through the 1967 season, the 910 coupes used the fuel-injected 2-liter flat-six developed from the 906 carbureted engines.

Ferry Porsche never intended to offer the 910 to privateers. He felt it would create a hardship for recent 906 buyers. Piëch entered the 910s only in prototype categories. Failures that his 906s did suffer came from metal fatigue. As Karl Ludvigsen wrote in *Excellence was Expected*, "This meant that the metal, which was strong enough to meet the needs of the parts as they were designed, developed cracks and broke when cycled [through] normal stresses too many times." Piëch quickly developed a new strategy of building new cars for each major event—and getting rid of "older" cars. Some of the 910s (at DM 60,000, roughly $15,000,) usually with only one race on their tube frame chassis, ended up with private racers who routinely ran them against the factory. At year end, the FIA decreased the requirement for Sports Car class from 50 cars to 25, and the Porsche 910, with 28 assembled in 1967, automatically achieved homologation as a Sports Car for the 1968 season.

Meanwhile, for the 1967 Targa, Piëch sent six cars, three with the 2-liter fuel-injected six and three with the newly enlarged 2.2-liter Typ 771 flat-eight. A 910/8 with Rolf Stommelen and Paul Hawkins alternating turns at the wheel won the event outright. The 910 proved evergreen. Over the next decade dozens of drivers won events all around the world in these cars.

In a manner typical of Ferdinand Piëch's drive for motorsports supremacy, and aided by a nearly DM 4 million (roughly $1 million) budget, his racing department brought a new car to Le Mans that same year. Airflow across the 904, the 906, and even the 910 had pleased no one, least of all Piëch. The new 907 arrived primarily to address that shortcoming. Porsche introduced it in long-tail form at Le Mans where, with their reliable fuel-injected six-cylinder engines, they reached 187.6 miles per hour (302 kilometers per hour) along the Mulsanne Straight. The car's cockpit, narrowed to interrupt less airflow, reminded Porsche's racers of a fighter jet. Engineers devised a new front suspension that allowed spring rate adjustment by angling the front spring instead of using variable-rate coil springs themselves. This also saved weight, as did using ventilated front discs. Engineers also gave the car right-hand steering, which drivers believed gave them an advantage in driving clockwise circuits. Hans Herrmann and Jo Siffert finished fifth overall, averaging 125 miles per hour (201 kilometers per hour) over the entire 24-hour race.

For 1968, Piëch fitted the 2.2-liter flat-eight Typ 771 in the 907s. This strategy paid off with overall wins both at Daytona and Sebring. At Daytona, he stretched another envelope by trying an aluminum tube frame version of the car fitted with numerous titanium parts. Mechanics nicknamed this the *Muletta*, the little mule. Had its generator not failed, the car would have won. Piëch also experimented with a brake-pad-wear warning system with a light mounted in front of the driver.

The 907s arrived after the 910s and represented Ferdinand Piëch's next step in aerodynamic attention to fiberglass-bodied racers. Drivers likened driving the coupes to flying fighter jets because of the near-central seating position and cramped quarters.

1967 911R

Dirty and tired didn't begin to describe the car. In late October 1967, a Swiss team started a series of records that culminated in using this R to run at an average of 130 miles per hour (208 kilometers per hour) for 10,000 miles (20,000 kilometers).

Immediately after Le Mans, the FIA changed its rules again, limiting the capacity of "prototype" cars to 3 liters. It increased the Sports Car engine maximum to 5 liters, still requiring a minimum of 25 identical models to be made for homologation. This led Piëch to develop two new cars, one for each class. Even with a slightly increased racing budget, above DM 4 million but not quite 5 (between $1 and $1.25 million), a complete new car could put a strain on things.

Still, Hans Mezger quickly produced a new flat-eight-cylinder 3-liter engine that Piëch introduced on April 6 at the 1968 Le Mans trials. Two long-tail 907s, still running 13-inch wheels, used the new engines identified by serial numbers 908-001 and 908-002.

The cars, now designated the Typ 908, suffered teething problems. However when they appeared at Nürburgring to contest the 1000-kilometer second round of the World Championship race, the cars rode on 15-inch wheels and tires. Despite challenging practice and qualifying sessions, Jo Siffert and Vic Elford brought their 908 home in first place. The aluminum tube frame cars boasted a new-for-Porsche aerodynamic feature, a movable rear spoiler. At full or steady throttle, the wings

Before the start of the 24 Hours of Le Mans, Porsche lined up its 908 entries and built a forbidding wall of raised long tails. Car number 33 ultimately finished third overall, while the other three failed to complete the race.

1969 911S-GT

The 84-hour-long Marathon de la Route made any 24-hour endurance race seem like a practice session. Here, 1968 event winner Herbert Linge headed for victory over the course that used both Südschleife and Nordschleife for a combined 19.1-mile (30.55-kilometer) lap at the Nürburgring.

1968 Typ 908 Long-Tail Coupe

After qualifying first on the grid, Jo Siffert (foreground) endured a frustrating race at Le Mans, failing to finish when his gearbox gave out after just 59 laps. Rolf Stommelen and Jochen Neerpasch in car number 33 finished third after the long rainy event, which ran in September after student and worker strikes disrupted life in France in the spring.

1968 Typ 908 Spyder/2 Flounder

This was a car and a race car design in transition. Undulating shapes with tapered "Coke-bottle" waistlines had been the state of the art for decades, but that thinking changed with later version of the 908s.

remained horizontal. Under braking, the wings swung up, holding the rear down against weight transfer and providing some air-brake effect. But the car still was far from "developed," and the Paris student riots in May 1968 that sent all of France out on labor strikes through June provided Porsche the chance to finish the cars for the by then delayed Le Mans race.

The rescheduled event ran on September 28 and 29 as the final round of the World Sports Car Championship. Piëch entered four 908s, and privateers filled in with three long-tail 907s, prepared by Porsche mechanics for the

1969 Typ 908/3

The third-generation 908s reflected current wind-tunnel developments in aerodynamics and downforce. These cars combined the 908 3-liter engine with 909 *Bergspyder* chassis and transaxles to move the driver further forward.

Driving a car literally *made* for the Targa Florio, Björn Waldegaard and Richard Attwood snuck past a twitchy-handling Ferrari 512 to capture fifth in the 1970 running. Porsche 908/3 models took first, second, fourth, and fifth, split only by another ill-handling 512.

race. This was not unwise; the Dieter Spoerry and Rico Steinemann 2.2-liter 907L took second overall behind a Ford GT40, and Rolf Stommelen and Jochen Neerpasch finished third overall in one of Piëch's 908s.

For 1969, the 908s were once again bridesmaids, but this time they worked in service to Porsche's ultimate weapon, the 917 "Sports Car." With prototype rules changed, Piëch introduced the spyder versions of the 908s.

Uncharacteristically, the racing engineers couldn't get enough testing time on the new spyders, designated the Typ 908/02. It was a cold winter with more snow than normal. Weissach's test track was a white wonderland. Exhaust systems and timing chains failed on all five Daytona entries, and at Sebring, aluminum tube frames broke on all four of the factory cars. Yet according to Jürgen Barth, the mechanics saved the race. They had gained so much experience repairing broken welds that they kept the Rolf Stommelen and Joe Buzzetta car together to finish third overall.

One of the most interesting 1970 entries at Le Mans was not its fastest 908, but its busiest. Jonathan Williams and Herbert Linge co-drove Steve McQueen's "camera car," a 908/2 that McQueen and Porsche modified to house two bulky motion picture cameras for McQueen to capture actual racing footage for his film *Le Mans*.

Engineers learned from their failures. By the time the new spyders reached Brands Hatch, Porsche 908s were "strong" enough to finish first, second, and third. Good, but this was not certain enough for Piëch, who authorized and directed creation of a new spyder. With its more undulating forms, mechanics quickly nicknamed it *Flunder*, after the fish, the flounder. They assembled it on a 908/02 chassis. Early Flounders crashed because of another aerodynamic misstep: too little downforce to the front end. Engineers fitted small winglets to the nose.

For Le Mans, Piëch chose to campaign 908 long-tail bodies and a long-tail *Flunder*, both with fixed rear wings. It was a risk. During the 1968 Spanish Grand Prix at Montjuïc Park in Barcelona two Formula One Lotuses fitted with high, movable wings crashed. The Commission Sportive Internationale, CSI, the group inside the FIA responsible for organizing races since 1922, banned the devices. Eugen Kolb's long tails brought a 12-mile-per-hour (20-kilometer-per-hour) advantage over standard-length 908 coupes at 195 miles per hour (312 kilometers per hour) despite the additional 22 pounds (10 kilograms) of weight, to total 1,550 pounds (705 kilograms) for the 908 Long Tail.

Porsche efforts to tame, manage, and win with its new 917 "Sports Car" racers proved an enormous challenge. As with other racers, aerodynamics was a cut-and-try practice in those days. The 917s required even greater efforts to harness their huge performance potential. At the same time, Piëch expended his effort in developing a third-generation 908. The 908/03 bore little resemblance to 908s that had come before it, except for its 3-liter engines that developed 350 or more horsepower. The new cars weighed just 1,199 pounds (545 kilograms). These racers, campaigned strategically, won the 1970 Targa Florio and the 1970 and 1971 1000-kilometer races at Nürburgring.

In hopes of keeping racing interesting, in 1967 the FIA rewrote the Sports Car rules for 1972. They limited displacement to 3 liters. Hans Mezger and his colleagues developed a new engine that retained air-cooled cylinders but fitted water-cooled four-valve cylinder heads. However, these engines never raced. After winning the World Championship in 1971, Porsche withdrew from the series. The racing department sold what remained of their eleven-car fleet of 908s at, according to Barth, prices ranging from DM 150,000 to DM 180,000, roughly $41,700 to $50,000 per car. As with the 907s, privateers competed regularly with 908s for another decade. The most successful of the private entrants, Reinhold Jöst, ran his 908/3 with consistent results through 1975. He told Barth his "main asset was the old car's reliability in long-distance races." ■

1970 911ST Monte Carlo Rally Winner

Björn Waldegaard was ready for another long drive as he glanced out the window of his slightly dented 911ST. Porsche produced these rally cars on lightweight but reinforced T chassis using sturdy S engines.

CHAPTER SEVEN

INVITING THE NEXT GENERATION

1970 Volkswagen-Porsche 914
Everybody was introducing mid-engine cars by the mid-1960s. Porsche, looking to expand its car line to include an entry-level vehicle, approached Volkswagen with the idea that became this 914.

SINCE THE CONCEPTION OF THE VOLKSWAGEN, Porsche had served as the design and engineering "department" for VW. The company had not achieved Adolf Hitler's goal of a Beetle in every driveway, but the car had sold well from its postwar reintroduction in 1948. By the early 1960s, however, VW no longer owned the market for small cars in Germany. Ford had a new Taunus, Opel had the Kadett, and by 1967, Fiat had slipped ahead of VW as Europe's largest car producer.

VW, in addition to the Beetle, offered the Variant as a two-door ("fastback"), sedan ("notchback"), or station wagon ("squareback") and the Karmann Ghia "sporty" car as a coupe or convertible. But all these

models were aging, especially the Karmann Ghia. Assembled by Wilhelm Karmann GmbH in Osnabrück from designs by Luigi Segre at Ghia Carrosserie in Turin, Italy, the car had evolved by 1966 into an edgy, sculptured coupe that paid only slight homage to its organic shapes at its introduction in 1955. VW's director Heinz Nordhoff asked Porsche to begin developing a replacement for the Beetle. (For VW, this was their Typ EA266; at Porsche, it was the Typ 1966.) Nordhoff deflected comments and criticism of his car's lineup but he understood that not only did they need a new

Part of Porsche's rigorous chassis and body durability testing involved driving hundred of miles over potholed and dimpled test roads. The 914 appeared in 1970 with a 1.7-liter flat-four-cylinder engine from the VW 411E model that developed 80 brake horsepower.

The 914's radical appearance grew out of a concept that Hans Gugelot created for BMW. Butzi Porsche took the idea further and incorporated his Targa roof treatment for the economy car.

small sedan, they needed a new affordable two-seater.

Porsche had a dilemma on its hands with its 912. In most markets it sold for around 15 percent less than the base 911, but it offered much less engine performance. Dealers complained about poor sales. Ferry Porsche recognized that his company could use a new affordable two-seater as well. But with racing sapping resources, Ferry knew he could not develop a new car line. But what if Porsche did the work for Volkswagen and then shared the body and chassis? Nordhoff liked that proposition, and Porsche's engineers set to work.

Mid-engine placement was the design and engineering vogue in the mid-1960s. Ferrari and Ford both introduced mid-engine racers in 1964, the 250LM from Italy and the GT40 from Detroit. Lamborghini introduced its showstopping Miura in 1966, and others followed in 1967 with Ferrari's 206/246 Dino, Matra's M530, the DeTomaso Mangusta, and the Lotus Europa. To Porsche, mid-engines were nothing new.

Ferry earlier had contemplated producing a run of 904s for the street, but fitting bumpers had been one of several challenges. Without a suitable project they could inherit from racing and revise for the road, everyone went to the drawing boards.

Ferry already had seen a proposal from Gugelot Design in Ulm, about 50 miles southeast of Stuttgart. Hans Gugelot was one of Butzi Porsche's instructors at the *Höchschule für Gestaltung* in Ulm. Gugelot's concept placed the engine in front, and he used composite materials for the body. Beginning in mid-1966, Butzi, fellow stylist Heinrich Klie, and body engineer Gerhard Schröder took what they could from Gugelot's ideas (he had died in 1965). They replaced the composites with steel panels fitted onto a welded pressed-steel chassis. Porsche designated the project the Typ 914, and Butzi gave the car a variation of his new Targa removable-roof treatment. Gugelot's concept featured a very low nose. To meet headlight standards, especially in America where he hoped his car would sell well, Gugelot had designed flip-up headlights.

Karmann fabricated and assembled the bodies with VW's flat-four. VW agreed to ship partially completed bodies to Zuffenhausen—at a reduced price—for Porsche to install its six-cylinder engines, finishing these 914/6 models on the same assembly lines as the 911.

Meanwhile VW prepared for a succession in management as Heinz Nordhoff readied

Fitted with the 1,991cc Typ 901/36 engine, the lightweight mid-engine 914/6s enjoyed 110 brake horsepower that got them to 125 miles per hour (201 kilometers per hour). Porsche sold them for $5,475 (about DM 19,980) at Zuffenhausen and manufactured 3,338 of the cars.

1972 Typ 916

Porsche planned the Typ 916 package to challenge Ferrari's 206 and 246 Dino models. With the 190-brake-horsepower 911S engine in a car weighing 165 pounds (75 kilograms) less than the S, performance was great. Unfortunately so was its proposed $14,100 price (about DM 45,000). The company assembled just 11, which became Porsche family cars and vehicles offered to factory friends.

himself for retirement in 1970. VW hired Kurt Lotz in June 1967 to learn from and succeed Nordhoff. At Porsche, the first drivable prototype VW 914 rolled out on March 1, 1968. But Nordhoff died only 42 days later, on April 12. Lotz barely had time to understand the personal relationships his predecessor had with other business leaders. Sadly for VW and Porsche, the verbal agreement on pricing and providing 914 bodies to Porsche was one of those.

Lotz and Ferry Porsche soon found a meeting point. Ferry established a marketing and distribution company, VW-Porsche *Vertriebsgesellschaft* GmbH, or V-G. This covered both VW cars including the 914s, and Porsche's 911s nearly everywhere but the United States, France, and Great Britain, where the two would remain separate entities. VW had acquired Audi-NSU. For American dealers, Volkswagen of America, which had sold, serviced, and stocked Porsche parts, gave dealers the choice of remaining VW dealers for economy cars or going to Porsche-Audi for performance sports cars and higher-end sedans. At home, Porsche purchased a headquarters site in nearby Ludwigsberg, and the V-G moved in.

At Osnabrück, production began in October 1969 for the 1970 model year using the engine from VW's Typ 411E (successor to the Variant), an electronically fuel-injected 1.7-liter flat-four. With 1,679cc, this engine developed 68 net horsepower. The injection system met emissions requirements throughout the United States and the rest of the world. With full tanks, fuel and oil, the car's weight balance was nearly 50/50. The mid-engine layout provided room for luggage front and rear and for a tall driver and passenger.

Porsche's 914/6 version used the 911T engine producing 110 net horsepower.

1974 Typ 914 2.0 Special Edition

Nicknamed the Bumblebee, the 1974 Typ 914 2.0 Special Edition cars commemorated Porsche's significant—and repeated—Can-Am championships. These cars used 2.0-liter flat-fours that developed 100 brake horsepower.

The five-speed transmission gave the Typ 914 2.0 a top speed of 118 miles per hour (190 kilometers). Full instrumentation was one of the features of the Special Edition package.

Zuffenhausen began turning out these models at year's end. It proved a mixed blessing for Porsche. Because the Nordhoff agreement dissolved with his death, the terms Lotz dictated cost Porsche nearly as much to buy 914 bodies from Karmann as it was paying internally for the more complicated 911 bodies from its Reutter division.

Sales and improvements grew steadily for the VW model. Porsche's first-year production of 914/6 models reached 2,657, along with two 3-liter flat-eight-equipped 914/8 prototypes, one in red for Ferdinand Piëch that developed 300-horsepower and the other a silver car that produced 260 horsepower, which was given as a birthday gift from Porsche to Ferry. For 1971 Zuffenhausen completed just 432 of the 2-liter 914/6 models, and that was roughly halved for 1972, with just 229 cars off the line. Porsche also assembled a run of eleven special 916 models. Viewed

122

CHAPTER SEVEN

1970 914/6R

In the U.S. Porsche+Audi referred to these as 914/6R models. Each came with the "R Competition Option Group." With widened steel fenders to accommodate 15x7 wheels in front and 15x8 Fuchs alloy wheels in back, oil cooling, 100-liter fuel tank, racing seats, "specific suspension," a "changeable gear transmission," performance exhaust, and the 911S brake system, Porsche charged $15,568 for this car.

To stiffen the car adequately to compete, Porsche inserted a reinforcing X brace inside the removable roof panel and then bolted the top in place. These GTs weighed 1,980 pounds (900 kilograms), nearly 200 pounds (90 kilograms) less than production 914/6 models.

initially as preproduction cars, these fixed-roof six-cylinder cars (priced between DM 46,000 and DM 50,000, roughly $13,200 to $14,400) received 2.4-liter 911S engines or the 2.7-liter Carrera RS engines. To strengthen these exclusive cars, Piëch's engineers reinforced the floor and welded the steel roof in place. Porsche planned to introduce the cars, with a top speed in excess of 150 miles per hour (240 kilometers per hour), at the Paris Salon in October 1971. Two weeks before the show, Porsche

Porsche put serious power into the GTs with big-valve heads and dual-spark plug ignition. These engines, nearly 906 racing motors, developed 210 brake horsepower.

engine for 1973 through 1975 and a 1,795cc 85-horsepower version for 1974 and 1975. U.S. cars rated 95 horsepower from the 2-liter four for 1973 and 1974, 76 horsepower from the 1.8-liter engine for 1974 and 1976, and finally 88 horsepower from the 2-liter for 1975 and 1976.

Postmortem discussions of the 914 acknowledged the loyalty of many Volkswagen purchasers who believed they were getting a Porsche in the 1970s for the price of one in the 1950s. Some 914/6 buyers felt they were getting a Volkswagen for 1970s Porsche prices. Magazine reviewers, subjected to an ailing prototype for their first drive, were not charitable, and the nickname *Volks-Porsche*, or *Vo-Po*, hurt both products. But it didn't hurt that badly. By the time the 914 went out of production, VW had assembled 115,597 of its four-cylinder models, and Porsche had produced 3,330 914/6s, 914/8s, and 916s, enough to establish another keystone in the company's legend.

Racers liked the handling and Porsche's engine interchangeability, and in late 1969 and early 1970, Porsche produced a series of 12 cars known as 914/6GT models. Stripped to bare essentials, these cars weighed 198 pounds (about 90 kilograms) less than series production 914/6 models. At the Nürburgring 1000-kilometer race at the end of May 1970, four of the factory 914/6GTs finished second, third, fourth, and fifth in the two-liter class. A single 914/6, which French importer Son-Auto entered,

cancelled the car. Costs, from importation duties to labor at Zuffenhausen, were too high to make sense for so small a market. Porsche stopped producing 914/6 models at the end of the 1971 model year.

Volkswagen continued with the 914 version, introducing a 1,971cc 100-horsepower

1970 914/6 "Sports Purposes"
One of Porsche's three factory-entered 914/6GTs charged along on the 84 Hours of Nürburgring on the grueling Marathon de la Route. The winner, this Group 6 prototype riding on 8-inch wheels to guarantee enough tire to last between pit stops, covered 6,293 miles (10,068 kilometers).

1976 912E Coupe

Porsche resurrected the 912 model for one year only, strictly for American customers, to bridge the gap between ending production of the 914 and beginning production of its replacement, the 924 model. Using a 2-liter four-cylinder engine derived from the 914 2.0, this model offered 86 brake horsepower.

Porsche quoted 912E top speeds at 109 miles per hour (176 kilometers per hour) and acceleration to 62 miles per hour (100 kilometers) in 13.5 seconds. The cars sold for $10,845.

With only 86 horsepower on tap, air conditioning had to be a bit of a drain. Porsche manufactured just 2,099 of these cars.

won the Grand Touring Class at Le Mans in 1970, averaging 99.27 miles per hour (158.8 kilometers per hour) for the entire race. A 914/6GT won its class in the 1970 Marathon de la Route, an 84-hour enduro run over the Nürburgring circuit, and the cars won the GT season championship.

For 1971, the factory took three cars, fitted with 160-horsepower 911S engines, to the Monte Carlo Rally. Porsche rally-master Björn Waldegaard finished third overall and first in class. On course racing, 914/6GTs had won the SCCA Class C championship in 1970, and they took the IMSA GTU (for cars under 2.5 liters displacement) for 1971. Motor racing at Porsche turned into a protest movement resulting from the FIA's decision to limit engine displacement to 3 liters. So Porsche's efforts with other cars turned to the United States and the Canadian-American Challenge Series, the Can-Am.

As production wound down, Porsche found itself with no product for the next year for its U.S. customers. The planned end of 914 manufacture and the arrival of a new front-engined water-cooled car to replace it, another VW-Porsche collaboration, left the company scrambling. Complying with American emissions and safety standards added to the stress. Porsche resurrected the 912, fitted it with the electronic injection 2-liter 86-horsepower four from the 914, and sold 2,099 of the 912E models, priced midway between the current 911S and the previous 914. ∎

CHAPTER EIGHT

THE WIDOW MAKER BECOMES A *LEGEND*

Wind-Tunnel Testing 917 Long Tail

Eugen Kolb's long-tail bodies gave Porsche racers greater top speed on long straightaway tracks such as Le Mans. The first generation long tails, or *Langheck* bodies, carried over the articulating rear wings from the 908 long tails, but Le Mans regulators tried to ban them.

It was right after Le Mans, round seven of the World Manufacturer's Championship, in June 1967. Ford had brought a seeming-military operation to the race to fulfill three commands from Henry Ford II: Win Le Mans. Win the World Championship. Kick Ferrari's ass!

With various subsidiaries and privateers, Fords accounted for eight of the starting spots, each with an engine larger than 5 liters in displacement. Ferrari countered with six of its 330Ps at 5 liters.

When the checkered flag fell on Sunday, June 11, Ford's Mk IV GT40 won. Ferrari took second and third, and another Mk IV finished fourth. A Porsche 907, a 910, and two 906s filled the next four spots.

Within days of the race, officials in the FIA began to leak word that for 1969, maximum displacement for Sports Cars would be 5 liters. Manufacturers planning to compete had to show 50 completed examples to FIA inspectors before the first race. Ford's 7-liter powerhouses were doomed, but almost everybody else's cars were just fine. The FIA hoped manufacturers would continue racing existing sports cars without the financial drain of producing more. The organization set a high production minimum specifically to discourage anything new.

Alfa Romeo's Autodelta racing organization convinced the FIA to reduce the number, according to historian Anthony Pritchard. Alfa had assembled some 27 of their Tipo 33/2 coupes and already had sold several to privateers. Porsche also sent a representative to Paris to appeal the number. The FIA agreed that 50 was high; it halved the requirement.

Racing spectators had packed circuits to watch the great Ferrari–Ford battles with Porsches, Alfas, and others mixing in additional drama. The FIA recognized that circuits, sponsors, and the sport counted on those crowds.

The FIA did not count on Ferdinand Piëch's ambition. It never expected the Typ 917. And the FIA could not possibly have known of the arrangement Porsche had struck with Volkswagen.

By 1965, VW had manufactured around 1.2 million Beetles. Nearly every decision-maker in the company felt sure the time for this car and its engine had passed. A successor for this profit-maker was nowhere in sight. VW hadn't yet authorized Porsche to begin design concepts on a replacement sedan. Porsche had not yet begun to develop the joint-use sports car, the Typ 914. Fearing an unknown future, VW's board felt it needed to sustain the positive image of air-cooled engines.

Ferdinand Piëch relates this story in his *Auto. Biographie*, published in 2002 by Hoffmann und Campe Verlag in Hamburg. Volkswagen board member Carl Hahn was head of the VW sales organization at the time. He contacted Porsche with an idea to promote the image of air-cooled engines. It took a while to hammer out details and arrangements, but by early 1968, Volkswagen had agreed to fund two-thirds of Porsche's racing budget. Their only condition was that all Porsche race cars must have an air-cooled engine.

VW set no limit. Under Piëch's direction, Porsche racing assembled 60 to 70 race cars per year over the three years of the agreement, from 1969 season through 1971. This backing, however, allowed Piëch and Porsche to proceed with its Sports Car entries. It was far from blind faith, however.

Ferdinand Piëch's father, Anton, became Volkswagen's Managing Director

1969 Typ 917 "Assembly Line"

It was a race to assemble 25 matching 917s for the FIA inspectors. Mechanics made certain the cars would start, drive forward in first gear, backward in reverse, and barely steer; then Porsche put secretaries, accountants, and everyone else to work attaching parts so the cars looked complete.

24 Heures du Mans 1970

"Quick" Vic Elford in number 25, raced Jo Siffert in number 20 from the start at Le Mans in 1970. Porsche had turned over "factory" racing efforts to John Wyer Racing with Gulf Oil sponsoring 917K short-tail cars, while Porsche Salzburg, the Piëch family team, ran Martini-sponsored long tails. Lost in the dust was eventual winner Porsche Salzburg number 23 with Richard Attwood and Hans Herrmann trading driving duties.

in 1941 at the height of World War II. He helped reassemble the company after the war ended. Ferdinand arrived at Porsche in the spring of 1963 and plunged into developing the 2-liter flat-six 911 engine for racing. His brilliant mind grasped details almost instantly. He pushed colleagues and even superiors to try his new ideas. His work on the 904/GTS6, the 906, and every racer that led to the 917s helped convince VW's board to invest in Porsche and in Piëch.

Engineers began planning the 917 in July 1968. Hans Mezger conceived a 4.5-liter opposed 12-cylinder engine. He based displacement on using the same cylinder dimensions, pistons, valves, and timing, and the same connecting rod lengths as the 908. Essentially, this engine added four cylinders to the 908. In fact, internal changes from the 908 to make the flat-12 were substantial. (Porsche homologated a 4.9-liter flat-12 late in 1969 by varying bore and stroke dimensions.)

Hans Mezger conceived a crankshaft with a spur gear in the middle that drove a vertical shaft up to a train of gears to two shafts operating the dual-overhead camshafts on each side. This also spun the distributors and the fuel injection pump. This concept enlarged on the idea Ernst Fuhrmann had originated with

During the long day's journey into night, Porsche Salzburg's long-tail entry failed to finish. After 225 laps, the engine in Vic Elford and Kurt Ahrens' car failed.

his Typ 547 Carrera engine to limit crankcase and camshaft flex at high speeds.

Mezger's engineers cast the interchangeable cylinder heads, cylinders and fins, the timing gear casing, and the camshaft boxes and their covers in aluminum alloy. They chrome-plated the cylinder bores. They split the magnesium-alloy crankcase at its center. This had the effect of making a big engine into two smaller sixes. Two valves per cylinder fed fuel and extracted exhaust, and two spark plugs ensured complete combustion, via two Bosch distributors. Dividing the crankcase also let Porsche's engineers initially split the exhaust with pipes from the front half exiting the car body ahead of the rear wheels and those from the back half coming straight out below the tail. Porsche's press information claimed the engine developed 520 horsepower at 8000 rpm.

The chassis was similar to the 908/02, an adaptation that saved design and development

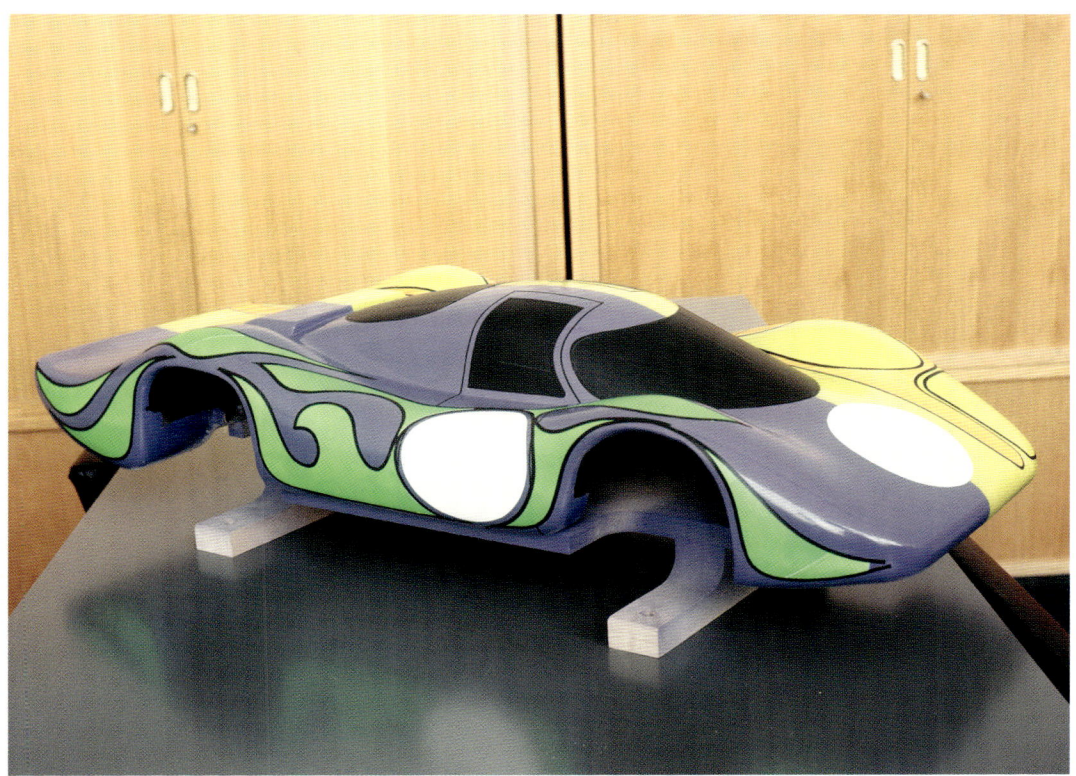

Scale Model 917 *Langheck*

One of styling chief Tony Lapine's more enjoyable tasks was to design paint schemes for the racers. This one-fifth scale model showed his concept for a long tail. It wasn't meant to be psychedelic: Lapine chose the colors of blue irises, his favorite flowers.

1970 Typ 917 *Langheck*

Photographers loved Lapine's paint schemes. Here, Gerard Larrouse and Willi Kauhsen shared driving duties and brought the Typ 917 "Hippie Car" to second place overall at Le Mans in 1970.

time. Piëch's engineers used aluminum-alloy tubing that they argon-welded together to produce a typical pyramid structure at the rear. It had been a sprint. Hans Mezger and another six engineers worked full-time on the engine, and seven other engineers labored on the chassis at the same time. Porsche debuted the car at the Geneva motor show in mid-March 1969. They posted a price of DM 140,000, about $35,700, for the car.

Inspectors arrived at Porsche in early March and found six complete cars and all the parts for the next 19. They approved this, but the FIA directors in Paris then declined. They had to see all 25. There had been too many instances of cars shown in mirrored halls or a manufacturer showing ten cars at breakfast, moving to another location and showing ten cars before lunch, then to another location showing ten cars, another show before afternoon coffee, a move again and again, and a show before and then after dinner. Of course, it had been the same ten cars all day.

To meet the FIA deadline, racing manager Rico Steinemann recruited secretaries, accountants, and others to assemble 917s on the 911 car line. Racing mechanics made sure the engines ran and the cars could engage first gear and reverse. He lined up 25 cars in the driveway of Werke I, parked so closely that they only could go forward or backward but not turn. The show car and a second development mule were complete and would run well on a race course. The others were there to pose for pictures, to start, roll forward five meters, and return.

The FIA came, saw, tested, departed, and then the 917 mechanics dismantled them all. Racers, as Piëch knew, were always modified up to the last minute before the race. Many of the cars returned to parts bins.

Engineer Helmut Flegl had worked on aerodynamic developments for the 917. He first gathered experience with the 907 long tails. He helped convert the 908 coupe into the 908/03 stubby roadster. He was part of the decision to conceive the 917 as a long-tail car with interchangeable short-rear bodywork. He and test driver Peter Falk put in hours at the wind tunnel testing long-tailed racers.

Wind-Tunnel Testing 917 Short Tail

Aerodynamics as it related to handling still was an imprecise science, and it took the fresh eyes of John Wyer's team manager John Horsman to understand what might improve the 917 *Kürz*, or short-tail cars. While testing at Zeltweg, Horsman and his mechanics grafted tin onto the rear of the cars, raising the bodywork over the rear wheels and developing the channel up the center of the rear deck.

1970 Gulf-Porsche 917K

John Horsman's observation that gnats hit the nose of the cars but missed the rear fenders told him air skimmed over those fenders too. He elevated the bodywork. In this photo the Gulf-Porsche 917K driven frequently by Pedro Rodriguez and Leo Kinnunen streaks along glued to the ground.

"But the short tail was never really tested in the wind tunnel," Flegl explained. "It was just put on the race car. And the aerodynamics were just wrong.

"The motivation behind the Nine-Seventeen was to go for the World Championship," he continued. "Mr. Piëch said, 'This is my goal!' Before those times, we had excellent cars. The Nine-Oh-Eight could win Le Mans. But, really to win the championship, you needed major luck. The Nine-Seventeen should be that car. It would be the luck."

Piëch provided his staff directives for the new racer. There was not enough development time through 1969 to achieve his goals. For 1970, they planned to conquer the racetracks where a short tail was right for the car. But, with Volkswagen's backing, Piëch had other

After its regular life as a factory backup car, Steve McQueen acquired this 917K to use in his film *Le Mans*. Several years later, McQueen sold the car to Californian Otis Chandler who, during a subsequent restoration, inadvertently gave the car number 1.

strategies in mind. After losing at Daytona with the 908s, he and Steinemann talked. Piëch excelled at race car development and believed that he and Porsche could accomplish more with the 917 given another two years.

Piëch, however, referred to his grander ambition: "To be the best," Steinemann recalled. "Everywhere. His strategy was to win the sports car world championship, win Le Mans, win the Formula One world championship, and then to go to Indianapolis.

"After the sixty-nine season, we would concentrate on developing these new things. We needed someone to race our cars in a way that we don't waste time. We needed somebody excellent."

John Wyer's Gulf Ford team had beaten Porsche's 908s at Daytona. Steinemann knew Wyer and his organization. Piëch encouraged a conversation. At Sebring in March 1969, Steinemann met Wyer and made his pitch. Wyer's Gulf Ford Mirages won again, and immediately afterward, John and Gulf VP Grady Davis flew to Stuttgart to meet with Piëch and Ferry Porsche, where they signed an agreement.

"They got the materials at no charge," Steinemann explained. "From the moment it left Stuttgart, it was on their expense. We split drivers, paying Jo Siffert and Brian Redman. Wyer paid Pedro Rodriguez and Leo Kinnunen."

After Le Mans in 1969, where Ford GTs, now with 5-liter engines and run by Wyer's organization, took a fourth consecutive victory, Piëch and Porsche knew they had to pay attention to the 917 handling. The car had won its first race at the Österreichring circuit near Zeltweg, Austria, in August. But it had been a handful for Jo Siffert and Kurt Ahrens. On October 15, about two months after the World Championship race there, Porsche returned to Zeltweg to examine the 917's aerodynamics under full scrutiny from Peter Falk (in charge of the test session), Helmut Flegl, and Wyer's team manager, John Horsman, and a few of his colleagues. Falk had brought along a 917 Spyder prototype. Its flat rear surface had emerged from Tony Lapine's design studio. It had evolved over a 10-week period during the summer, resulting from work on the 908/02, the *Flunder*. The spyder was four seconds quicker around the track, no matter who drove the coupe or the open car. It stood to reason that the body configuration made the difference. The Porsche engineers had added vertical spoilers onto the rear of each of the two test coupes, but they had no effect on handling. It was mid-fall, and there were clouds of gnats in the air. The fronts of both cars were splattered with their bodies.

1971 917 Experimental Flat-16-Cylinder Spyder

When the first Can-Am Spyder engine tests revealed just 580 brake horsepower from the 4.5-liter flat-12s, Ferdinand Piëch welcomed any new idea. One result was this 7-liter flat-16, which developed 755 horsepower and convinced Piëch to pursue the idea of turbocharging as the "more technically interesting" approach. This car never raced.

"I noted there were hardly any dead gnats on the rear spoilers," John Horsman wrote in his biography, *Racing in the Rain*, "Since they are very small and light, I knew the gnats would flow over the bodywork exactly as the air flowed, and similar to the smoke from wands used in wind tunnels. Any gnat remnant on the white paint would indicate the air had touched that surface. I knew immediately that we had to raise the rear deck and then attach small adjustable spoilers to the trailing edge. It was obvious to me," he added, "that if the whole rear body surface was in the airstream, it would be able to exert some downforce."

Horsman borrowed one of the two coupes from Falk and Flegl and got some sheet aluminum, tin snips, and "racer tape" from the Porsche transporters. With his team manager, David Yorke, and master mechanics Ermanno Cuoghi and Peter Davies, they fashioned bodywork that extended from the back of the doors up to the top of the extended vertical spoilers, relying on them for rear support. Using track Armco safety barriers as a hammering form, they pounded and bent the aluminum to the contours Horsman wanted. It took them the rest of the afternoon and into the night.

"To the horror of the German observers," he wrote, "Ermanno and Peter snipped and riveted the rest of the afternoon. . . . Back at their garage in town, we completed our desecration of the 917, wheeling it out the next morning for testing. This was the moment of truth for all engineers. . . . It looked very ugly and Brian Redman was rather rude about it."

On the way to victory there were a few stumbles. Porsche engineer Helmut Flegl (blue jacket at far left) walked around the rear of the car while driver George Follmer waited patiently for mechanics to adjust the fuel injection.

138

CHAPTER EIGHT

1972 917/10 Porsche+Audi L&M Can-Am Turbo

Mark Donohue started the 1972 Can-Am season in this 917/10 but crashed, and George Follmer stepped in. Follmer caught on quickly and won the final four events to capture the series championship in this car.

George Follmer's office included a variable boost knob in the upper right. He ran between 13 and 19 psi of boost, between 0.9 and 1.34 bar, good enough for 211 miles per hour (338 kilometers per hour) on the long straight at Riverside.

When George Follmer turned up the boost, the 5-liter fuel-injected twin-turbocharged flat-12-cylinder engine developed 910 brake horsepower. It provided sufficient performance in a car weighing just 1,720 pounds (782 kilograms).

Redman was first to drive it. The day before he had gone out, run two or three laps, and returned, announcing, "No better." On this day, "Brian stayed out," Horsman recalled, "lapping a little faster each time around. At the end of [seven] laps he came in and said, 'That's it—now it's a racing car!'" Contrary to popular myth, it was Austrian gnats, not the shape of the 917 Can-Am prototype, that inspired Horsman to change the shape of the coupes. More modifications followed, including forming a valley between rear venders to better manage airflow over the car and a new nose. But, as Horsman wrote, "After months of being a monster, the 917 was tamed."

At the 1970 Daytona 24-hour event, Wyer's team with the new improved 917Ks (for *Kürz*, or short) took first and second. By the end of 1971, when new FIA rules restricted all cars to 3-liter maximum displacement (matching contemporary Formula One rules in the hopes of standardizing engines), Porsche had entered 24 World Championship racers over the two years. The 908s scored 4 victories, while 917s won 15; John Wyer's Gulf team took 11 of them, the Piëch family Porsche Salzburg entries took 1, Le Mans in 1970, and the Martini team won 2 more for the Piëchs and a third for privateer Hans-Dieter Dechent at Le Mans in 1971. Porsche's racing department had assembled five 917 long-tail cars, 36 short-tail versions, and two spyders.

The 917 program cost Porsche close to DM 15 million, approximately $4.2 million, or roughly DM 349,000 per car, about $98,250. Porsche had increased the price of the 917K from DM 140,000 in 1969 ($35,700) to DM 280,000 in 1971 ($80,500 at the 1971 exchange rate). The company sold its 917/10 Spyders for DM 325,000 ($93,400) and its turbocharged 917/30s went for DM 450,000, or $129,300. Not surprisingly, the 908 campaigns had cost nearly as much.

Even with support from Volkswagen, the nearly DM 30 million racing program had left Porsche with expenditures that nearly doubled its previous racing budgets of DM 5 million per year. VW's help was pivotal in achieving the World Championship. But it had cost too much. When VW CEO Kurt Lotz retired in early 1971, Rudolf Leiding succeeded him. Leiding had no faith in air-cooled engines, and he was shepherding the development and introduction of the Golf as a water-cooled Beetle replacement. He ended Porsche racing financing soon after he arrived while planning for the 1972 racing season was under way. Porsche retired from the series. But it did not retire from racing the 917s.

Jo Siffert had become enthralled with the American Can-Am championship, and he

Whether Willi Kauhsen pulled over to let the Mercedes-Benz motorcade go past or to let the snowstorm blow over is unclear. This photo gave new meaning to the term "Winter Testing" for Kauhsen and his 1972 European Interserie entry.

believed that the 917 would be competitive. In the summer of 1969, Piëch's engineers quietly prepared a prototype spyder (the one at the test at Zeltweg that brought 917-coupe handling under control). Entered by Porsche's U.S. marketing arm, Porsche+Audi, Siffert ran 7 of the 11 races in the only 917 P+A, but it was enough to wake up the motorsports world.

Porsche didn't compete in the Can-Am in 1970 because of its efforts to win the World Championship with 917 coupes. The 3-liter limitation for the 1972 season of World Championship of Makes made it clear that if Porsche were to capitalize on its developments, it must return to America. They ran a limited season in 1971, a season that ended when Jo Siffert died in an F1 crash at Brands Hatch.

For 1972, Porsche "hired" Roger Penske to run the Can-Am campaign with sponsorship from Liggett and Myers Tobacco Company (L&M). For this series, Porsche launched its turbocharged 917, the 917/10, and later the 917/30. Turbos had done well at the Indianapolis 500 (a unique form of racing where drivers are at full throttle nearly all of each lap). On a road circuit, with acceleration and braking taking the engine on and off the turbo's boost, it was a different challenge altogether. Hans Mezger and fellow engineer Valentin Schäffer introduced reliability and reduced turbo lag, the lapse of time between pressing the accelerator and the highly pressurized fuel mixture reaching the cylinders. Courageous drivers learned to operate counterintuitively, braking hard into

1972 Typ 917/30 Experimental

Herbert Müller commanded the same respect in the 1972 European Interserie with this 917/30 as Mark Donohue earned in the United States. This racer also was an experimental test bed that Flegl equipped with variable-length tubes behind the driver to change its wheelbase from 2300mm to 2400mm or 2500mm to determine the best handling.

Not everyone was turbocharged back in the wildest days of North America's Can-Am Challenge. With close to 20,000 horsepower heading south from Riverside's Turn 5, the noise brought everyone to the fences.

the the turn but mashing the accelerator long before the apex, relying on the lag to carry them safely to the point at which horsepower could double or even triple on leaving the turn.

By the time Mezger and Schäffer had the twin-turbocharged 917s dialed in, they saw 850 horsepower from the 4.5-liter engines for the European Can-Am equivalent, the Interserie races. For the U.S. Can-Am racers, the unlimited regulation let Porsche go to 5 liters, and they got nearly 1,000 brake horsepower from these engines in 1971. Mark Donahue dominated the series. An accident early in the 1972 season left him seriously injured, and George Follmer stepped in. Driving the L&M 917/10, he won the championship for Penske and Porsche. Donahue returned for 1973 in the 5.4-liter 917/30, which developed 1,100 brake horsepower at race boost levels. Porsche constructed a test-and-development car with the potential to vary its wheelbase to determine the best handling, and a primary race car and a backup for the Can-Am series. In the cockpit of the 1,764-pound (800-kilogram) car, Donahue could control boost pressure to as high as 2.8 bar, 39 pounds per square

1973 Porsche+Audi Sunoco 917/30

Porsche and team-owner Roger Penske built the 917/30 to fit Mark Donahue's capabilities and endowed it with one of Porsche's wildest engines ever, the 5.4-liter twin-turbocharged flat-12. It developed 1,500 horsepower in the form used by Donohue to set a speed record of 220.6 miles per hour (352.9 kilometers per hour) after the season ended.

inch to increase horsepower momentarily, and he could adjust rear anti-roll bar stiffness. At full boost, he reportedly had 1,560 horsepower available.

Racing rule makers and promoters are a fickle lot, happy when the racing is even, happier when the grandstands are full. The unequalled success that led the FIA to rule against 7-liter Ford GTs, and then 5-liter 917 coupes, led them to hobble turbocharged engines in the American Can-Am series for 1974. Officially, concerns over high speeds (Donohue's car hit 245 miles per hour, 394 kilometers per hour) and high fuel consumption of these lower-compression engines led to a rule requiring 3-mile-per-gallon fuel economy. (In October 1973, the Organization of Petroleum Exporting Countries shook the world with production reductions and an oil shipment embargo to the West.) But, as Jürgen Barth observed, "Instead of re-energizing the Can-Am by encouraging more racers using less expensive technology, the anti-turbo rules were the series death sentence. The Can-Am died after nineteen seventy-four for a lack of spectators." ∎

CHAPTER NINE

NECESSITY IS THE MOTHER OF INVENTION

1973 911 Carrera RS 2.7 Lightweight

Under challenges from Ernst Fuhrmann, Porsche engineer Tilman Brodbeck devised the front lip air dam, and about a year later he created the rear ducktail, or bürzel, to control airflow over the car and improve handling at speed. Here, Jürgen Barth drove a preproduction prototype with an early version of the side graphics.

PORSCHE'S RACING DEPARTMENT ALREADY HAD LEARNED THE IMPORTANCE OF CAREFULLY READING FIA REGULATIONS. For engineers such as Piëch, Bott, Flegl, Mezger, and a recent hire named Norbert Singer, rules created the 917 and regularly led them to the winner's podium. It was a talent among engineers and project directors that approached fine art. Jochen Neerpasch and Michael Kranefuss became masters at it. Unfortunately for Porsche, these two worked for Ford.

In 1968, Ford of Germany went racing with their new Capri coupes. These were the Mustangs of Europe with water-cooled front engines underneath long hoods, with small cockpits, and short rear decks. The first several years passed like any fledgling program. Development took time, and victory was elusive. But they did win, and that tantalized the designers, engineers, managers, and especially the board members who funded the next year. By late 1971, the car that first appeared with a 170 horsepower 2.3-liter V-6 had grown to 2.9 liters pushing out 280 horsepower. Neerpasch and Kranefuss widened wheelwells, gave it a broad front spoiler, and a nowhere-near-stock configuration rear suspension than helped it win every race but one for the season. For 1972, although Ford's Zakspeed operation lost Neerpasch and engineer Martin Braumbart to a new motorsports operation beginning at BMW, Kranefuss took the now 300-horsepower Capris with Formula One car–sized brakes to the championship a second year. Then he started selling cars to privateers.

By early 1973, Kranefuss had 320-horsepower Capris with wild aero-package bodywork. Neerpasch had turned BMW's luxurious 2.8 coupe into a fearsome CSL model for teams like Schnitzer and Alpina. FIA's Group 3 racing was intensely competitive. Against them in the same events on the same weekends, Porsche 911s competed in Group 4, not directly, but appearance was important.

"I was just standing in the pits," Ernst Fuhrmann recalled in an interview in May 1991. "I watched many Nine-Elevens. And the Fords and the BMWs were passing them. Even our fastest Nine-Eleven, I think it was lapped by a Ford and then a BMW!" The appearance at the Hockenheimring or anywhere else that a compact Ford had lapped a 911, flustered Fuhrmann. In its own classes, Porsche GT racers found themselves fighting to stay ahead of Ferrari 365GTB/4 Daytonas and Ford V-8-engined DeTomaso Panteras. "I went looking for one of our engineers, Mr. Singer, or Mr. Falk, to ask him why this happened. I found another one, younger, one of Mr. Singer's protégés."

Wolfgang Berger, the protégé, explained that Ford's racing director in Cologne, Michael Kranefuss, had produced a small group of *rennsport* models that really were prototypes that bent FIA rules. For a production-based class, Kranefuss had pulled everything not needed for racing from the car, cutting its weight greatly. The 1972 Capris weighed 1,980 pounds, the class minimum of 900 kilograms. Large wings and spoilers improved their aerodynamics, and wide tires further enhanced handling. FIA rules had not specifically forbidden such changes. Fuhrmann recalled that Berger went further, explaining what Porsche might do to win. "'Your analysis is interesting,' I told him," Fuhrmann said. "Think about it, and then tell me what you will do."

1973 911 Carrera RS 2.7 Touring

In Lightweight (M471) or Touring (M472) trim, the 1973 RS Carrera became one of Porsche's most sought-after driver's and collector's cars. Porsche produced 200 lightweights and 1,308 touring models with the 210-brake-horsepower, 2,687cc flat-six-cylinder engine.

The 2.7-liter engine used bore and stroke of 90x70.4mm and Bosch mechanical fuel injection to generate 210 brake horsepower. This was good enough to get the 2,112-pound (960-kilogram) car from 0 to 62.5 miles per hour (100 kilometers per hour) in 5.8 seconds and to a top speed of 152 miles per hour (245 kilometers per hour).

Soon after returning to Porsche in 1971, Fuhrmann appointed Helmuth Bott to head all development, including design and testing. Aerodynamics had plagued Porsche's 911 shape since Butzi created it. Bott had assigned a newly hired aerodynamicist, Tilman Brodbeck, to keep the Porsche noses on the ground. Brodbeck's efforts in Stuttgart University's wind tunnel developed the subtle chin spoiler that first appeared on the 1972 911S. Within days of the Hockenheim race, Bott called Brodbeck into his office again.

"'Porsche Nine-Eleven drivers,' he said, 'have a lot of trouble when they go for the curves on the racetrack. Even the Ford Capri and the BMW coupe are quicker through the curves. You must do something. Anything! Without changing the whole car, it must be possible that these racers can buy something to make the car better. Think about it!'

1972 911 Carrera RS

Running a preproduction model, Polish rally driver Sobieslaw Zasada, shown here in the mud, is on his way to second overall in the 3,310-mile (5,300-kilometer) 1972 East African Safari Rally. Weather was always unpredictable, with dry weather bringing choking dust and rains leaving all of Kenya in mud.

During the East African Safari Rally, pits were wherever crew members—or racers themselves—could escape from mud or dust. Drivers and co-drivers often changed tires with an audience of Kenyan spectators.

"I'll never forget it," Brodbeck recalled. Now, as head of Porsche *Exclusiv,* he is surrounded in his office in Werke I by options and accessories that boulevard racers buy to make their cars look and perform better. "It was a time when people really didn't know about spoilers. On normal cars, nearly nothing. On racing cars, not much."

In 1968, during his last year at school, he owned a Fiat 850 GT coupe. He liked it because it had 5 horsepower more than the standard 850 coupe he owned, and it had a small lip on the rear. He asked a professor about it. "Perhaps it has to do with aerodynamics," the man told him, "but I think it is more something from design."

"We went back into the Stuttgart wind tunnel," Brodbeck said, "the same one where we had done the front lip for the Carrera. Now we started with welding wire to make a form. The front had needed such a little bit. We thought about how to change the shape of the rear. Over the next three days we formed this new shape. It was trial and error. It

1973 911 Carrera RSR 2.8

Jürgen Barth and Georg Loos co-drove this RSR at Le Mans in June 1973, finishing tenth overall. They drove 312 laps, 2,656 miles (4,249 kilometers), averaging 111 miles per hour (177 kilometers per hour).

changed things so much with the lift. But you know, in those days, it was still just theory. We had to have a real driver take the car out and test it."

Günther Steckkönig, a Porsche test driver since 1953 and a factory racer by the mid-1960s, took the welding-wire-and-sheet-metal structure onto Weissach's track. After several laps, Steckkönig came in and announced that the car felt much better. Brodbeck then took the wing to Lapine's styling studios. "'You have to do something that is smoother.' We told them the important points for the aerodynamics, where they have to be. Then they made this little thing, this ducktail, the bürzel."

Bott sent a mocked-up prototype to VW's test track in Ehra-Lessien. In the 1950s, working with Zora Arkus-Duntov, the two had developed handling tests intended to unsettle a car. One of these involved a violent lane-change maneuver. Bott's standard tolerated three fishtail swerves before the car either stabilized or else went back for more work. Bott invited Brodbeck to accompany him for the first ride of the day.

"The first time," Brodbeck recalled with a laugh, "he was driving about one hundred eighty kilometers [roughly 112 miles] per hour on a straight. And then suddenly he yanked [the steering wheel] hard to the right. You can imagine what that does. I got pale. Without the spoilers it was awful what this car did. With the spoilers, it was amazing."

"Everybody said, 'Well, something else must be changed, tires, suspension. It cannot just be these two small spoilers.' But Mr. Bott used the same car. He only had technicians change the front panel and the rear deck lid. The difference was so great. With the spoilers it did three swings and then it went straight ahead."

In the meanwhile, Wolfgang Berger also had made progress. Fuhrmann had given him direct access, eliminating normal chain-of-command reporting hierarchy. Porsche

1973 911 Carrera RSR 3.0 IROC
Roger Penske ordered 15 identical RSRs and instigated the International Race of Champions by culling drivers from Indianapolis, NASCAR, and sports car racing to run a four-event series. At the first race at Riverside, California, in late October 1973, Bobby Allison (number 11) and Emerson Fittipaldi (number 12) cornered two abreast ahead of David Pearson (number 9) and Gordon Johncock (number 10).

racing engineers learned from Piëch's 911R models, and they applied the same thinking now. First Berger gutted a 911T. In the engine the Biral cylinders used on production 911s nearly had reached maximum bore at 88mm before making cylinder walls too thin to be reliable. Helmut Flegl and Hans Mezger had used a nickel-silicone carbide called *Nikasil* for liners on 917 cylinders. This allowed a few extra millimeters of bore. Mezger increased the dimension to 90mm from 84. This brought displacement to 2,687cc and moved the 911 up to the next racing class, under 3 liters. Porsche quoted output at 210 brake horsepower compared with the 911S output at 180.

The FIA regulations allowed wider wheels. This let Berger extend rear fenders and fit 917 brakes with a prototype anti-lock system (ABS) from Teldix. A front spoiler that Falk, Singer, and Mark Donahue had developed for the Can-Am 917/30 had incorporated a low-mounted oil cooler, and its shape channeled air off

1974 911 Carrera RSR Turbo

Ernst Fuhrmann was so worried by the size of the rear wing, or *eindecker*, that Norbert Singer used to keep the RSR Turbos on the ground that he ordered them painted black so people would not notice them. Manfred Schurti and Helmuth Koinigg finished sixth in the 1,000-kilometer race at Nürburgring in car 9, right behind van Lennep and Müller in the identical number 8.

the nose. Berger adapted this and created a larger version of Brodbeck's *bürzel*. This one reached the height of the rear window. Then, according to Porsche historians Thomas Gruber and Georg Konradsheim, Porsche asked old friend Paul Ernst Strähle to enter the new car as his own Group 5 Prototype in the 1000 kilometers at Österreichring on June 25. Fuhrmann hoped this diversionary tactic might avoid revealing that the new car was a factory prototype. Brodbeck's test driver Günther Steckkönig, along with 1969—and 1970—Monte Carlo Rally winner Björn Waldegaard, drove the prototype to tenth overall, finishing just behind open sports racers.

The 911 was back.

It was a crucial test for Fuhrmann. He had no money and no 911 replacement. He needed to rekindle interest among racers and customers in a car he thought was slated for extinction. Racing could accomplish that. But this was racing at its best since it cost so little. A production option that reflected the character of this

1976 Typ 934

These Group 4 turbocharged cars appeared in time for the 1976 racing season, and many owners campaigned them into the early 1980s with great success. In 1982 at Le Mans, this particular car finished first in Group 4 and 13th overall with Richard Cleare, Tony Dron, and Richard Jones driving.

1976 Typ 935

Jacky Ickx and Jochen Mass debuted the 935 at Autodromo di Vallelunga north of Rome on April 4, 1976. This early car used air-to-air intercooling, a technology that progressed quickly into liquid intercooling, but not before Ickx and Mass claimed first overall with the new Group 5 racer.

new racer would excite buyers just as Fuhrmann's Carrera 356s had done.

Porsche regularly proved two of motoring's oldest maxims: Racing improves the breed; and race wins on Sunday bring sales on Monday. Norbert Singer was assigned to take competition development and racing programs for the 911 as far as he could. The full force of Wolfgang Berger's small production engineering staff along with Tony Lapine's styling studio would work on this new car called the 911S 2.7. The target was to produce a Group 4–legal production model devoid of anything that did not help racing, yet that would still—somehow—appeal to 500 paying customers. But "S Two Seven?"

Marketing grumbled that numbers had no charisma. Oddly, no one had challenged the appeal of "911."

Within days, they resurrected a popular name, reaching into their racing past, and christened the car the *Carrera*. Marketing had anticipated using the name over future generations. They added RS, *rennsport*, to the name, and Tony Lapine's staff created a script logo that was striped across the bottom of the doors in colors that matched the Fuchs five-spoke wheels.

Fuhrmann planned the 911S 2.7 as an addition to the production line, above the 2.4-liter 911S already in production. Timing was crucial; he knew BMW had a 3-liter

Leaning hard through the Karousel, Porsche's new Group 5 titan—the 935—made its debut at the Nürburgring. For drivers Rolf Stommelen and Manfred Schurti, it was a short race, however, lasting only nine laps before Schurti suffered a broken distributor rotor.

CHAPTER NINE

1977 935/77 2.0 "Baby"
While Porsche's 935s cleaned up in over-2-liter racing categories, Ernst Fuhrmann complained that Ford and BMW still triumphed in under-2-liter classes. This prompted Norbert Singer's engineers to create "Baby," based on a 1.4-liter turbocharged flat-six with 20 psi boost (1.4 bar) developing 380 horsepower. The car earned its nickname when mechanics trimmed 400 pounds of weight (182 kilograms), bringing the car to just 1,599 pounds (727 kilograms). It finished its single race half a lap ahead of second place, just to show competitors Porsche could win there, too.

coupe coming in late 1972. Fuhrmann was motivated: What if Zuffenhausen assembled the required 500 cars, each stripped (and striped) as Norbert Singer needed them for homologation? In a peace offering to sales and marketing, Fuhrmann created a second trim and option level to broaden the car's appeal. Singer's engineers created the RSH homologation version with narrow wheels and no sway bars. The M471 package, the sports version, fitted wider tires and thick anti-sway bars. The "Touring" version, M472, provided appointments near the 911S production run, offering the style of the new Carrera RS without sacrificing comfort. For Norbert Singer's factory racing purposes and customer sales, the M491 option, the RSR, or *rennsport rennen* version, gave buyers a 2.8-liter racing engine, a factory-installed roll bar, 11-inch-wide rear tires, and flared fenders.

Wolfgang Berger completed his prototype in April 1972. He used a 1972 E-series body that still had the external oil filler cap on its passenger side. It lacked even preproduction versions of Brodbeck's front and rear spoilers and Lapine's script logos. Another eight prototypes emerged before the 500-unit production run began in October. Fuhrmann pressured sales, and they shifted into high gear. They had a single prototype but stacks

1978 911SC East African Safari Rally

Porsche had tried its hand at Africa's Safari rallies since the mid-1960s, but it always was a bridesmaid and never the bride. The 26th running of the Safari rally in 1978 through 3,125 miles (5,000 kilometers) of mud and dust was the same story with Björn Waldegaard fourth in this car, behind Vic Preston who finished second in number 14.

of brochures, and they called personally on likely 911S customers to encourage an RS purchase instead.

Fuhrmann set the Paris Auto Show on October 5, 1972, as the public debut. According to Karl Ludvigsen, Porsche's sales staff already had recorded 51 orders for the M471 sport versions by opening day. Porsche listed this car at DM 33,000 (roughly $10,350 had it been available in the United States). For another DM 2,500, about $785, a buyer got the Touring package with full 911S luxury. Orders flooded in. Within a week of the end of the Paris show, Porsche had sold all 500 it needed for homologation. Fuhrmann kept the order books open, and demand finally trickled out at 1,580. He raised the price DM 1,000, about $315, after completing number 500, but no one complained. With those extra sales, the FIA reclassified the car as a Group 3 Grand Touring. In that class, it owned the field.

Porsche made no effort to meet U.S. emissions standards with a car it intended only for racing in Europe. As a result, Porsche did not offer Carrera 2.7 RS models in America. These cars were unavailable for years until EPA standards relaxed on older cars.

While demand for these cars surprised Ludwigsberg sales staff, they did not miss the lessons. Porsche owners were loyal; buyers recognized and valued something unique. They were willing to pay a premium price to be part of a small group that could own a limited edition model.

With fuel injection, the 3-liter 250-brake-horsepower SC engines were strong enough for East Africa. But it was the weather that engineering could not factor with the rear-drive 911s.

Porsche assembled 20 of these SC-RS models to meet FIA regulations for Group B for the European Rally Series. The 3-liter engines developed 255 horsepower in cars weighing 2,112 pounds (960 kilograms).

Norbert Singer's racing department assembled 55 of the RSR 2.8-liter models (achieved by enlarging bore another 2mm to 92mm). These sold for DM 59,000, about $22,265 delivered to the United States. These cars started life as plain RSH models that came off the new Zuffenhausen assembly line without engines or transmissions and went to the former racing shops in Werke I where they received Hans Mezger's 2,806cc engine. Porsche rated these engines at 300 brake horsepower in a car weighing 1,875 pounds (852 kilograms).

Between Le Mans trials in April and the race in June, Singer changed rear tire widths from 12 inches to 15. Fuhrmann, an engine man, objected to the drop in top speed of about 10 miles per hour (6 kilometers per hour) due to wind resistance. But cornering and tire life improved with the wider wheels and tires.

"I remember Mr. Fuhrmann was really disappointed about the top speed," Singer

158

CHAPTER NINE

recalled. "On the morning before the race, he came up and said, 'Okay, tell the driver we race flat out from the first lap. Twenty-four hours.'

"I went to Herbert Müller," Singer continued, "'You can make your dinner reservation. Mr. Fuhrmann wants 'flat out.' It'll be a short race.'"

But Müller's car, shared with Gijs van Lennep, running a near sprint around the clock, had no problems. It finished fourth overall behind two pure sports racers and a prototype. Other RSRs took eighth and tenth. By season's end, Porsche's road-car derived 911 Carrera RSR 2.8 was class champion. In answering Fuhrmann's question, Wolfgang Berger and Norbert Singer had resuscitated the 911. This was the car that Porsche management had sentenced to die at the end of 1973. From here, the 911 took off with the vigor of a successful heart-transplant patient.

With the RSR homologated for Group 3, Porsche's next step was back to Group 4. Singer's competition department assembled an initial group of 30 cars using a turbocharged version of the 3-liter RSR engine. Porsche called this series the Typ 934. The factory offered these to privateers at DM 108,000, about $41,850 in 1974 dollars. The 911 silhouette grew wider with bolted-on wheel arch extensions (fender flairs) and a distinctive front spoiler that fed air to a central oil cooler, intercooler radiators, and both front brake ducts. Based on the planned series production 911 Turbo model, FIA rules set minimum weight at 2,470 pounds (1,120 kilograms). This gave Singer and his engineers leeway in relocating the oil tank and battery.

While most Group B cars were turbocharged, drivers competing in the SC-RS models enjoyed not having to work against turbo-boost lag. The rear engines made the cockpits slightly cooler as well.

They placed extra ballast into corners where it best served handling. Though Singer gutted the interior, he kept stock door panels and even the electric window lifts because they weighed less than manual regulator cranks.

The turbocharged engine introduced Bosch's K-Jetronic electronic fuel-injection system to Porsche's racing program. The fuel charge passed through a large intercooler, this one cooled by water pumped through twin radiators in the front spoiler. This system dropped fuel temperature from about 300 degrees Fahrenheit to about 125 degrees (150 degrees Celsius to 50 degrees). Porsche used the same turbocharger it had chosen for the 917s but installed two for the 934s, operating at 1.3 bar of boost, about 18.5 pounds per square inch. The

2,993cc engine initially produced 485 brake horsepower. By late 1976, 934s raced with more than 580 horsepower operating with 1.7 bar of boost, about 24 psi. A few years later, 934s routinely exceeded 600 horsepower and, depending on gearing, reached 190 miles per hour (305 kilometers per hour). This was remarkable performance considering the car's weight and its large frontal area and wind resistance

While customers raced the 934s, Singer's factory efforts went into Group 5 racing with another 911 derivative, the 935. One of Norbert Singer's greatest talents was reading FIA regulations and discovering not only what was allowed and what was not, but also what went unstated. If something was not expressly permitted or banned, it might not be legal, but it was not illegal. FIA rules for World Championship events called for production-based cars. These were the so-called "silhouette" rules. These saved Singer the expense of developing a new prototype that Porsche

Porsche built cars to stay together, but team manager David Richards rebuilt his Rothmans entries to come apart quickly for repairs when needed. After each event, his mechanics largely rebuilt every car.

CHAPTER NINE

still could not afford. It also let them capitalize on knowledge that Mezger and Valentin Schäffer had gained from the 917 Turbos. At the last minute, the FIA delayed Group 5 rules until the 1976 season. Porsche's factory efforts went toward supporting 934 privateers and further honing what became the 935.

"But," as Jürgen Barth explained, "this time was not wasted because the regulations for Group Five turned out to be different from what we expected. And so this allowed us to change specifications for the series production model Nine-Thirty on which we based the Nine-Thirty-Five."

As had happened with the 917s, again Porsche was not the only manufacturer that developed a new car for the series.

1978 Typ 935/78 "Moby Dick"
Norbert Singer's creative interpretation of the rules scandalized and antagonized the FIA. Again, they were stumped, and Porsche's ultimate cheater—nicknamed "Moby Dick" when it still was unpainted in white because of its size and its high, wide tail—went to the races.

Porsche developed a new 935 engine for this car, the 935/71, using water-cooled twin-cam cylinder heads and twin turbochargers. The engine displaced just 3.2 liters, yet with full boost it developed nearly 900 horsepower.

BMW hurriedly revised its CSL coupes with 3.5-liter motors and more. These gave Porsche a run for the championship, going all the way to a rain-soaked Watkins Glen six-hour race to give Porsche the title.

Because Fuhrmann was unsure just how successful Porsche's Group 5 car would be, and indeed, how successful the new Group 5 series would be, he challenged Singer and the others to come up with an open prototype for Group 6 to compete against the French Alpine Renault open sports racers. Fuhrmann also had heard rumors that Alfa Romeo might have a prototype.

He raised the idea in a meeting, and the engineers fired back excuses: other

162

CHAPTER NINE

At Le Mans, along the Mulsanne Straight, Rolf Stommelen touched 227.5 miles per hour (366 kilometers per hour) in practice with full boost delivering 900 horsepower. For the race, drivers dialed it back to 750 horsepower, and drivers Bob Wallek, Jürgen Barth, and Jacky Ickx brought the car home in second overall.

1976 Typ 936

Ernst Fuhrmann's affinity for black cars spilled over to Count Luigi Rossi, who authorized painting his own colors on top of Fuhrmann's black for the 1976 300-kilometer debut race at Nürburgring. But photographers couldn't see the car, and few photos made the newspapers. The Martini cars immediately went back to white.

911-derived projects, supporting privateers, developing 935s, no time, no money. . . ."

Fuhrmann listened and then reminded them, "We have a lot of spare parts from the Nine-Seventeen in stock," he said. "It should be easy to make a sports prototype car out of the parts . . . make a new space frame, a new body. . . ."

Singer, master of the loophole, thought he had found one: "A new body meant air tunnel time," he remembered telling his boss.

"You have a lot of experience," Fuhrmann said. "You don't need a wind tunnel. Just make it!" That was November 1975, and for the next six months, engineers already pressed with other projects slept even less. Helmut Flegl, the project director, ran the new car, the Typ 936, for the first time in late March. It used

1976 Typ 936/81

After winning Le Mans in 1976 in Martini colors, a Typ 936 took the race in 1977, also for Martini, then second overall for Porsche in 1978, and then returned in 1981, sponsored by Jules men's cologne, to win again.

a turbocharged 2.1-liter they had developed for the Carrera RSR that developed 520 new horsepower. This was more than adequate for the 1,540-pound (700-kilogram) open racer. Technicians formed the fiberglass body by hand blending features from the long-tail 917s with tricks from the Can-Am 917/30s. Most notably, they adopted the large horizontal rear wing from the Can-Am cars.

It failed to finish its first outing. But then it won at Monza, Imola, and Enna-Pergusa in Sicily. For Le Mans, Flegl's hard workers finished a second car, so Porsche entered two cars. It was a valiant effort: Jacky Ickx and Gijs van Lennep won in the second car. Rolf Stommelen and Manfred Schurti drove a factory-entered/Martini-Rossi–sponsored 935 and took first in Group 5. Three privateers brought home their 934 in first place in Group 4. It was the beginning of a series of individual race and seasonal triumphs for the 935 and 936, at Le Mans and elsewhere. It would continue until the FIA changed the rules again. They created a new sports prototype category based on fuel consumption for 1982, Group C. They no longer knew what to expect from Porsche. ■

CHAPTER TEN

NECESSITY IS *STILL* THE MOTHER OF INVENTION

1973 911T Targa

The 1973 model year brought many changes to the 911 line. Black rubber bumper guards and sealed beam headlights appeared on U.S. cars, and, midyear, Porsche introduced a new Bosch fuel injection system, the K-Jetronic.

THE EARLY 1970S WERE STRESSFUL FOR PORSCHE. The company had completed an 18-month-long construction project expanding the Zuffenhausen assembly facilities by about 160,000 square feet (roughly 14,880 square meters). The complex incorporated new paint and interior trim shops. Ferry Porsche had moved his stylists and engineers into the new design, engineering, and technical center at Weissach. While the company had revenue from car sales around the world and from its research and development projects for VW and others, motorsports expenditures had been colossal, and from 1965 to 1972 the rising value of the German mark against the U.S. dollar had affected sales seriously. Total 1971 production reached just 11,715 cars, the lowest in five years.

Ferry had done a careful job of controlling costs on production cars. But he understood clearly how forces beyond his control affected sales to his largest single market. The dollar, which had traded for DM 3.99 in 1965, slipped to DM 3.48 in 1971 and DM 3.19 in 1972.

After the family left Porsche management, Ernst Fuhrmann returned to the company in charge of all things technical from engineering and design at Weissach to racing and production at Zuffenhausen. He and the board quickly promoted Helmuth Bott to head development, including design and testing.

Board member Heinz Branitzki stayed on to manage commercial and financial matters, and Ferry remained as chairman of the supervisory board.

But four weeks after Fuhrmann arrived, VW's board forced out its chairman, Kurt Lotz, replacing him with Rudolf Leiding in October 1971. Leiding promptly examined all

1974 Carrera 2.7

New crash safety laws in the United States forced Porsche to redesign its front and rear bumpers to accommodate 5-mile-per-hour (8-kilometer-per-hour) impacts with no visible damage. Accordion-like rubber bellows sealed the resilient bumpers to the bodies.

CHAPTER TEN

1975/6 Typ 930 3.0
Porsche widened the bodywork of the 911 Carrera by nearly 5 inches (120mm) to accommodate 185/70 VR 15 tires on 7-inch wheels on 21mm track spacers at the front and 216/60 VR 15s on 8-inch wheels on 28mm spacers at the rear. Along with its "whale-tail" rear wing, all this gave the car an aggressive, grounded appearance.

valve that dumped boost back into the duct running from the exhaust to the turbine. This maintained rotor speed when the driver lifted off the accelerator briefly.

Porsche introduced the 930 Turbo coupe at the Frankfurt show in September 1973. The brilliant silver car boasted RSR-type flared front and rear fenders over the widest tires the company ever had offered on a series car, Dunlop 215/60VR15s. (Porsche switched to 225/50VR15 Pirelli P7 tires for production.) A graphic "Turbo" stretched like an elastic overlay from the top of the rear wheel arches

K-Jetronic mechanical fuel injection that Paul Hensler had introduced on the 911T in late 1972 and into America as a 1973 1/2 model. The Bosch system spread across the full 911 lineup starting with 1974 models for the base 911, the S, and the Carrera.

Schäffer made the turbo work. He pulled in outside air upward through the K-Jetronic past its metering valve and into the compressor side of the exhaust-driven turbocharger. From there the rotor forced condensed fuel-air mix to the throttle valve on top of the engine's new cast-aluminum intake manifold. Schäffer and Mezger turned the project over to Herbert Ampferer and Robert Pindar to make it production ready. Their challenge was no less difficult.

Ultimately, Ampferer and his colleagues engineered not only the typical waste-gate arrangement familiar to racing applications, but also a spring-loaded vacuum-controlled

The Turbo used a 2,994cc engine with compression reduced to 6.5:1 to accommodate the pressure developed by the Kühnle, Kopp & Kausch (KKK) Typ 3LDZ turbocharger. Porsche quoted engine output at 160 brake horsepower with 11.3 psi of boost (0.8 bar).

to the taillights, which sat beneath a large flat rear wing. For motor show patrons who had attended Interserie events and watched the 917s, this new car was irresistible. It bothered no one that Porsche again showed a car long before a buyer could get one. The 901 introduction in 1963 had served to warn people to save their money. The October 1972 launch of the Carrera RS told them to order now and wait patiently. Sales had learned its lessons well, and according to the printed materials, here was this 930, not really a 911, but a companion model, a turbocharged car with 260 brake horsepower from 3 liters. This was race car stuff, and Porsche's regular customers could own it!

Originally conceived as a homologation special, Fuhrmann hoped Porsche might sell the 200 copies necessary to legalize it for racing. Bott told Ampferer he didn't need to worry about air conditioning or allowing room for a rear wiper, whose motor took more precious space in a cramped compartment. By the end of 1976, however, the company had turned out 1,300 of them. And lessons learned from RS Lightweight versus RS Touring models taught sales to encourage luxury. The Turbo moved to the top of the range, fitted with a full leather interior and air conditioning (and the rear wiper) as standard equipment. Ampferer had to redesign the engine configuration. None of this came cheap: Porsche sold the 1976 model for DM 65,000, $25,800 on the U.S. east coast.

About two years before Porsche introduced the Turbo, back when Hans Mezger, Valentin Schäffer, Herbert Ampferer, and Robert Pindar were toiling to make a turbocharged car roadworthy, the Volkswagen company had gone through its management struggles. New board chairman Rudolf Leiding wanted to broaden VW's product line, however. At the least, that meant finding a replacement for its sports car, the 914. With the two remaining years on Porsche's contract, he asked Ernst Fuhrmann to create a new water-cooled car, but only from existing parts.

"So this time," Tony Lapine recalled, "Porsche had a freer run of the shelves [than it had with the 914] and there were more shelves to pick from. Look at the engines available, the transmissions! There was Audi, VW. And that was the beginning of the Nine-Two-Four." For Volkswagen it was the genesis of the EA425, the code by which Leiding and his board referred to the new sports car.

"A task force came out with the idea," Harm Lagaay recalled. "The Nine-Eleven is on the brink. Why don't we do two cars for the future, a Nine-Two-Four that we will do for VW and a Nine-Two-Eight for us. The technical people at Porsche were convinced

Harm Lagaay Prototype Volkswagen EA425

This was the car that Volkswagen approved but that Lagaay felt needed improvement as it grew from small-scale models to full scale. Vents below the rear hatchback expelled interior air.

that rear engines were passé. We have to go for front engines with transaxles. They looked into the VW and Audi spec box division, and they found the engine and they found a gearbox. That's how the package was decided. So they said, let's take this particular sports car and go to VW and promote it. We'll give it to them. For reasons unknown, Leiding said, 'that's okay, show it to me.'

"The styling studio made three proposals. One came from Dick Soderberg. One came from Dawson Sellar, a Scotsman. And I did the third," Lagaay said. "These were fifth-scale models. In those days, it was all very practical thinking. You put the models into a VW [van] and drove up the seven hundred kilometers to Wolfsburg and you put them into 'Valhalla,' their huge presentation hall and we offered them, together with the package, to Leiding.

"Maybe he felt sorry for Porsche. Maybe he felt that killing his four-seater with the under-floor engine was sad. But he said, 'Keep on going, but I want this model.' He chose my model. He pointed to my car. I was stunned.

"We went home. We had a car. The next step was to go to one-to-four scale. Then comes a moment—it must have been spring nineteen seventy-two—that VW said 'No thank you, after all that, we don't need it.' Because they had the front-engine/front-wheel-drive Golf, they wanted a sports car with a front-engine/front-wheel drive.

"So there you are," he continued. "Suddenly Porsche had a sports car *back*.

1976 Typ 924 2.0

As an entry-level Porsche, the Typ 924 became a sports car for the masses—exactly what Volkswagen had hoped the car would do for them. The 1,984cc water-cooled inline four-cylinder engine developed 125 brake horsepower, and the car sold initially for $9,220 (about DM 23,240) at the factory.

We decided 'We'll take it. We'll use it for ourselves.' We have, however, VW parts, so then people responsible for contracts had to do their work. They had somehow to negotiate Volkswagen door handles and other bits and pieces and an engine and transaxle from Audi.

"When the car came out in 1976, everybody had noticed how many Audi and VW parts were there but it had a Porsche brand name on it. This was how *it* got the image of the Volks-Porsche. In the meantime, they still have the Nine-Fourteen, which nobody was happy with. It didn't sell. It looked awful. It wasn't fast.

"From a personal point of view, I was completely unaware of all the things that I needed to know to develop a car. So Richard Soderberg helped me a lot. My car was chosen and I, as a young man, said, 'Oh,

1981 Typ 924 Carrera GTS Club Sport

Walter Röhrl captured the attention of every young man in his audience at this stream crossing in his GTS. His four wins in the car caught Porsche's attention and launched a long relationship. The company assembled 406 of these 210-brake-horsepower turbocharged and intercooled cars, equally at home on paved roads as crossing shallow rivers.

wait a minute. I didn't mean it exactly like that! I meant it to go a little bit like this and they said, 'No, no. Exactly that way.'

"I said 'No, no, please!' It was unfinished. But Leiding had said, 'This is what I want.' So they kept on giving him that car and they didn't want to deviate on my first design. I said, 'But you can't leave it like that, you need to change . . . change . . . change.' Growing from one-to-five up to one-to-four, the mistakes grow! I wanted to change so many things."

But within a year, VW ended project EA425. Leiding had anxiously awaited its delivery. He personally had chosen Lagaay's concept, and Leiding anticipated that this new car would improve VW's image in the world. But his ambitions began to trip themselves up, and expansion began to cost too much. Then, just as currency exchange problems had up-ended Porsche's plans earlier, another outside influence made sports cars suddenly more risky. The Organization of Petroleum Exporting Countries, OPEC, formed in 1960, staged an embargo on oil shipments to Western countries in October 1973. Leiding was relieved of his job at VW a year later. VW named Toni Schmücker to replace him in early 1975.

"Schmücker saw the car," Lapine explained, "and said, 'Well, it's a lovely car, but you know we have some other problems which we will have to solve and we will not be building this automobile, at least not right now.'" VW had huge expenses from developing its new front-drive cars, the Golf,

1979 Typ 924 Turbo 2.0

Porsche introduced the Turbo for model year 1979, giving it a row of ventilation slots above the front bumper to help cool the engine compartment. The Turbo developed 170 brake horsepower. The rear spoiler helped reduce lift anc dropped the drag coefficient to 0.33.

the Passat, and the Scirocco, that had yet to return any of their investment.

"Lapine said," Harm Lagaay continued his story, "that going from one-to-five, to one-to-four, and up to full size, you need to adjust all the proportions. So the first cars, they were terrible. It was so embarrassing.

Everybody knew it was wrong. They weren't adjusted to the size.

"When the car was not wanted by Volkswagen anymore, we said, 'Thank God! Now we can make the changes!' We could re-proportion the car. The first ones looked like potatoes."

175

1973–1981

Then it became the 924 for Porsche.

Ironically, another one of VW Chairman Tony Schmücker's problems was excess production capacity. As he began choosing sites to close, he added a former NSU plant only 27 miles, (43 kilometers) north of Zuffenhausen at Neckarsulm.

"The capacity for building this car," Lapine explained, "was reserved right from the beginning, planned for Neckarsulm. And so a labor situation popped up. What was going to happen to this factory, to these workers, now that VW does not build this car. Well, the upshot was that Porsche bought the project back."

It was an interesting opportunity. As Jeff Daniel explained in his book, *Porsche— The Engineering Story*, "In the early 1970s it was Porsche's intention, so far as its own range was concerned, to diversify upwards and sideways rather than downwards. Thus the program to develop the big 928 actually began before a start was made on the EA425/924." But after the OPEC oil embargo, Porsche slowed work on the 928 because the market for fast, exclusive sports cars seemed in jeopardy. The 924's aspirations were more modest.

Porsche began series production of its Typ 924 in November 1975. An inline four-cylinder engine, derived from an existing Audi power plant bored out to 1,984cc, developed 125 net horsepower that had already been used in the Audi 100 sedan and VW LT van (*Lasten-Transporter*, or cargo van). Weissach engineers adopted an Audi gearbox and final drive transaxle and installed it at the

Porsche produced enough examples of the 1981 Typ 924 Carrera GTS Club Sport to qualify it for Group 4 racing. It tantalized its few customers with what the 924 replacement would look like. Its 1,984cc engine got the car to 62 miles per hour (100 kilometers) in 6.9 seconds and gave it a top speed of 149 miles per hour (240 kilometers per hour).

rear of the car to improve its balance and interior space. Six months later, production reached 60 cars a day, including a series for the U.S. market. Porsche introduced the car in Germany at DM 23,240, about $9,220. U.S. dealers sold the cars for $9,395. Just as Porsche had introduced on the 914, Harm Lagaay's 924 design adopted the pop-up headlights. Just as Butzi Porsche had hoped for the 911, the 924 also incorporated a large rear hatchback window. To hold Lagaay's low hood line, engineers set the engine 40 degrees off vertical, canting to the right.

For the 1979 model year, Porsche offered a turbocharged version of the 924, with 170 net horsepower, and at the same Frankfurt auto show, the company showed the racing version 924 Carrera GT. Porsche assembled 400 of these 210-horsepower models with gutted interiors, and an intercooler as well as the turbo. The GT weighed 2,596 pounds (1,180 kilograms). This was 330 pounds (150 kilograms) less than the series production Turbo and qualified it for FIA Group 4 racing.

Fuhrmann wanted to take the car further. He asked Norbert Singer to create a 924 Carrera for Le Mans under the new GT Prototype category. Singer constructed four cars for 1980, each weighing 2,046 pounds (930 kilograms) without oil. The cars, with 310 horsepower under the hood, reached 178.1 miles per hour (285 kilometers per hour) along Mulsanne in practice. Despite engine problems that slowed the cars, the three entries finished the 24-hour race, in 6th, 12th, and 13th overall.

Glistening in the sun, the 928 raw body awaits completion. The car measures 175.1 inches (4447mm) long and 72.3 inches (1836mm) wide, and it stands 51.7 inches (1,313 mm) tall. In its first year 1977, it sold for $23,700 (roughly DM 55,000) at the factory.

1979 928 Coupe

To many viewers, the 928 car arrived looking like something from the future. Under styling chief Tony Lapine's direction, designer Wolfgang Möbius invented this all-new take on Porsche's traditional forms.

For 1981, Porsche went again with two 924s, one a previous year entry and the other an all-new car under the skin. This was a prototype of the 924 successor, the 944, using an engine that was literally half a 928 V8 block, 2.5 liters with 100x78.9mm bore and stroke. This 2,196-pound (998-kilogram) Le Mans GTP developed 420 horsepower. At the end of the 24 hours, Jürgen Barth and world rally champion Walter Röhrl finished seventh overall. They had pitted only for fuel.

Unlike the 924s, Fuhrmann never planned the more luxurious 928s to race. Because of the work necessary to take over and bring the 924 to market, Ernst Fuhrmann delayed introduction of the V-8-engine sports car a year.

"We all know that part of the Nine-Eleven success was its uniqueness," Helmut Flegl explained. "What is unique? Rear engine, air cooling, its sound." But that uniqueness was under threat, and not only from American legislators promising to keep every driver safe.

"The customers were complaining all the time," Flegl continued. "'You have to improve this and that, fix more and other things.' From time to time there was the issue of so many problems, questions of people not liking this Nine-Eleven any more! They seemed to kind of want to get away from it." Between this and the noises from the U.S. Congress, the feeling grew within Porsche that it must make this front-engine car. Flegl managed the project for the two years of prototype testing that preceded manufacture. He took over from Wolfhelm Gorrison, who had been design director through the drawing board stages right up to running prototypes. Gorrison worked closely with the 928's designer, Wolfgang Möbius, and studio chief Tony Lapine.

With the Porsche design legacy very much in mind, the heritage of the 356 and the 911 to live up to and to absorb from, Möbius and his team began work on this flagship front-engine car. To meet performance expectations, the engine had to be a V-8. Fuhrmann planned to introduce the car with an all-aluminum 5-liter engine. (Sensitivity to world politics and oil issues scaled it back to 4.5 liters.) Water-cooling was part of its specification. New engineering technologies had to work in a car that anyone immediately would recognize as a Porsche. One of those legacies was the bumper.

"Porsche very early in the game," Lapine explained, "through an aesthetic sense from Mr. Komenda, Mr. Rabe, Mr. F. A. Porsche, decided to continue the 'illusion' that the bumper was part of the body, because the bumper was the same color as the body.

"The bumper, as such, was not a thing of beauty. When you finish a body outline as a designer, you have to say, 'Oh, and now the bumper . . .'"

Lapine's concept was to make the body be the bumper. The engineering was challenging. GM had tried to integrate a deformable bumper into the front end of the 1968 Pontiac GTO. It still was a separate piece with a noticeable seam between it and the car body. But more difficult was controlling paint and eventual discoloration. Elasticity was another concern. How could the material dissipate the energy of impact over a large enough area to not crack or permanently deform the material? Porsche settled on polyurethane mounted on collapsible struts for European customers. U.S. buyers got the integral bumper mounted on self-restoring shock absorbers, since U.S. regulations required the car suffer no visual damage after a 5-mile-per-hour (8-kilometer-per-hour) impact.

Opulent—if psychedelic—was a decorating scheme appropriate to the 1970s. More conservatively, the 928s used a water-cooled 4,474cc V-8 engine that developed 240 brake horsepower and could propel the car to a top speed of 143 miles per hour (230 kilometers per hour).

1981 911SC Coupe

Had Ernst Fuhrmann remained at Porsche and things gone his way, this would have been the final 911. His plans called for ending production when sales fell below 6,000 units a year or the 1981 model year ended, which ever came sooner.

CHAPTER TEN

While the car's looks astonished viewers, its handling stunned buyers and journalists. The secret was its double wishbone suspension up front that Flegl and his engineers fitted to provide an automatic stabilizing effect and anti-dive characteristics under acceleration or braking. Flegl's team introduced the "Weissach axle" at the rear. This took advantage of a tendency of soft suspension bushings to induce rear-steering tendencies. Two rear suspension links, one a transverse member and the other a semitrailing-type configuration, connected to the wheel hub using bushings positioned to compensate for the force acting on the wheels. This worked whether the car was cornering, braking, or in any combination. The effect on the driver was that, unlike most rear-drive cars where the rear axle seems just along for the ride or to transmit power to the ground, this system aided in turning by cocking the wheels into the turn.

Although its siblings, the 911 and the 924, got turbochargers, the 928 never would. Its engine grew in size and power. Introduced with 4.5 liters developing 240 brake horsepower, the next version, the 928S in 1980, had 4.7 liters and developed 300 horsepower and then 310 in the S2, though U.S. cars only developed 292 brake horsepower due to full emission controls.

Cars destined for the United States still had 85-mile-per-hour (140-kilometer-per-hour) speedometers and catalytic converters and oxygen sensors to meet growing concerns over exhaust emissions.

Production of the 928 reached 4,510 in 1982, the best of any year till 1985 when it finally cracked Ernst Fuhrmann's expected rate of 5,000 cars a year. Still, in 1982 Porsche manufactured 11,144 of the 911SC models, and then in 1985, it produced 13,007 of the Carrera 3.2 models. For a company planning to end its manufacture, the 911 refused to die. Fuhrmann had announced that when production dropped below 6,000 cars a year, he would discontinue the 911. It pleased Ferry Porsche, who never had wanted to stop the 911. In late 1980, he took the opportunity instead to release Ernst Fuhrmann. In his place, he hired a German-born American with an impressive background in diesel truck and engine manufacturing.

CHAPTER ELEVEN

RACING TO NEW HORIZONS

1981 Interscope Indianapolis Series car

Porsche developed a 2.65-liter engine, the Typ 935/75, which developed 630 brake horsepower running on methanol and using boost set at 54 inches of mercury. Porsche welded the dual-overhead camshaft four-valve per cylinder heads onto the block.

INDIANAPOLIS HAD BEEN A TARGET ON FERDINAND PIËCH'S MASTER PLAN: Win the World Championship of Makes, Le Mans, Formula One, and the Indy 500. But that had been in the early 1970s. Now it was 1978; Piëch was gone, and Ernst Fuhrmann was running things. Fuhrmann understood the wisdom of participating in a highly visible contest: In some recent years, more than half of Porsche's revenue had come from U.S. sales. Appealing to that audience was important to Porsche.

Jo Hoppen, competition director for Porsche+Audi Division of Volkswagen of America, knew what the Memorial Day event meant to the American racing enthusiast. He also understood selling racing.

"The American public," he explained, "liked to see it fast, furious, close, exciting, and still heavily populated at the checkered flag." Perhaps most importantly, he recognized that it took lots of someone else's money to sell a racing program to Porsche's management.

In California, Hoppen's friend Vasek Polak had a solid relationship with Ted Field, whose Interscope Racing Panasonic–sponsored 935s were doing very well in IMSA. (Field co-drove his own 935 with Danny Ongais and Hurley Haywood to win the Daytona 24-Hours in January 1979.) Field already had ventured into Champ Car racing, as it was known at the time. With Ongais driving Field's Cosworth-engined Parnelli, Ted Field grasped the potential of a Porsche Champ Car effort. His Interscope team eventually could dominate the Indy car series.

"But that was an uphill battle," Hoppen recalled. "Open-wheel racing was not highly regarded at the factory. Their past involvement had been more as a result of momentum rather than any clearly planned strategy." From its beginnings in 1958 with center-steering RSKs for Jean Behra and Carel de Beaufort up to the full factory effort in Formula One in 1962, Ferry Porsche had been a reluctant leader, not really sure why his firm was spending the money on something that bore no resemblance to anything he sold to the public.

Hoppen was prepared. Field was able to pay the project's costs. All Porsche had to do was develop an engine program to fit into Field's chassis. The obvious choice was the water-cooled cylinder head 935 engine from Le Mans in 1978. It fit the United States Auto Club (USAC) sanctioning body's displacement regulations. Its development was well along.

Hoppen argued effectively. The company sought to sell more cars in the United States. Racing every other Sunday in an IMSA event before a crowd of 60,000 spectators was nothing compared with the Indianapolis 500, which, in 1978, drew 400,000 in the gate and some 60 million television viewers.

Hoppen was asking Ferry Porsche only to revise an engine that was basically done. Yet, for Hoppen, his easiest sell proved to be Ernst Fuhrmann, the "engine" engineer. Fuhrmann liked the idea. Porsche would go to Indianapolis. This was early in the fall of 1978. Unfortunately, it also was early in the fall of USAC.

In those days, some Indy 500 entrants were marginal organizations of rugged individuals who built their Champ Cars in their home garages.

However, Indy also attracted Roger Penske, Pat Patrick, Jim Hall and his Chaparrals, and Dan Gurney and his Eagles. These organizations showed up with transporters,

The 2.65-liter Typ 935/75 engine developed 630 brake horsepower. Operating the engine on methanol fuel, Porsche hoped to use a boost of 54 inches of mercury.

With the Porsche engine, Ted Field's Parnelli-chassis Interscope racer weighed 1,496 pounds (680 kilograms). It was a power-to-weight combination good for a few laps averaging 192 miles per hour (307 kilometers per hour).

teams of drivers, support personnel, and armies of mechanics to tend the Cosworth-powered cars.

The USAC was a "democracy." Its members elected its president, Richard King. The majority ruled, and it could thwart the efforts, topple the ideas, and frustrate the ambitions of the few, the rich, the organized.

That is why in late summer of 1978 Dan Gurney, Roger Penske, and Pat Patrick founded Championship Auto Racing Teams, CART. Then they approached USAC and expressed their members' concerns. CART represented the teams with substantial investments. CART understood "where USAC was coming from." But CART, on the other hand, hoped USAC understood that the team owners with valuable sponsorships who were spending vast amounts of money, who had specific needs—better promotion, larger purses, and a meaningful national championship— wanted their concerns satisfied.

USAC refused to change. CART warned that a split was eminent. USAC believed a split was impossible. With USAC controlling the tracks, where would they race? Parking lots? City streets?

USAC overlooked something. They never had convinced Indianapolis to take its 500-mile race date off the FIA calendar. Any driver with an FIA license could run it. New CART members joined SCCA and got SCCA-issued FIA licenses. Indianapolis denied their entries in spring 1979. In court CART reminded the judge that Indiana was a right-to-work state, that Indy had the date, and its members had the licenses. The verdict was as near a death sentence as could be. In a court sympathetic only to the rule of law and the right to work, USAC had lost.

Meanwhile, in Weissach, Hans Mezger's staff was testing engines. Oil could not get to the number one cylinder. Connecting rods separated from crankshafts and punctured crankcases.

In his dealings with USAC, Hoppen had negotiated turboboost. The four-cylinder Offys were allowed 60 inches of mercury, about 2.0 times barometric pressure, roughly 29.4 pounds per square inch; USAC allowed the eight-cylinder Cosworths 48 inches, 1.6 bar, or 23.5 psi. Porsche's six straddled the middle at 54 inches, 1.8 bar, about 26.5 psi boost. But Hoppen never got that in writing.

USAC was struggling at this point to keep its part of the Champ Car series alive. CART was proving to be a formidable force. While Hoppen had made appearance promises for both USAC and CART events, it was USAC who attended Porsche's public unveiling. With Porsche, USAC now had two jewels. The other was A. J. Foyt.

Foyt was very curious about Porsche's efforts. He had a similar grasp as Ted Field did of Porsche's potential. When Foyt won at Le Mans in 1967 with Dan Gurney in a 7.0-liter Ford Mk IV, he beat two 330-P4 Ferraris and another Mk IV. But it was 2.0-liter Porsches that followed in fifth, sixth, seventh, and eighth. Foyt knew what Porsche could do given an even chance. He did not want

The state of the art in 1980 meant fairly clean and simple bodies. A front and rear wing were about as sophisticated as air management got in those days at Indianapolis.

that to happen; Foyt wanted the 1980 Champ Car title for himself.

"Which is why," Hoppen continued, "I took USAC technical director Jack Beckley to Stuttgart to see the engines on the dynamometer. Accompanying Beckley was Howard Gilbert, the man who built engines for A. J. Foyt."

Foyt ran a four-cylinder Offy in those days. He had told Beckley and King that USAC's boost rules allowed too much leeway. He suggested they simplify the rules, setting 60-inch boost for four-cylinder engines and 48 inches for engines with more than four cylinders.

On the day of their visit, the two Americans saw another steaming, broken engine with one more punctured case. But before it failed, Mezgers' technicians achieved nearly 630 horsepower out of the engine. That was the message Foyt got when Gilbert and Beckley returned home. Rumors circulated that Foyt threatened to join CART if USAC didn't "simplify" the boost rule.

"Interscope had begun chassis tests," Hoppen explained, "running on the Ontario Motor Speedway oval east of Los Angeles. Engines still blew. But enough laps were done to indicate the car had serious competitive

This was neither Interscope's nor Porsche's last attempt at Indianapolis. But a chain of events left bad tastes in many mouths.

1980 Typ 924 Carrera GTR/944GTP

Is it coming out of hiding or going back under wraps? While Peter Schutz felt Porsche should do better than merely going for class victories, the three 924s acquitted themselves handsomely at Le Mans with number 3 finishing 13th overall, number 2 coming in 12th, and number 4 ending the race in 6th overall.

potential. In tests watched from helicopters high above the oval, the car ran faster than Field's Cosworth-powered Parnellis. And in the end, duplicating the Indy 500 four-lap qualifying series, the Interscope Porsche lapped with an average speed of 192 miles per hour [307 kilometers per hour]."

USAC was not concerned about losing the German manufacturer. Porsche had come into the series to run Indy. Losing Foyt was another matter. With one month till the track opened, USAC "simplified" the rule. Porsche's six-cylinder racing engine was limited to 48 inches of boost.

Hoppen remembered Ferry Porsche's reaction: "'How can you change the rules with one month to the race? We cannot test and develop a new engine in one month? We cancel the project!'" Hoppen, however, was as wily as Foyt, and as experienced as Norbert Singer. Everyone knew that rules are meant to be changed. Hoppen had advocated developing the engine at 48 inches of boost as well. His strategy was to huff and puff, bluster and threaten, and then show up at the brickyard and run. In that strategy, too, Ernst Fuhrmann was his ally. And yet, it never happened.

"Porsche management never wanted the program," Hoppen said.

"They said, 'Great! No one knows what we could do with a forty-eight-inch boost engine. Therefore, our public excuse is we simply cannot do it at all in the time remaining!'"

Without telling anyone, without informing its "partner" Ted Field, Porsche simply shut the program down. Field had constructed four cars for 1980. They all went into a warehouse.

For Ernst Fuhrmann, it was one more checkmark on a list that Ferry Porsche had begun making. The 928 had failed to meet Fuhrmann's sales predictions, the 911 oversold his production projections, and he had led the company away from the direction Ferry Porsche still believed it should head. Ferry had expressed to fellow board members, and they to him, a growing dissatisfaction with Fuhrmann's behavior in assuming the public face and voice of Porsche. Now this ill-fated racing program had wasted time and resources.

Was Fuhrmann fired? He said, in an interview in 1991, that he told Ferry that he wanted to retire in 1980 because, with 924 and 928 programs on target, he knew Porsche

1982 Typ 956-001

In its first test at Weissach, Norbert Singer, on right, headed to test driver Jürgen Barth's door on the right to get his assessment. Barth was accused of going off course because of the debris the car's undercarriage tunnels had sucked off the track surface.

1981–1985

needed a new car and that would take five to seven years, a period he preferred to spend at home in Teufenbach, Austria, with his wife, Elfreida. He left quietly before the end of 1980. Just a few months later under the new leadership of chairman Peter Schutz, Porsche then launched one of its most successful racing programs ever to begin in 1982.

"I must say," Paul Frère admitted several years before his death in 2008, "that I was eighty percent responsible for the nineteen eighty-two Group C regulations which specified completely free engines and restricted fuel consumption. It was a responsible thing and a good engineering challenge."

"I hated it!" Derek Bell said. "We're in show business. The public cannot understand that we go around Silverstone in one minute fifteen to qualify and then in the race go one minute twenty-four. Just to conserve fuel? I mean, bloody hell, nine seconds off the pace is a bit of a joke!" For 625-mile (1,000-kilometer) events, the new regulations allowed 148.4 gallons (600 liters) of fuel. For Le Mans, contestants could consume 686.4 gallons (2,600 liters).

Porsche engineers looked at the water-cooled 2.65-liter Indianapolis project engine, the Typ 935/78, and saw the possibilities. Porsche designated this as the Typ 956. Hans Mezger and his staff first had developed it as the 935, the Typ 935/71. They used a KKK turbocharger and an air-to-air intercooler for each cylinder bank. For Indy, the car burned methanol fuel. For Europe, Mezger converted it back to gasoline. With compression set at 7.2:1 to avoid detonating the engine, Porsche got 620 brake horsepower at 2.2 bars, about 32.3 psi boost.

Regulations dictated that the cars had to weigh at least 1,760 pounds (800 kilograms) dry and stand between 1.1 and 1.2 meters in height. Specifications prescribed maximum width at 2 meters, length at 4.8 meters (189 inches). Overhangs, too, were to be between 15 and 20 percent of the car's wheelbase of 104.3 inches (2,650mm).

Rules also required what are known as crushable structures surrounding the driver ahead of the firewall or bulkhead. The minimum windshield height of one meter at the top eliminated Porsche's chances of re-using the 936 from Group 6. Norbert Singer, questioning the difficulty of accommodating effective "crushability" in a tube frame, set out to produce a new chassis. The result was Porsche's first monocoque structure of riveted and bonded sheet aluminum. The torsionally stiff body was the sole load-bearing member absorbing all suspension and drive loads without needing separate subframes. Singer's engineers placed the fuel tank behind the cockpit and, allowing space for the engine and transaxle, positioned the driver's feet ahead of the front axle.

Racing body aerodynamicist and designer Eugen Kolb had created both short- and long-

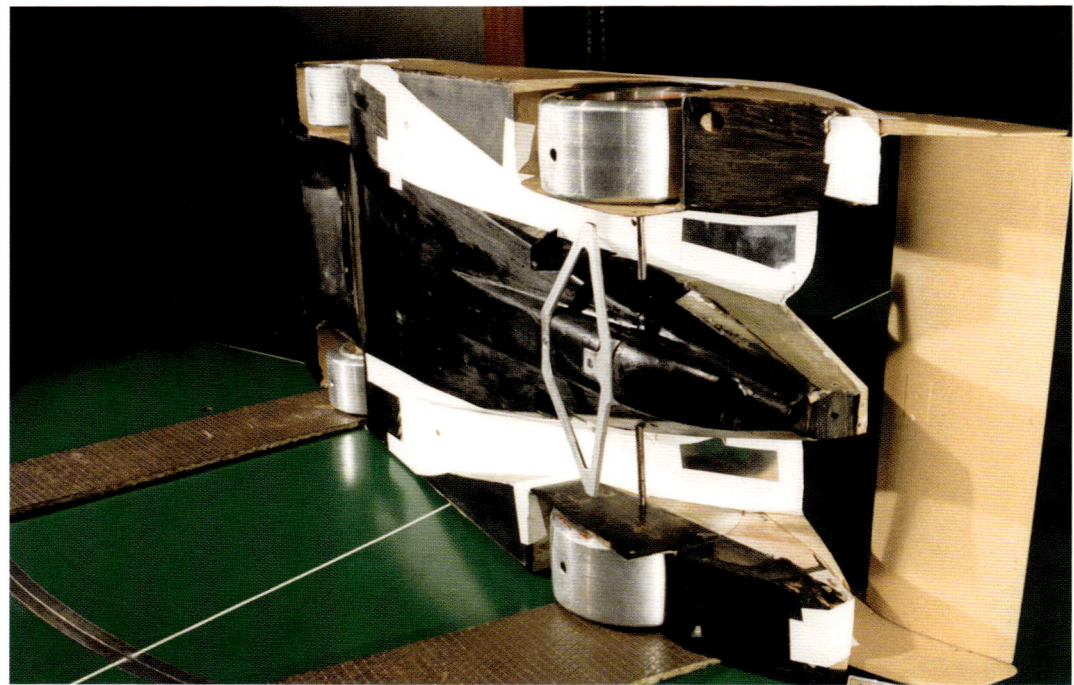

The magic of downforce required essentially turning the underside of a car into an inverted airplane wing. As Norbert Singer and others devised the underside of the 956, this was one of several configurations they tried on models in their wind tunnel.

CHAPTER ELEVEN

tail and short- and long-nose variations for this new car. Based on his experiences with the 906 long-tail and the 917s, his versions of the 956 were the most subtle he had done.

Jürgen Barth, as factory test driver, was first to drive the 956. "The cornering forces were simply incredible. You see, no one had driven ground effects sports cars yet. I went out and did about five laps and came in to check the fluids. Professor Bott looked around the rear of the car and asked me if I had gone off the road.

Porsche recycled the 2.65-liter 935/71 engine it used for the ill-fated Indianapolis project to develop the Typ 935/76 for these 956 models. Using Kugelfischer mechanical fuel injection and twin KKK turbochargers with air-to-water intercoolers, these engines with water-cooled heads developed 620 brake horsepower.

1982 Typ 956 with Techniques Avant Garde Twin Turbo Engine

In one of several efforts to determine the potential of their other engines in this Group C endurance racer, Weissach engineers installed the 1.5-liter twin-turbocharged flat-six engine from the McLaren Formula One racers. With nearly equal horsepower, the lesser stresses on the 2.65-liter engine made it a better choice than this engine.

"I said no, and he pointed to the dust. We realized the tunnels under the car had vacuumed the track!" For Barth and his colleague Roland Kussmaul, the new experiences were only beginning. On orders from racing director Peter Falk, they drove a 625-mile (1,000-kilometer) test session over Weissach's "rough road," the cobblestone track, to challenge chassis durability. "With my knees smashed under the cowl, it was brutal," Barth recalled. "We could only go for a couple hours each and when we got out we couldn't walk. With ground effects the suspension is extremely stiff. So the driver absorbs a lot of the shock through his body."

Sports director Manfred Jantke brought in sponsorship from Rothmans International, a British tobacco company. The first race for the Rothmans 956 occurred at Silverstone, the six hour endurance event in May 1982. Regulators imposed the 600-liter/1000-kilometer fuel allocation on the race. The 956s ran against Lancia's turbocharged LC-1 Spyders, and they qualified fast, but raced slow. As a result, Jacky

CHAPTER ELEVEN

Cockpits on the 956s bore a family resemblance to the endurance racers that had come before: 907, 908, and 917. The tight fit badly bruised the knees of development drivers Jürgen Barth and Roland Kussmaul.

Ickx and Derek Bell finished only second, three laps down. Bell's frustration at competing against the more fuel-frugal Lancia and driving nine seconds off his normal pace founded his hatred of Group C regulations.

At Le Mans, Kolb's long-tail 956s hit 216.9 miles per hour (347 kilometers per hour) along Mulsanne. Yet this was 13.8 miles per hour (22 kilometers per hour) slower than the 936/81 cars had run the previous year with a similar engine. The ground effects reduced the 956's top speed slightly even though lap times were quicker.

Porsche 956s finished first, second, and third in their inaugural year at Le Mans. They were the only three Group C finishers out of 29 entries in the new class. The year before, Ickx's and Bell's winning Porsche 936/81 had consumed a gallon every 4.54 miles (52 liters per 100 kilometers). In the new consumption formula, the same 956 drivers won the race at 4.95 miles per gallon (48 liters per 100 kilometers), a 10 percent improvement.

1985 Miller High Life Typ 962C

Streaking to victory through the infield road course at Daytona International Speedway, co-drivers Bob Wollek, Derek Bell, and John Andretti shared duties to win the Rolex 24 Hours event. Thick fog stopped the race for four hours early in the morning after which the rest of the event became a sprint.

In 1983, the 956s swept Le Mans again, cementing in place the 956 legacy. Porsche had produced nine additional cars intended for customers, and during the 1983 season the company saw private 956s beat the factory cars at Monza and Brands Hatch. For 1984 the factory withdrew from the season when the FIA's ruling body, Fédération Internationale du Sport Automobile, FISA, chose not to implement a new fuel economy regulation that Porsche had met but others had not. The others gained performance and endurance advantages. Successful outsider Reinhold Jöst's "New Man Jeans" 956 led eight other 956s across the finish at Le Mans. Jöst won the 24-hour race again in 1985.

Porsche had to create a 956 variant, the Typ 962, for the IMSA championship starting in 1984. IMSA's directors had feared a rerun of the late 1970s in which nearly every race and almost every championship went to a 935. IMSA required that the driver's feet were to be behind the hub center line of the front wheels. As had happened with many other sanctioning bodies in the past, IMSA did not expect the 962. For Singer to lengthen the wheelbase by 4.72 inches (120mm) meant only that he had to revise the aerodynamics and retune the high-speed balance.

IMSA also required different engines, based on a scale of engine capacity to car weight (1,914 pounds, 870 kilograms). The water-cooled four-valve 956 engine was not legal, so Mezger provided American racers with a two-valve air-cooled single-turbo engine developing 680 brake horsepower from the 2.85-liter engine and 720 brake horsepower from a 3.2-liter version. As if there were not enough challenges, the FIA announced it would require the same driver's foot location for its European racers, a change that led to the "Group C IMSA car," the 962C. Development continued. Al Holbert in America and John Thompson in England used aluminum honeycomb to further stiffen the 962s. Brothers Erwin and Manfred Kremer in Cologne, Germany, who had stretched the shapes and aerodynamics

CHAPTER ELEVEN

of 935s in the late 1970s and early 1980s, developed a full carbon-fiber monocoque for the 962 in 1989, designated the 962CK6.

The arrival of Jaguar and then Mercedes-Benz into Group C and Jaguar and Nissan into the IMSA GTP series made the racing more interesting for spectators but marked the beginning of a long end to 956/962 supremacy. It was not the last enthusiasts heard of the 962 models, however.

A number of successful 956/962 racers went into the road car business when Norbert Singer discovered yet another loophole in the rules of the 1994 Le Mans. This quirk in the regulations allowed a car to compete in the GT category provided the manufacturer had produced and registered at least one street-legal model of the same car. Jochen Dauer, the Kremers, Vern Schuppan, and Willy König all developed road-going models. Most of Singer's behind-the-scenes encouragement and assistance went to Dauer. This rule led to a flurry of new cars derived from older race cars incorporating engineering changes and creature comforts required to make them manageable, comfortable, and desirable supercars. This resulted in prices around $1 million. With engines producing 600 horsepower and top speeds in excess of 220 miles per hour, some of the cars sold, some got stolen, and the rest disappeared in the blurry history of supercars. Dauer's Le Mans effort met better success as his two 962LMs finished first and third overall.

Turbochargers led Porsche back into Formula One in the early 1980s. McLaren International's co-managing director Ron Dennis (he shared the title with Teddy Mayer, who also was company chairman) knew he needed the high horsepower of a turbocharged 1.5-liter engine to race competitively after the FIA banned movable side-skirts as aerodynamic devices. The only way to achieve high cornering speeds under these new regulations was to use large front and rear wings. Renault had introduced an engine in 1979, and both BMW and Ferrari were working on their own. Rules allowed for normally aspirated 3-liter engines, and McLaren, of course, operated its own Ford Cosworth engine shops. Cosworth vigorously believed their 3-liter DFV could match the performance, but Dennis wanted to investigate all possibilities.

For most of the previous decade Ernst Fuhrmann had danced around Formula One participation even as the engineers behind him worked on one turbo project after another. They were eager to get involved. But with the 956 Group C car and racing versions of the 924, the GTS and GTR in works as

Starting in late 1984, these engines produced 820 brake horsepower at 36 psi of boost, 2.55 bar. During the 1985 season, the engines saw 860 brake horsepower during races. Output reached 910 for 1986. By 1987, the 1.5-liter V-6 turned out 960 brake horsepower.

1984 Porsche-TAG Marlboro McLaren Turbo

Niki Lauda, number 8, led the crowd of Formula One racers at the European Grand Prix at Brands Hatch in September 1983. Lauda was a huge fan of the Porsche TAG engines, and he pushed for their use prematurely, which gave him a frustrating end of season. At Brands, he retired with engine failure after 25 laps.

well, and a new boss, Peter Schutz, in charge, engineers had plenty to do.

Dennis met with Helmuth Bott, who politely deflected his requests until Dennis returned with an offer that McLaren would pay for an engine program. McLaren's chief engineer John Barnard joined the meeting with Hans Mezger in late 1981 and hatched a two-year plan. Porsche set a cost to provide and rebuild engines at DM 165,000 each, roughly $73,000 at 1981 exchange rates. But that didn't cover design, development, manufacturing, and testing the engines prior to the first race. That figure ultimately reached DM 14 million, more than $6 million during the terms of the contract.

Mezger had conceived a V-6 to allow venturi tunnels underneath the rear of the car. With a commitment from Ron Dennis to fund the engine design study, Mezger set to work on project number 2623. He and his staff conceived an 80-degree V that allowed room for the intake manifold and injection equipment between the cylinder banks. Barnard, as chassis designer, imposed other restrictions on the outside of the engine so it would fit deeply and cleanly into the well between the tunnels.

To fund the next phase of the engine project, Dennis appealed to Techniques

Avant Garde (TAG) co-founder Mansour Ojjeh. This Saudi businessman and his family ran a company that brokered imports and exports between France, Britain, and Saudi Arabia. TAG already sponsored Frank Williams' Formula One team, but Dennis offered Ojjeh ownership of the engine and its intellectual rights, something TAG then could sell to other automobile companies after the contract with McLaren expired.

Once TAG was on board, it assisted Dennis in buying out former partner Teddy Mayer. Peter Schutz joined the program. They arranged a meeting with Ojjeh's father and TAG founder Akkram Ojjeh and Ferry Porsche at the Paris auto show.

Engine development proceeded, now identified by the TAG name and logo on the cam covers above the legend, "Made by Porsche." The first engine ran in mid-December 1982, achieving 550 horsepower at 10,500 rpm. The 1.5-liter 90-cubic-inch engine weighed just 330 pounds (150 kilograms). Within a few months, the engine developed 640 to 650 horsepower, Dennis's target for qualifying. Niki Lauda debuted the TAG-Porsche engine McLaren MP4 (with full carbon-fiber monocoque chassis) in August 1983 at the Dutch Grand Prix at Zandvoort. With 715 horsepower available, Lauda retired with exhausted brakes.

For 1984, the FIA outlawed aerodynamic tunnels, forcing flat-bottom cars on designers and rendering moot Mezger's and Barnard's effort to design a narrow engine. Barnard designed a new car, MP4/2, again using a

Alain Prost is known as "The Professor" for his driving skill and analytic mind. A good engine helped him accomplish unusual back-to-back world championships driving for McLaren with the TAG-Porsche twin-turbo engines.

carbon-fiber tub. Running 2.4 bar of boost, 36 psi, the Porsche engines produced 820 brake horsepower at 11,200 rpm in race tune. The effort paid off that year. Lauda or his new teammate Alain Prost won 12 of the 16 Grand Prix races, earning Lauda the driver's championship by 1/2 point over Prost. McLaren-TAG blitzed the manufacturer's championship, scoring nearly three times what second-place Ferrari earned.

For 1985 and on through 1987, TAG-McLaren won more Grand Prix races than its competitors while Porsche's engine output rose to 860 horsepower in 1985, 910 in 1986, and 960 for 1987. Boosted for qualifying in 1987, engineers and drivers saw 1,060 brake horsepower from the highly evolved 1.5-liter powerplant.

For 1988, FIA regulations reduced turboboost. This dropped Porsche's TAG-P01 engines to between 600 and 700 horsepower, comparable to what regulators expected from the normally aspirated 3.5-liter engines also legal for the series. McLaren looked elsewhere and TAG and Porsche sought other uses for the Formula One engine. But its power came as a result of too high a boost to apply successfully to series production cars. TAG ultimately sold about 50 engines as décor pieces for the dens, studies, and recreation rooms of wealthy enthusiasts. Porsche had scored 25 wins in 68 starts. Weissach expected someone would approach them to do a 3.5-liter racing motor. A V-12 seemed logical. A client approached. ∎

CHAPTER TWELVE

FROM **OBLIVION** TO THE **ULTIMATE** DRIVING MACHINE

1983 911SC Cabriolet

For countless reasons, it took Porsche 20 years from introducing the 911 to bring out a true cabriolet. It marked the last of the SC generation and the return to open-top motoring.

"When I walked in, I saw a big chart on Mr. Bott's wall, a bar graph." The speaker was Peter Schutz, hired by Ferry Porsche to replace Ernst Fuhrmann. Schutz had come from industrial diesel engine manufacturing, including K.H.D. in Germany, Cummins in the United States, and Caterpillar before that. He had no experience in the car business, a fact he pointed out to Ferry during his interview with the family.

"No, Herr Schutz," Porsche replied. "You don't understand our problem. We have people who know how to design automobiles, how to build them, to sell them and service them. Our problem is that we're not making any money," Ferry said. "When we explore the reasons for our poor earnings, we see that people in our organization are simply not working together. . . . We are looking for someone who can get this whole organization unified and working together."

Before accepting the job, he did his homework. Before starting, he dug deeper. Dealers in the United States and Europe consistently voiced two complaints: The cars were too expensive and they had serious quality-control problems. Schutz heard that morale at Porsche was poor because the company planned to discontinue the 911 while pushing the 924 and 928. Routine development, upgrades, and improvements for the 911 ended in Fuhrmann's last years as he waited for production to dip below 6,000 cars per year, his endpoint for the life of the car.

"Every Monday, Porsche's top managers have lunch together," Schutz recalled. "This has been going on forever. So the first Monday I was there, I went to the lunch. It was a mixed bag of engineers, sales people, manufacturing, and I listened to the conversations. After a while, I asked these folks one question: 'What is going on is this company right now that is so exciting that you can hardly wait to come to work?' You could hear a pin drop. 'Okay, everyone, thank you.' I heard what I needed."

The next day he went to Weissach to discuss company racing plans for Le Mans with Peter Falk, Norbert Singer, and their staffs. They were entering three 924 Turbos.

"What are your chances of winning?" he asked.

"'There is no chance of winning,' they told me. 'This is a modified production car. It's good for the sales department but we are going to be competing against full racing cars, prototypes. . . .'

"Then why are we going?" Again, he could hear a pin drop.

"Okay," he went on, "as long as I'm in charge of this organization, we will never go to any race without the objective of winning it." More pins dropped. "Since I do not know how you do this, I'll return at ten o'clock tomorrow morning and you'll give me your plans."

The next morning, everyone in Porsche's competition department along with engineers from Bosch, Dunlop, Shell, and Bilstein filled the conference room. "'There were these Nine-Thirty-Sixes in the museum,' they told me, 'retired from racing three years ago. There were turbocharged flat-six engines we developed for the American Indianapolis series but we never used. . . . We could pull the museum cars out, recondition them, install the Indy motors. . . .'

"The excitement in that room was electric," Schutz remembered. "Word got out. Porsche

Peter Schutz, Porsche's CEO, was the prime reason that Porsche put its long-awaited cabriolet into production, and here he stood smiling in front of his own prototype "Turbo-Look" Cabriolet. Schutz, a man with great motivational skills, arrived at Porsche to find the 911 headed for extinction.

was going to Le Mans to win. I got phone calls from Jacky Ickx, Derek Bell, and Hurley Haywood, offering their service."

Schutz heard the 911 camshaft drive chain tensioners failed, the major source of quality control complaints. He challenged the production engineers. "Do you know how to fix this problem?"

"Oh yes," they all said. "But we're not going to. This car is going out of production. Repairs kits are a profit source." This struck Schutz as shortsighted and incorrect. Quality problems negatively influenced future buyers' perceptions. A reliable fix would yield more car sales as owners remedied the problem once and for all. But it was the engineers'

second sentence that plagued him. Porsche's finance people had shown him that the 911 was Porsche's most profitable car.

Schutz had met Helmuth Bott at the Monday lunch. He called on the director of engineering the next evening at Weissach. The bar graph on Bott's wall caught Schutz's attention immediately.

1982–1989

1984 Carrera 3.2 Coupe

The new Carrera 3.2 line offered coupes, cabriolets, and Targa bodies, and between 1984 and 1989 Porsche manufactured more than 74,000 of these models in all body styles. Tony Lapine's stylists integrated the fog lights into the lower front valance.

"The Nine-Two-Eight ran out for four or five years. The Nine-Twenty-Four became the Nine-Forty-Four and it ran out several years. The 911 stopped in 1981. It quit.

"That was just a few months away. I thought of everything I had heard. So I walked to Mr. Bott's desk and picked up a crayon marker. I extended the 911 line off the end of the chart.

"I pushed the line onto the wall, over to the corner, around the corner, and on to the next wall.

"I wrote on his wall with an indelible marker. And I said, 'Mr. Bott, do we understand each other?'

"He was beaming. 'You can do this, Herr Schutz?'

"I can do this, Herr Bott."

Bott recalled in an interview in 1991 that after Schutz drew on his wall, they wondered how to let the world know. Bott had ideas, notes, drawings, and proposals he never could show Fuhrmann. An open car? All-wheel drive? Bott took Schutz to a garage below his office where he had hidden a car he called the Speedster. In 1979, Fuhrmann threatened to terminate him if Bott put more effort into it. Under Fuhrmann, no one worked on 911s unless it was critical.

Thus Porsche's 1980 and 1981 models received only minor running changes. "Spring" clutches replaced the failure-prone but gentler operating rubber-centered versions. Bosch and Porsche reprogrammed the K-Jetronic's cold-start mixture. Backfires on start-up often had destroyed air boxes.

The heart of the new car was its 3,164cc engine, with bore of 95mm and stroke of 74.4mm. A Digital Motor Electronics unit (DME) managed fuel injection and ignition, a system that evolved from Bosch's L-Jetronic and helped the engine develop 231 brake horsepower for European models, 207 brake horsepower for U.S. versions.

But these subtle improvements gave no hint of the indelible trail on Bott's wall. This line told everyone in engineering the 911 had turned a corner. It was running again.

Frankfurt's influential motor show arrived again in September after its usual two-year hiatus. Porsche had introduced the 901 there in 1963. Now, 18 years and nine shows later it was time to recapture the public's imagination of what the 911 was and could be. Bott and Schutz showed a 3.3-liter turbocharged all-wheel-drive cabriolet. It sat on a mosaic of mirrors that reflected the car's undercarriage. Weissach began work on a production cabriolet in March. On April 15, Schutz and Bott saw a white prototype with red interior. A day later, Bott drove it, and 18 days after that, Porsche's board approved production.

Schutz knew that board chairman Ferry Porsche moved out of Zuffenhausen and into a small workspace in Ludwigsberg as much to be away from Fuhrmann, who had marginalized him, as to work in privacy and peace. Schutz saw accountants working across from his own office. He moved them and remodeled the space into a large glass-case-lined office for Ferry.

"It was a lot nicer than mine and I was purposeful in that," he explained. He invited Ferry back to Werke I and each morning at nine o'clock, he would arrive. Shortly after

1984 Carrera 3.2 Cabriolet

A year after introducing the Cabriolet to the 911 series, Porsche brought out its new 3.2 Carrera series. This new model provided a new engine and a higher level of driver and passenger comforts and capabilities.

that, Schutz walked across the hall to have coffee together. Everybody in Porsche knew this was a routine.

About three months after his first Monday lunch with the manangers, Schutz showed up again. He asked the same question. "Everybody burst out laughing," he said.

At Le Mans in June, one of the museum-piece 936s took first overall. The second finished 12th. It was Porsche's 30th anniversary at Le Mans, and it represented Ickx's fifth and Bell's second victory. The two 924GTP cars finished seventh and eleventh overall.

In his first six months, Schutz accomplished Ferry's mission of getting the organization working together. The two continued morning coffee, and one day Schutz pressed an old question on Porsche.

"Whatever got into you," he asked the chairman, "to take a Volkswagen Beetle, remove the body, replace it with a streamlined two-seater and charge five times as much money for it?

"Without hesitation, he looked me in the eye and said, 'Herr Schutz, I didn't listen to anybody. I simply built my dream

Customers could order new Carrera 3.2 models with flat Turbo-style rear wings and polyurethane front "chin" spoilers as regular production options. Tony Lapine's stylists toned down nearly all the "bright work" to anodized black.

car and thought that others would share my dream.'"

"Often people think you go in a wrong direction," Helmuth Bott explained years later, "because you have an air-cooled engine, because you have the engine in the rear.... But Porsche always had an outstanding concept, different from others. And that's the key for Porsche, even in the future.

"If you have a water-cooled engine in the front, that's a system everybody can do . . . cheaper than we can do it. But the exciting things are sometimes more difficult for the engineers, and in the end you have advantages others do not. And with the advantages you can motivate customers. That is the secret of Porsche. We do things other people cannot."

Gerhard Schröder, who had designed mechanisms for Butzi Porsche's cabriolet concepts in 1963, resumed the assignment two decades later. Ferry wanted an electrically operated top. Engineering had a prototype working by March 1982, but its mechanisms needed more development. On the production cabriolet, Porsche settled for a top that owners opened or closed

1984 Carrera 3.2 Targa

With the Carrera 3.2 models, Porsche pushed its "Sonderwunsch" (special wishes) and "Exclusiv" options capabilities. Among many other things, these departments offered Fuchs wheels in contrasting colors and exteriors and interiors painted and upholstered to match buyers' samples.

by hand, zipping a plastic rear window into place.

Porsche again made only minimal improvements to the 1982 and 1983 SC models beyond introducing the cabrio. These were the last run of Fuhrmann's second-generation 911s. Tony Lapine's stylists continued toning down brightwork by painting the Fuchs alloy wheel centers black. For 1983 the U.S. Department of Transportation (DOT) allowed Porsche to return to 160-mile-per-hour speedometers from its previous 85-mile-per-hour instruments.

Porsche introduced the Carrera 3.2, its third-generation 911, for 1984. The designation came from the new engine displacement whose stroke now matched the Turbo's at 74.4mm. Bore remained 95mm for total displacement of 3,164cc. Bosch's latest L-Jetronic injection system worked together with its new Digital Motor Electronics (DME) Motronics 2 engine management system to boost performance and fuel economy and reduce emissions. Both Carrera 3.2 and the 3.3-liter turbocharged

1984 Typ 953 Four-Wheel-Drive Rally

This may have been one of the Paris-Dakar Rally's few stable and reliable river crossings. For 1984 Porsche entered three non-turbocharged 225-brake-horsepower prototype Typ 953 four-wheel-drive platforms racing engineers fitted under modified SC-RS bodies.

engines received new oil-fed camshaft drivechain tensioners.

Expecting 911 production to stop at the end of the 1981 model year, Porsche had withdrawn Turbo sales from the U.S. market starting in January 1980. Tighter exhaust emissions limits required catalytic converters to meet the regulations. Porsche reviewed catalyst technologies available up to that time. Combined with the quality of unleaded gasoline available in the United States, it estimated a constrained Turbo would develop only 240 brake horsepower, which offered little appeal. Schutz's arrival in 1981 put the Turbo back on Bott's wall chart, but it was not until the 1986 model year that Porsche sold them in America.

Better catalytic converters and higher-octane unleaded fuels made it possible. The 1986 models offered 282 horsepower, closer to European versions with 300 horsepower.

Throughout this time, however, Bott and his colleagues worked on the ultimate 911. The concept had begun life as an all-wheel-drive model for competition in 1984, known as the Typ 953.

Bott had a willing collaborator in Peter Schutz. The new chairman was born in Germany in 1930. His family emigrated to the United States in 1939 ahead of the war. Schutz graduated with a mechanical engineering degree from Illinois Institute of Technology. He understood and spoke German, and he quickly became fluent with

Porsche. To him, all-wheel-drive technology belonged beneath a Porsche 911.

The FIA's 1982 Group B was an umbrella classification in which manufacturers could create a racer in advance of series production. It incorporated the earlier Groups 4 through 7 and called for closed two-seaters with production of at least 200 examples over 12 months. Ferdinand Piëch's all-wheel-drive Audi Quattros often had won European rallies, and they demonstrated the value of this new drive system.

Bott's racing engineers wanted to do a mid-engined car for Group B, building something based on the 914. Jürgen Barth knew that 80 percent of Porsche's customers participated in some kind of paved-road competition, but just 20 percent rallied. Bott argued against both groups. Porsche did so many mid-engine race cars he felt the engineers would not learn anything new. Their 956 had succeeded from the start. He worried if Porsche built a mid-engine Group B car and no one else entered the category, would there even be a class?

"If you have to do a car which you must build two hundred times," he said, "you can also build one thousand times. If we do build a Group B car, let's have a look at the future of the 911." In early January, he formalized his concept on paper, envisioning a pure competition version first, with series production later that utilized technologies they developed for the competition car.

Bott completed his first prototype all-wheel-drive 911 in late 1981. He and his staff constantly upgraded it. In 1983, Porsche

953, 959, 961

In its three guises, the all-wheel-drive 959s set benchmarks that no other car has matched. The Paris-Dakar Rally version, the Typ 953 (left), won the event in 1986. At right, the Typ 961 all-wheel-drive Le Mans entry demonstrated the value of the technology so capably the FIA has never allowed all-wheel drive again.

racer Jacky Ickx entered and won the Paris-Dakar Rally driving a Mercedes-Benz factory-prepared 280GE Gelandewagen. Ickx brought practical knowledge to Bott's program. In advance of the 1984 run, they took Bott's own four-wheel-drive 911 to Africa. On the third day, a front axle broke. Bott's mechanics disconnected the other to make the car drivable. It was a revelation. Ickx had negotiated passages between dunes with 6 inches (15 centimeters) on either side of the car because he could place the car precisely. With only rear drive, Ickx needed nearly 7 feet (2 meters) on each side.

"We thought," Bott said, "if a car is so much better under bad conditions, than you must feel it on the dry road. . . . Our concept with the 911 always has been that it's an all-around car. With very few changes you can drive a desert rally and then to the racetrack at Le Mans. Without changing the concept, this 911 is capable of completely different things.

"So we thought, let's see if there is anything against our building this car for the next ten years, fifteen years. It was a goal, a task much greater than to build a race car."

Bott's concept went long range. There would be a desert rally car, the Typ 959, developed by Manfred Bantle, followed by 20 copies as a road-racing Typ 960 and then the next generation series Turbo as the Typ 961.

Bantle's version, the Typ 953, went straight to victory in 1984, finishing first

The "road" from Paris, France, to Dakar, Senegal, on the African Atlantic coast seldom was paved, but when it was, drivers made good use and crowds quickly learned to stand clear. The Paris-Dakar Rally, known as "The Raid," proved Helmuth Bott's statement that the 911 was a car that could do anything.

at the end of the 7,500-mile (12,000-kilometer) event. The race was more frustrating in 1985, and none of the three cars finished. But 1986 made up for that. Jacky Ickx captained three 959s to finish first, fourth, and sixth.

Stylist Wolfgang Möbius, who had designed the 928 and made 911 safety bumpers look attractive for U.S. customers, asked Dick Soderberg to create the look of this 911 of the future. Soderberg had worked with Norbert Singer on Moby Dick, the radical 935/78, and he understood how Singer interpreted rules. His Group B show car greatly advanced Moby's appearance. He retained the existing roof and doors as he had to do with Moby. Unable to design a more aerodynamic roof, Soderberg and Möbius, and Bott and Bantle accepted that a large rear wing was necessary. Soderberg developed a design icon with an elegantly integrated wing that morphed into the widened rear fenders. This elevated structure effectively lengthened and flattened the roofline. It treated detached airflow as if it were still laminar and attached to the car body. Two years after Bott's all-wheel-drive cabriolet startled Frankfurt show visitors, the September 1983 offering—a pearlescent white painted coupe—again stunned the audience.

Paul Hensler's production engine group devised a 2,849cc engine, using 95mm bore and 65mm stroke. Hensler employed two sequential turbochargers to develop 450 brake horsepower. But development costs and delays were affordable in the early 1980s when U.S. dollars bought DM 2 1/2 or DM 3. Porsche's profits for 1984 finished 33 percent higher than in 1983. Schutz's projections suggested another 30 percent improvement for 1985. Cars produced with costs in German marks seemed cheap to purchasers in the United States. American sales consumed two-thirds of Porsche's total output. Model year 1985 saw factory production reach a record of 54,458 cars.

At the Frankfurt show in 1985, Porsche announced two versions of the 959, a Sport with cloth interior (of which it produced only 37 examples) and a Comfort model with leather trim and heated leather seats. Porsche priced these at DM 420,000, about $142,850 at the time of the show, but they approached $200,000 as deliveries began. After struggling to meet U.S. DOT and EPA safety and emissions standards, Schutz and Bott concluded that they could not make the costs work for U.S. markets. They sold the entire series throughout the rest of the world without absorbing additional charges and delays to meet U.S. regulations despite having accepted 50 U.S. deposits. Production totaled 337 cars, including prototypes, development models, and those manufactured in 1987 and 1988, as well as a small run of eight fabricated from extra parts in 1992.

Regular production for 1987 upgraded all 911 models. Cabriolets got Ferry Porsche's long-desired power top. The company offered the Turbo Cabriolets and Targas, and option M506, a slant nose similar to the racing 935s, became a factory designation called the 930S. Turbos outside the United States ran with 330 brake horsepower, but horsepower was not the biggest concern of customers in America. The exchange rate buying power that had made Porsche's desirable and affordable in the early 1980s had reversed. Where first trade-day rates in 1985 had been DM 3.17 to $1, they dropped to DM 1.92 in 1987. A year later in 1988, four months after the Dow Jones Industrial averages plummeted 508 points in one day, the mark opened at DM 1.59 to the dollar.

Through this period, 928 models grew more powerful and aerodynamic. Porsche introduced the S model in 1980 with 300

1983 911 AWD Gruppe B Studie

Designer Richard Soderberg had collaborated with Norbert Singer on his 1978 Moby Dick racer, and he applied many of those racing aerodynamic aids to this Frankfurt auto show concept car. Adapting the concept to reality preserved most of Soderberg's imagination.

1987 959

Its 911 origins still are visible behind widened fenders and extended front and rear bodywork. Porsche's first supercar grew out of racing applications and helped define the genre with its limited production (337 examples) and its exclusive price of $200,000 (approximately DM 560,000).

Power for the 959 came from its Typ 959/50 engine, a 2,850cc flat-six with water-cooled cylinder heads (similar to the 935/78 and the 956/962 racers) that developed 450 brake horsepower. Acceleration from 0 to 62 miles per hour was 3.9 seconds, and several enthusiast magazines reached top speeds of 197 miles per hour (315 kilometers per hour).

To be legal for Group B racing, the roof, windows, and doors had to remain essentially "stock 911." Standard 911 bodies offered drag coefficients of 0.39, but the smooth, well-managed forms of the 959 brought its drag down to 0.32.

horsepower from 4.7 liters. This matched the 911 Turbo at the time. Its most significant visual features were black polyurethane front and rear spoilers; this intrusion on Wolfgang Möbius' clean form frustrated Tony Lapine deeply. By 1986 Porsche developed a four-valve 5-liter engine tuned for lead-free regular-grade gasoline rating 288 horsepower primarily for the American

Once Peter Schutz authorized production, Zuffenhausen moved quickly. The 959s emerged in many colors from Porsche shops and from a former bakery in the neighboring Reutter facility.

market. Almost 70 percent of 928 buyers opted for the automatic transmission.

European models in 1987 got four-valve heads with engines developing 320 horsepower in cars that reached 168 miles per hour (270 kilometers per hour). This made it the fastest series production Porsche yet.

U.S. specification cars held steady with 288 horsepower output.

As with the 928, Porsche updated the 944, and by 1985, the company had sold 60,000 of the popular cars. That year the 944 Turbo arrived with a newer, more aerodynamically efficient nose reducing its

already decent coefficient of drag from 0.35 to 0.33. With its KKK turbocharger the Porsche-designed in-line four developed 220 brake horsepower. Hensler's engineers had conceived and developed the engine package with a catalytic converter. The 944 Turbo became the first German production

1988 928S4

The next-generation 928 offered four-valve cylinder heads on a new 4,957cc V-8 with 100mm bore and 78.9mm stroke. Engine output of 320 brake horsepower would accelerate the car from 0 to 62 miles per hour in 5.9 seconds and reach a top speed of 168 miles per hour (270 kilometers per hour), making it Porsche's fastest regular production car up to that time.

vehicle to provide identical acceleration and top speed capabilities on unleaded and leaded fuels. Porsche listed the top speed as 152 miles per hour (245 kilometers per hour) and acceleration from 0 to 62.5 miles per hour (0 to 100 kilometers per hour) took 6.3 seconds.

The 944S arrived in 1987 with four valves per cylinder and developing 190 brake horsepower. Anti-lock brakes appeared as options on all 944 models, base, Turbo, and the S. For U.S. markets, Porsche provided dual air bags standard on the Turbo and optional on the base and S.

During 1988, Porsche manufactured its 100,000th 944 model. A new top-of-the-line model appeared, the 944 Turbo S, known internally as the Typ 951. The engine evolved

Body changes were evolutionary including a new rear polyurethane spoiler mounted up and away from the body. At the front, a new more-rounded nose provided a new spoiler and air intakes for brake cooling. The drag coefficient dropped from 0.38 to 0.34.

1984 944 Coupe

Porsche introduced the 944 in late 1981 as its replacement for the 924, and its resemblance to the earlier 924 Carrera GT sparked sales. The engine, a Porsche design, came from half of the 928 V-8 motor, with 2,479cc displacement, developing 163 brake horsepower.

This cast-aluminum cylinder block took its cylinder heads from the 928. Balance shafts inside the engine turned at twice the crankshaft speed to even out engine vibration, resulting in smooth performance that felt like the work of a much larger displacement engine. Zero to 62 miles per hour took 8.4 seconds, and Porsche quoted a top speed of 137 miles per hour (220 kilometers per hour).

1989 944 Turbo S

Porsche's final incarnation of the 944, these Typ 951 Turbo S models, brought performance of the 2.5-liter water-cooled four up to 250 brake horsepower. Acceleration to 62 miles per hour took 5.9 seconds, and Porsche quoted a top speed of 162 miles per hour (260 kilometers per hour). The company assembled just 1,635 of these.

The 944 and 951 model lines were tremendously successful for Porsche, and the company manufactured 111,500 of the cars in all variations. The final-generation Turbo with its name emblazoned onto its fender grew out of the 944 Turbo Cup series.

1985 944 Turbo Coupe

Porsche introduced the Typ 951 turbocharged 944 in January 1985. The 2,479cc intercooled engine developed 220 brake horsepower and got the car from 0 to 62 miles per hour in 6.3 seconds and up to a top speed of 152 miles per hour (245 kilometers per hour).

from the 944 Turbo Cup cars, and it developed 250 brake horsepower through turboboost set at 0.7 bar, 10.3 psi. Weissach gave the five-speed transmission its own oil cooler and reinforced the limited-slip differential. It was an exclusive offering in Silver Rose Metallic exterior paint and burgundy interior. Standard equipment included power steering and windows, automatic climate control, "Comfort" seats, and headlamp washers. The 0-to-62.5-mile-per-hour (0-to-100-kilometer-per-hour) acceleration run took 5.9 seconds, and Porsche published the top speed at 162 miles per hour (260 kilometers per hour).

It was the last year for the 2.5-liter four-cylinder 944s. Production had fulfilled Porsche's expectations, totaling 143,786 cars, including 1,635 of the highly desirable Typ 951. For 1989, a new engine took the 944 further and changed its designation.

Porsche, the company and the man, had begun this period in turmoil. These years ended the same way. People significant to the peaceful and profitable days in the middle had left, disappointed and discredited. But the idea that the 911 had a life beyond 1981, beyond 1985, beyond a closed coupe with rear-wheel drive, was the legacy that carried the company into a new century. ∎

CHAPTER THIRTEEN

EXTENDING LINES ON THE WALL

1989 Carrera 3.2 Speedster

The Carrera line culminated in the 911 Speedster, which Porsche offered both in normal bodies or Turbo look. This is one of the 171 normal, or "narrow body," Speedsters.

SOON AFTER PETER SCHUTZ ARRIVED AT PORSCHE, when calling on Helmuth Bott in his office at Weissach, Bott showed Schutz a dream car of his, one he called the Speedster. With all those other projects these two men put in motion, it took eight years to bring the Speedster to the market. It arrived in late 1988 as a 1989 model. It was nearly a year after the U.S. stock market had convulsed, sending stock prices down almost 23 percent in a single day. Recovery was slow.

Schutz saw exchange rate difficulties coming. He cut production severely, interrupting manufacture for a week or more every month. In this way, he kept employees on the job and the company alive.

But neither Bott nor Schutz was there to see the Speedster leave Zuffenhausen. Bott took the brunt of the criticism for the 959's failure to make money. According to historian Karl Ludvigsen, Ferdinand Piëch learned through his position on the supervisory board that each 959 had cost the company DM 1.3 million, about $730,000 in 1987/1988 exchange rates. This was about three times the delivery price. Schutz took responsibility for high costs and overruns. Several of the company's ten Porsche/Piëch family owners were unhappy as their share value dropped 30 percent when effects of the 1987 market crash reverberated around the world. Schutz resigned in early December 1987.

Helmuth Bott, an outcast after the abrupt change of management, remained at work at Weissach until late 1988 to see the 959s out the door. Then he retired at age 63. He had tamed the handling of the 356s at one end of his career, brought generations of new cars into existence, and shepherded the creation of dozens of race cars worth dozens of championship victories and titles. At the end of his career he established a new automobile category with his 959, one that became the ultimate target, the "supercar."

1989 Carrera 3.2 Speedster Turbo Look

The Turbo look Speedster was 69.9 inches (1,775mm) wide, compared with the standard body at 65 inches (1,652mm). Porsche used the 3,164cc flat-six that developed 231 brake horsepower or 217 brake horsepower for U.S. customers.

CHAPTER THIRTEEN

One of the Speedster's most significant design features, beside its wide stance, was the fiberglass tonneau that covered the rear parcel area. Porsche conceived the car as strictly a two-seater and used this cover also to cover the manually operated cloth top.

Supercar capabilities that had cost buyers hundreds of thousands of German marks quickly appeared in Porsche's next 911 model line. The Typ 964, introduced as a 1989 model, offered all-wheel drive in a car known as the Carrera 4. For Porsche it was the perfect marketing move. As Peter Schutz said in an interview in 2005, "Porsche is in the business of selling memberships in a dream." If a buyer could not get (in the United States) or could not afford a 959, the new C4 offered much of the same car for a fraction of the price, opening membership in that dream to a wide audience.

Under Schutz's direction, Bott had planned the next 911. Bott assigned Manfred Bantle and his series production car counterpart Fritz Bezner to develop two new lines. The 964s were normally aspirated, and the 965s had turbos. They utilized Typ 959 innovations including self-leveling suspensions, ABS, and all-wheel drive.

At this time Porsche still enjoyed a favorable exchange rate of around DM 3 to $1. Bott took some of this profit and installed a wind tunnel at Weissach. Based on financial strength and the look of the 959, Porsche's board approved Bott's new unitized body. However management allowed styling only to update the body. Wolfgang Möbius and Dick Soderberg could not revise it as radically as Soderberg had done with the 959. Fenders, headlights, and the broad, expensive roof panel remained off limits.

Bott's project notebook on the new car, the *Lastenheft*, set a drag coefficient target

1989–1995

at 0.32. The 959 had achieved 0.31. Current production 911s lagged behind competitors at 0.395. To make this jump, Soderberg and Möbius fine-tuned valences, flush-mounted front bumpers, and fitted a belly pan under the nose of the car shielding the new front differential and driveshaft tunnel.

At the back Bantle, Bezner, and the Weissach engineers collaborated with designers on an electrically operated rear spoiler providing lift control. Above 50 miles per hour (80 kilometers per hour), the spoiler rose from the rear deck lid and reduced rear lift to zero.

As the 964 came together, Bott and Bezner configured its weights and balances with 59 percent of the weight on the rear, which received 69 percent of the power allocation. Bott hoped "to provide our customers handling characteristics that felt familiar to them . . . but with the benefit of additional traction in poor conditions."

1989 Typ 964 Carrera 4 Coupe

All-wheel-drive technology from the 959 reached the regular Porsche customers in the Typ 964 Carrera 4 models. The new front end, more aerodynamic rain gutters, a completely flat undertray, and an automatically elevating rear spoiler helped reduce its drag coefficient to 0.32.

CHAPTER THIRTEEN

1991 911 Turbo 3.3

Porsche stylists and engineers had in mind an all-new Turbo, the Typ 965, to accompany the new normally aspirated 964s, but budget considerations stopped the project. The 3.3-liter intercooled engine developed 320 brake horsepower and initially only was available for European customers.

1992 964 Carrera Cup

At the start of the race at Norisring, traffic always jammed up. The benefit for spectators of this series was that even as the race progressed, the field remained clustered together and the cars passed each other, winning only through driving skill.

The front differential forced Bezner and Bott to develop a new rear suspension because the driveshaft running forward from the engine would have penetrated directly through the tube traditionally housing torsion bars. That transverse tube had provided much of the car's stiffness.

Another compromise arose when Paul Hensler committed to using twin spark plugs per cylinder. This would burn fuel more efficiently to meet California's ever-tightening nitrogen-oxygen (NOx) emissions standards. However twin-plug heads compromised room for cooling fins. Hoping to transfer cylinder head heat to the heavily finned cylinders, Hensler's engineers eliminated the gasket between them. This eventually caused leakage problems that later engineering efforts had to solve.

New computers, electronics, and other features and their wiring added 500 pounds (227 kilograms) of weight to the car, making it almost 20 percent heavier than the 3.2 Carrera. To meet their performance targets, Bezner, Bott, and Hensler developed a new 3,600cc engine by increasing bore 2mm to 100mm and lengthening stroke 2mm to 76.4mm as well. This engine developed 250 brake horsepower. Marketing named the new cars the Carrera 4 for the all-wheel-drive version introduced for 1989 and the Carrera 2 rear-drive version for 1990.

Efforts to develop the 964 effectively sent the car overbudget and caused management to postpone its introduction by a year, making matters even worse. These problems compounded the effects of a falling exchange rate, the departure of Peter Schutz, and the board's selection of frugal business manager Heinz Branitzki as chief executive officer.

The 964 eventually cost much more than anticipated. The number of parts the 964 shared with either the previous 3.2 Carrera or the new 944 Turbo was so small that when production manager Wendelin Wiedeking examined parts lists, development costs, and production revenues, he concluded that no one was monitoring engineering. Historian Ludvigsen reported that Wiedeking accused Bott of destroying the company through his financial practices. When Wiedeking observed that no one cared about his discoveries, he left. Bott followed him a few months later, just before the 964 Carrera 4 introduction and two years before his scheduled retirement.

Branitzki, cash and cost sensitive, killed some projects. Variations on the 928 that styling and engineering had proposed, including a cabriolet and a four-seater, went first. Sales of the luxury sports car had fallen

so low that new variations no longer promised new sales. Bott's all-wheel-drive Typ 965 Turbo survived a bit longer.

Bezner and Bott experienced cooling and horsepower output problems similar to those Paul Hensler suffered developing the 3.6-liter 964 engine. They contemplated alternatives that included adapting the latest Indy V-8 engine with four valves per cylinder and dual overhead cams or developing a six-cylinder version. Those options were expensive and time-consuming. By late summer 1988 water-cooling the flat-six was the favored solution.

Then Schutz resigned, and Tony Lapine and Bott retired early. Engineer Ulrich Bez, who had quit Porsche in 1978 to join BMW, came back to succeed Bott. He brought with him Harm Lagaay, who had designed the 924 with Dick Soderberg but who also had ended up at BMW in the interim.

Bez recognized that water-cooling the flat-six would take years to develop properly. With Branitzki's approval Bez launched a program to install the 3.3-liter 930 Turbo engine in the new all-wheel-drive Typ 965 as a 1991 model. Engineering then proceeded with two V-8 versions, one with turbos and the other without. They investigated larger displacements. Would 3.6, 4.0, even 4.2 liters work for 1993 or 1994 as well as for the new car line, a four-door sedan designated the Typ 989, a logical step considering Bez's background at BMW?

Yet through November and December, everything changed. Stylist Tony Hatter's sensational 965 concept was toned down and then killed. "We had to redo it completely," Hatter recalled, "take off all the aggressive-looking hoops and things and make it a reasonable car."

To make it reasonable, Bezner and Bez filled the gap Porsche created when it discontinued the Typ 930S. They adopted its 3,299cc engine and installed it in a real-wheel-drive 964 body. Production started in May 1990 as a 1991 model. The body incorporated pieces from the former "Sportkit" option that boosted output to 320 brake horsepower.

In late 1988 customer sports department manager Jürgen Barth proposed the idea of building just two or three rear-drive 964RSR racers using 3.4-liter engines to enter the 24-hour endurance race at Nürburgring. Worldwide currency exchange rates had seriously depressed Porsche sales of both series production and race cars. Barth sought a project to develop. Years earlier, Norbert Singer had created a graphics demonstration showing that when Porsche raced, sales increased.

1992 964 Carrera Cup

Porsche Cars North America intended to bring the Carrera Cup series to the United States, but after importing 45 cars, plans collapsed. Andial, the southern California Porsche specialists that had converted 25 of these cars to racing specifications, undid their work and returned most of them to street trim.

Barth got tentative approval for his idea and a second one as well, creating a customers-only car on the new platform using some exotic spare parts Weissach had in storage.

When Porsche builds new-technology race cars, it seldom assembles only those few examples competitors and the public see. For the 1986 Paris-Dakar, Porsche entered three 953s. But it assembled about 30 sets of all-wheel-drive running gear. Its high clearance meant the 953 was strictly an off-road racer. But Barth envisioned constructing perhaps a half-dozen new cars with lower ground clearance for circuit racing.

He had been at Porsche as it created the 1973 911RS Carrera 2.7 and its 2.8- and 3.0-liter RSR versions. He knew the 911R models. These cars played with the rules. Current competition regulations had no opening for all-wheel-drive racers, but Barth knew from past experience that if Porsche pushed it, venues and series opened up.

A curious quirk of economics came into consideration here to further this project. Porsche dealers had trouble selling Carreras for $60,000, yet "investors" with no racing experience or interest bought 908s for

1992 964 Carrera 4 Lightweight

This car grew from customer racing engineer Jürgen Barth's imagination after learning that Porsche still had some two dozen sets of Typ 953 racing all-wheel-drive running gear. He built the cars hoping the FIA might create a series in which these would be eligible.

Weissach's rough road was the destination at some point in development for any and every car that came out of Porsche. The C4 Lightweights got the same destructive test time that 917s got and future 911s will get.

$400,000 one week and sold them for $700,000 a week later. In private club locker rooms, speculators showed snapshots of their latest deals instead of bragging over recent stock trades. Legitimate racing cars, even those with no competition history, became an investment target.

Barth gutted the 964 interior, installed 953 running gear, and created the 964RS. While he contemplated a run of 10 or 12 cars, Californian Kerry Morse immediately committed to the first one. Barth estimated its price at DM 200,000, between $110,000 and $120,000 at the time. With a solid order, Barth knew he could move his project forward. He pared 700 pounds (350 kilograms) from the series car. He replaced doors and front and rear deck lids with thin aluminum panels. Side windows became Plexiglas. A roll bar surrounded the interior. Two large knurled knobs set off the instrument panel. Racers recognized these as turboboost controls on 935s. But this car used normal aspiration. These controls shifted differential bias from left-to-right and front-to-rear. The 2,430-pound (1,105-kilogram) "race car" achieved 265 horsepower using modified electronics and a stainless-steel dual exhaust system that scarcely muffled noise. Visually, the car appeared stock and quite tame. It ran on stock-width wheels and tires.

Helmut Flegl, now number two to Ulrich Bez, questioned the project. He was involved in developing the 964 Carrera Cup model with Roland Kussmaul. Barth answered each question and kept moving forward. He

1992 964 Turbo Look Cabriolet

Because it had worked so well for the 1989 Speedster, Porsche introduced a variety of Typ 964 models using the wider body shells. Top speeds were slower than narrow bodies due to greater wind resistance, but few buyers of these 702 cabriolets were speed-oriented. Cars such as this green model sold for about $112,000 (roughly DM 175,000) at the factory.

1993 964RS America

Porsche couldn't export the lightened 260-brake-horsepower 1992 911RS models to the United States because they lacked air bags. To appease American customers, they developed these RSA versions for 1993 and 1994 using 3.6-liter engines that developed 247 brake horsepower in a car about 80 pounds (36.4 kilograms) lighter and $10,000 less expensive than standard C2 coupes.

got the car, now called the C4 Lightweight, or *leichtbau*, serial-numbered as a racer with numbers beginning with 964-001 rather than the 17-character VIN number, an important benefit for a collector market valuing rarity and to the U.S. DOT and EPA, who felt duped by private owners attempting to import luxurious 959s as "race cars."

Word spread through the world of Porsche race car devotees. Here was a car that might never race, but it was rare and available. The run grew from 10 cars to 21 and sold out quickly. Intriguing internal politics drove the price up from Barth's second estimate of DM 225,000 to DM 285,000, nearly $176,000 plus a $24,000, DM 39,000 value-added tax (VAT) assessment.

U.S. buyers (there were a half dozen) could apply for the tax refund, but the U.S. EPA and DOT decided to admit the cars as racers only after individual inspections of each car.

The price jump raised eyebrows. Any one of the 70 starting-flag-ready 964 Carrera Cup cars that Helmut Flegl and Roland Kussmaul had developed sold for about $76,000,

CHAPTER THIRTEEN

DM 123,000 at 1991 exchange rates. People wondered aloud if 953 running gear was worth an extra $100,000. C4 Lightweight deliveries continued through 1991, but the collector car world was teetering on the brink of disaster.

The car-as-investment boom burst in 1992. Prices for Porsche 908s had reached $1 million, and deals for 917s approached $5 million. Prices had swollen preposterously, but sharp speculators already were out. This left hundreds of latecomers with cars attached to huge loans. It affected racing dramatically. The 24 Hours of Le Mans had fielded starting grids of 50 to 60 cars during the 1980s. Just 28 cars started in June 1992. Barth sent letters to buyers reminding them about their commitments.

The last C4 Lightweight left Weissach in June 1992. The project made money just as most all Barth's ideas had done. It had cost Porsche nothing to delete sound insulation and little to add running gear from storage and a fixed wing it already had in stock. Another lesson came clear: Limited edition special cars such as the 1973 RS or even the 1989 Speedster carried strong appeal to loyal customers. Perhaps not at the nearly 30 percent markup that some in Porsche's management cynically had applied to this car, but Porsche now knew that its customers would dig deeply to be the only one in town with something unique.

The C2 and C4 series production models for 1992 were most recognizable because of their new 16-inch "Cup-design" wheels and outside mirrors. Porsche's *Exclusiv* Department, the in-house boutique service for customers to personalize their cars, offered performance boost packages for Turbos that modified the intake manifold and cylinder heads and altered timing to deliver 355 brake horsepower and a top speed of 174 miles per hour (280 kilometers per hour). At the Geneva show in March 1992 Porsche introduced its Turbo S. Engineering reduced weight by 396 pounds (180 kilograms) using lightweight plastic doors and front deck lid, and thin-gauge glass for side windows. Revising camshafts, intake ports, and ignition and injection systems, as well as increasing turboboost 0.1 bar, raised output to 381 brake horsepower. Acceleration to 62.5 miles per hour (100 kilometers per hour) from 0 took 4.2 seconds, and Porsche quoted top speed at 180 miles per hour (290 kilometers per hour). The company manufactured just 86 of these cars.

Porsche created a new enthusiast's car for 1992, the Carrera RS, on the C2 chassis. Using the 3.6-liter engine with alterations to the control unit and a 98-octane requirement, gave them an extra 10 brake horsepower. To save weight, Weissach engineers relieved the

Porsche manufactured just 702 of these models in white, black, red, silver metallic, or midnight blue metallic, selling them for $53,900 apiece. The few options included air conditioning, a limited-slip differential, and a power sunroof.

1989–1995

interior of every accoutrement except leather bucket seats. The car weighed 2,684 pounds (1,220 kilograms), which was 286 pounds (130 kilograms) less than the stock C2. Eliminating air bags helped reduce weight, but this kept the car out of the United States. Porsche offered three versions, a spartan base model, a touring version with electric windows, and a racetrack model N/GT. Acceleration to 62.5 miles per hour (100 kilometers per hour) from 0 took just 5.3 seconds. Top speed was rev-limited at 161 miles per hour (260 kilometers per hour).

For 1993, Porsche offered the new 3.6-liter Turbo. A few months later at the Frankfurt auto show, it debuted the 964's replacement, the Typ 993. In early 1993, the company released a 30th anniversary commemorative 911 model in the C4 wide-body configuration. For customer racers, Weissach offered a 911 Carrera RS 3.8 in limited quantities for competitors entering the new Supercup series accompanying Formula One races.

Porsche resurrected a two-time winner again in 1992 and 1993 with a new Speedster on the 964 platform. For 1993 and early 1994 model years the company manufactured a run of 930 narrow-body Speedsters on C2 platforms. These sold for DM 134,000,

The new "Symphony" model radio offered real-time traffic reporting and station identification. The four-speed automatic was optional at no extra charge and cost acceleration to 62 miles per hour only 0.2 seconds—5.9 seconds instead of 5.7. Top speed was 171 miles per hour (about 275 kilometers per hour).

1994 928GTS

Porsche introduced the GTS for model year 1992 with a redesigned V-8, which had its stroke enlarged to 85.9mm (with bore at 100mm) to increase overall displacement to 5,397cc. Styling cleaned up the exterior by removing all side moldings even while slightly widening the rear wing.

CHAPTER THIRTEEN

$80,720, at the factory. Following that, the factory assembled 15 Turbo-Look Speedsters, also on the C2 running gear. As with Bott's Speedsters in 1989, narrow- and wide-body cars offered a manual top with a plastic fairing covering the rear parcel shelf. Porsche quoted a price of around DM 18,000, nearly $11,000, to convert narrow-body Speedsters to the Turbo-Look.

To make up for denying American customers an RS, the factory produced a run of 701 RS America models for 1993. This slightly lightened C2 coupe featured most distinctively the fixed rear wing of the Carrera 3.2. By removing air conditioning, using manual seats and a simple cloth interior, Porsche reduced the price to $53,900 for the U.S. market only. The 247 brake horsepower U.S. 3.6-liter propelled the car from 0 to 62.5 miles per hour in 5.6 seconds. Top speed matched the European RS.

From 1989 to the end of its life in 1995, the 928 continued subtle development improvements. Porsche offered the 1990 and 1991 S4 only with a four-speed automatic. The GT model got a five-speed manual. In 1992, Porsche introduced its most refined and powerful version of the 928, the GTS. A new 5,397cc engine with four-valve heads and LH-Jetronic fuel injection developed 350 brake horsepower. It needed just 5.7 seconds to reach 100 kilometers per hour, and Porsche quoted the car's top speed at 171 miles per hour (275 kilometers per hour). When Porsche ended production of the 928, it had assembled 2,831 of the 928GTS and a total of 61,056 of 928 models in all. In its last days, the fast, elegant, luxurious GTS sold for DM 167,890, or $117,400.

1993 968 Coupe

Stylistically, there were just subtle changes in profile from the final 944 to the 968. Technologically the car was a big step forward with Motronic ignition and fuel-injection management and the versatile VarioCam induction system delivering broader, smoother performance from the engine.

1993 968 Cabriolet

The 968 provided an electric mechanism that retracted the cloth top once the driver released it manually from the windshield header. Headlight washers, air conditioning, a leather interior, and a variety of audio systems were optional on the 3,959 Typ 968 cabrios Porsche produced between 1992 and 1995.

Production of the 944 model proceeded steadily from 1983 through 1988. The 190-horsepower 944S arrived with four-valve heads for 1987, and the two-valve 250-horsepower 944 Turbo S reached markets in 1988. But new engines were coming.

For 1989, the base 944 ran a new 2.7-liter four-cylinder engine developing 165 brake horsepower. The S2 replaced the 944S model and introduced a new 3-liter four with 211 brake horsepower at 5800 rpm. The Turbo, no longer designated the Turbo S, carried over its 250-horsepower 2.5-liter four. Porsche sent S2 coupe bodies to American Sunroof Corporation's (ASC) subsidiary in Weinsberg north of Zuffenhausen to convert them to cabriolets by removing the roof, trimming the windshield, and adding a second floorpan. Its 2,990cc in-line engine was the world's largest-displacement automobile four-cylinder and got the car from 0 to 100 kilometers in 6.9 seconds and to a top speed of 149 miles per hour (240 kilometers per hour).

Porsche dropped the 2.7-liter base 944 for 1990 but gave the Turbo a new hoop spoiler. The S2 got standard anti-lock brakes. For 1991, the final year of 944 production, Porsche offered a limited run of 944 Turbo cabriolets. Porsche's manufacturing contract with Audi's plant at Neckarsulm expired in April 1991, which took 944 Turbo models out of production a month before Zuffenhausen ended assembly of the S2 models. The 944s had been very successful for Porsche, selling 163,302 units between introduction in late 1981 and its demise in early 1991. For fans of these nimble front-engined water-cooled cars, the successor Typ 968 was only months away and carried over many 944 body parts.

The smart-looking nose of the new 968 loosely resembled the 928. Porsche offered coupes and cabriolets from introduction. While it was the company's least expensive model, there was nothing entry-level about is appointments, with leather on the steering wheel, gear lever, and handbrake. The 968s included tinted glass, power steering and windows, dual front air bags, central locking with an alarm, and heated, remotely operated outside mirrors. The coupe got an electric rear wiper while the cabriolet used an electric hood mechanism.

The six-speed gear shift lever, steering wheel, and handbrake were leather-covered as standard equipment, as was power steering, electric windows, front air bags for both driver and passenger, electric seat adjustment, and electrically adjusted and heated outside rearview mirrors.

The heart of the 968 was its new 2,990cc water-cooled four-cylinder engine with bore and stroke of 104x88mm. The Typ M44/43 developed 240 brake horsepower and propelled the car to 62 miles per hour in 6.5 seconds and on to a top speed of 157 miles per hour (252 kilometers per hour).

Porsche improved performance of the 3-liter four it had introduced in later 944s increasing output to 240 brake horsepower as it carried them into the 968 models. Paul Hensler's staff incorporated two counter-rotating balance shafts to smooth four-cylinder operation to something more like a six-cylinder or an eight-cylinder engine. Performance improved as well, with 0 to 100 kilometers per hour requiring 6.5 seconds and top speeds of 157 miles per hour (252 kilometers per hour) for six-speed manual transmission cars.

For 1993, Porsche introduced a lightened (110 pounds, 50 kilograms less) 968 Club Sport version. Riding on 17-inch Cup wheels, engineers lowered the car roughly 0.8 inches (20mm) for better handling and a firmer ride. One weight-saving decision removed air bags, a choice that kept the car from U.S. customers. However, buyers everywhere opted for the new Turbo S package that rode on 18-inch wheels and tires. A single KKK turbocharger boosted engine output to 305 brake horsepower, propelling the car to 100 kilometers per hour in 5 seconds on the way to a top speed of 174 miles per hour (280 kilometers per hour).

Porsche made few changes in the 968s either for 1994 or its final year 1995. The company offered heated leather seats starting in 1994 and introduced an optional Sports package, a Comfort package, and a Safety package for Club Sport models sold in Europe and Asia. Production ended with the 1995 model. Porsche had manufactured a total of 11,425 of the 968s. The most desirable and rarest of these models was the Turbo S coupe, with production reaching only 14 examples.

An era ended when Porsche took the 968 out of production. Beginning in 1975 with the first four-cylinder transaxle 924, two decades of water-cooled front-engine models had introduced tens of thousands of enthusiasts to Porsche. What few outside Porsche knew was that a replacement was coming, and its configuration and shape would open an entire new audience to what Porsche could offer. ■

CHAPTER FOURTEEN

THE END OF AIR-COOLING ON ROAD AND TRACK

1994 993 Preproduction Prototype Coupe

Porsche takes cold weather testing seriously. This was one of a fleet of preproduction prototypes that froze above the artic circle and baked in American and African deserts.

"WHEN I ARRIVED, THERE WAS NOTHING GOING ON IN THE ADVANCED DESIGN STUDIOS!" That was how Harm Lagaay remembered his first impressions of Weissach in late 1989. While Ernst Fuhrmann was long gone and the inertia of rest surrounding the 911 had been overcome by Peter Schutz's inertia of enthusiasm, Schutz was gone, too. The 928 soldiered along with the 944. In Schutz's place, another "inertia" had assumed control: Heinz Branitzki and the practice of caution.

"We have here," Branitzki stated in the press kit introducing the 964 in 1989, "the Nine-Eleven for the next twenty-five years, the concept that will help our favorite model to reach its fiftieth anniversary!" The 964 provided technology and styling improvements over the 3.2 Carrera. However, engineering and design compromises forced on Weissach had made the car less of a success than their creative minds had wanted. The 944 had a cabriolet, and there were sketches for a 928 open car as well. But no engineering upgrades loomed on these horizons. With fresh minds, Ulrich Bez and Lagaay examined the flaws of the 964 and accepted their mission from the supervisory board. "Get it right," was the way Lagaay remembered it. He put Tony Hatter to work sketching concepts for a 964 replacement.

"With the Nine-Sixty-four," Hatter explained, "the Nine-Eleven had kind of gotten out of balance with its big fat bumpers in the front way up in the air, and the rear end hanging down. We addressed the complete proportional balance of the car. That was the main goal."

While Hatter and his design team worked to examine form and proportion, Bez asked his

1995 911 Typ 993C4 Coupe

Porsche introduced the Typ 993 as a rear-drive Carrera Coupe in 1993, and the cabriolet followed in early 1994. The companion Carrera 4 arrived in the fall of 1994 in both body styles as well. Virtually everything about the car was different from the previous-generation 964s.

engineers to consider what the 911 should be. Peter Falk was the soft-spoken competition director with decades of experience in racing and series car development. He succeeded in verbalizing what Bez sought. Falk used the word *Wendigheit*, meaning "agility or nimbleness." In a 20-page paper, he contrasted maneuverability with agility, concluding that agility had more to do with responsiveness while maneuverability referred to controllability in direction change. Falk suggested that agility had been disciplined out of the 964s in their attempts to tame handling quirks. Georg Wahl, present-day General Manager of Chassis Development, Axles, remembered the time clearly.

"The idea was to concentrate on the Nine-Eleven with the model Nine-Nine-Three as a short-term solution. We designed it with a complete new chassis front and rear."

Wahl and his engineers changed the front axle system from the 964 to the 993. The wheel carrier for the 964 was a steel forging; for the 993 they die cast it in aluminum. With every successive generation, Porsche engineers worked to remove weight and increase strength and stiffness.

"The Nine-Sixty-Four had the so-called 'Wonder Bushing' which we used to 'educate' this axle to the ride, to toe in with braking. But this bushing also was expensive, and we thought that with the *Nine-Nine-Three*, for this amount of money we can do a more perfect axle. A rear engine car needs the best rear axle for this weight distribution." The axle system Wahl advocated, one he himself

Engineers extensively redesigned the 3.6-liter flat-six, eliminating the crankshaft torsional vibration damper used in the 964 version. Countless improvements, upgrades, and updates increased output to 272 brake horsepower.

1997 Typ 993 Cabriolet

Porsche introduced the 993 Cabriolet in early 1994. Opening the power top no longer required turning off the engine; it merely required the driver to stop and apply the parking brake, which served as the interlock device.

had designed, ironically came not from a rear-engined Porsche, but from a front-engined prototype and a mid-engine concept he had developed.

Through 1984 and 1985, Wahl worked on the Typ 984 project. Chairman Peter Schutz was a flying enthusiast, and he and Helmuth Bott had adapted the Porsche flat-six 911 engines to aero uses. Bott thought that it would be sensible to offer a flat-four as well. If they had a flat-four for airplanes, they also could use it for a car.

"The thought was to be a small two-seater under Nine-Twenty-Four at the time with a mid-engine flat-four. We started a project and I was responsible for the complete chassis. Front axle, rear axle. I designed the rear axle myself. We did one prototype.

"This rear axle was the first multilink axle at Porsche. At the time, Mercedes had a multilink in the C-class. Until this time we didn't believe in a series production car, with these high production numbers, that we could do one economically. Our own calculations told us everything about it was too expensive, too many linkage pieces, too many joints. But the kinematics are the best you can imagine."

As with other projects Weissach undertook, the 984 was ahead of its time. Development costs for the flat-four proved too costly, as did those of the car, nicknamed the "Porsche Junior." But engineers, designers, and planners at Porsche do not lose or discard good ideas. The multilink resurfaced under Ulrich Bez as the rear-axle design of choice for his 989 sedan.

"The Nine-Eight-Nine," Wahl continued, "was, if I look back, maybe twenty years too early. We worked on it through nineteen ninety-one, ninety-two, and then we stopped the project. The costs were exploding. We thought that, with the competition of other cars, we had to get everything money can buy into this car: Rear-axle steering, all-wheel drive, everything that we could do. That was the problem regarding the growing cost and weight of the vehicle. We had enormous costs developing those systems for the car."

But with the 993, "It was clear that we had to do a real big step in the development. When I came up with the presentation for Mr. Bez, we had two versions. One was a further development of the 964 axle. The other was the multilink. At the time this was a shared part with the Nine-Eight-Nine! That both cars shared this part was a big advantage. We lost the Nine-Eight-Nine later, but we got the axle!"

Meanwhile Hatter, who had worked with Dick Soderberg on the 965 Turbo body, adopted some of the shapes and air inlets from that project. A few of these already had transplanted onto the 968 as it entered final design phases. Lagaay gave some thought to linking the 911/968 designs closely. Another good idea not lost, this concept reached maturity with Porsche's next generation 911, the Typ 996.

Hatter fine-tuned his design, working painstakingly to make this new Porsche very much a Porsche. "We really work surfacing to perfection," he said. "You can't do it in an afternoon or a week. There are no shapes or forms on the cars that don't have to be there. The bulges are where the wheels are. You can see where the people sit. It's such a tightly packaged vehicle that it's like a trained athlete shape."

Engineers addressing engine questions reviewed 964 and 965 proposals for water-cooled engines. Porsche was developing a V-8 for Bez's proposed 989 sedan. The current

Revisions to the Digital Motor Electronics (DME), the Motronics, and the VarioCam system as well as introduction of the Varioram induction system increased horsepower output from 272 up to 285 for 1996 and 1997 models. The 993 marked the end of the air-cooled Porsche engines.

From the start of the 993 line, Porsche provided American, Swiss, and Austrian purchasers with a six-speed transmission with higher gears than "Rest-of-the-World" buyers to improve fuel economy and reduce engine and exhaust noise. In 1997 all cars got this transmission, which brought top speeds up 4 miles per hour to 171 (275 kilometers per hour) while improving 0-to-62-mile-per-hour acceleration from 5.6 to 5.4 seconds.

1994 993 Supercup

The line-up of cars awaiting delivery showed a who's who of racers in the series. In the white row, German driver Uwe Alzen won in 1994, and Frenchman Jean-Pierre Malcher took the title for 1995.

Indy V-8 for the Quaker State and Foster's Lager Typ 2708 entries provided ideas as well. But the board concluded that developing a new engine was too costly, so engineering returned to the 3.6-liter flat-six of the 964.

Project manager Herbert Ampferer and his staff rid the crankshaft of the torsional vibration damper that the 3.6-liter engine initially required for smooth running. They incorporated self-adjusting hydraulically operated valves into the heads and reduced valvetrain weight. They revised the entire exhaust system, ultimately obtaining 272 brake horsepower. It was quieter than any 911 engine to that time.

All-wheel drive had been Helmuth Bott's priority with the 964 C4. Bez and his successor Horst Marchardt reexamined the concept to provide superior handling. The 993 configuration replaced computer-controlled differentials and heavy planetary gears with a viscous coupling connecting a torque tube to a much smaller front differential. The new configuration cut the weight in half.

One of Hatter's toughest assignments he got when he started the 993 was that this new car, whatever it looked like, had to be less expensive and take less time to manufacture. Bez had pounded design and engineering staffs to complete the car quickly. His intolerance for delays incited a lobby against him. They dissuaded management from renewing his contract, and Bez left in late 1991.

Wendelin Wiedeking had returned to Porsche by now, arriving several months earlier. He was dedicated to streamlining procedures and reducing costs. He knew about Toyota Motor Company's legendary efficiency and its practice of the Japanese philosophy of continuous improvement, *kaizen*. He invited another Japanese legend, *Shin-Gijutsu*, a company established by two former Toyota executives that taught "new technology," to Zuffenhausen. The executives inspired Wiedeking himself to take a power saw to parts bins standing 10 feet (3 meters) tall after they shouted at him in Japanese, "We said, 'Bring us to the factory. This is a warehouse!'"

Wiedeking reduced assembly floor inventories from 28 days on hand to 30-minute supplies by instituting just-in-time inventory delivery to Porsche from its suppliers. It was not easy, but Wiedeking and his staff forced smaller companies to rethink their own traditional techniques or lose business to organizations more adaptable.

As Porsche prepared the 993 launch, the company faced another change in a weakened, shaky economy. Sales through 1992–1993 had reached only $1.18 billion, DM 1.9 billion. Zuffenhausen produced just 9,648 cars (119 of the 928S4 models, 1,188 coupe and cabriolet 968s, and 8,341 of the 964s, whether coupe, cabriolet, or turbo). The company lost $157 million, DM 253 million, a record for any fiscal year. In retrospect, Ferry Porsche's nervousness over his DM 15 million investment in the new 901 seemed nothing compared to the $310 million, DM 500 million, that Ulrich Bez and short-time chairman Arno Bohn had committed to the 993.

With 2,374 of the 993 coupes (and only 22 cabriolets) assembled by New Year's Eve 1994, Porsche considered the two-wheel drive Carrera 911 to be a 1994 model for Europe. Americans waited until April to receive first-year 1995 model 993s.

Creating the cabrio was a challenge, "tricky," as Tony Hatter referred to it. "The first cabriolet that Porsche did was the D Program [1983 911SC]. They used the same roof on the 964. I never liked the look for the early cabriolets. The classical 911 shape is the coupe. With the Nine-Nine-Three we tried to get some form into the roof. It was the first time, I think, that we tackled the roof."

Porsche introduced the much-improved 993 Carrera 4 in mid-1994 worldwide as a 1995 model. Buyers hankering for a turbo accepted 964 carryover cars through 1994 when the new 3.6-liter twin-turbo version appeared along with the C4. Raising the excitement level for all buyers, this 408 brake horsepower automobile

arrived with all-wheel drive and the new six-speed G50 gearbox.

The 993 was a success. The factory manufactured 7,865 coupes and 7,074 cabriolets as well as one hundred new 305-horsepower 993 Carrera Cup cars to compete in the ongoing series in Europe and the United States. Because of Bez's relentlessness (engineering succeeded in reducing manufacturing time from 120 hours per 964 to around 85 hours for 993s) and Wiedeking's watchfulness, Porsche lowered the base price by $5,000. At the end of 1994's fiscal year, accountants put away their red pencils.

On the heels of Jürgen Barth's frustrating efforts with the 964 Carrera 4 Lightweight, he and new motorsports director Max Welti found a more international form of competition than the Carrera Cup events. They created a 911S LM based on the 964 with twin turbochargers for Le Mans in 1993. Barth had helped establish

1994 993 Carrera Cup/Supercup Pace Car

Porsche assembled 35 of these 3.8-liter racers to run in support of Formula One events. Fitted with adjustable anti-sway bars and shock absorbers, the cars weighed 2,425 pounds (1,100 kilograms).

1998 911 GT2 Evolution

To help its private customers battle Ferraris and McLarens racing in BPR's GT1 category, Porsche engineer Roland Kussmaul developed what he characterized as a GT 1.5, an Evolution package of body and running gear parts for the GT2. Rear fender extensions accommodated 14-inch-wide wheels and reinforced transaxles delivered the revised engine's 600 brake horsepower.

Porsche's reputation for customer race cars: They delivered tested, proven automobiles that did not break.

One factor helped Porsche define the new car, helped it achieve success, and helped initiate a resurgent interest in Gran Turismo, GT-class racing for closed cars. Through the early 1990s as the economy ground to a halt, the FIA ended the Group C series. With only 28 cars starting at Le Mans in 1992, FIA officials imagined that times would get worse before they improved for expensive prototype racers. Yet nearly every country had its own rules for GT cars, rendering it a gamble to

1995 993 Carrera RS 3.8

The 3,746cc flat-six in the 1995 Carrera RS 3.8 developed 300 brake horsepower in a vehicle lightened to 2,794 pounds (1,270 kilograms). Porsche quoted acceleration figures for 0 to 62 miles per hour (100 kilometers per hour) at 5 seconds and a top speed of 177 miles per hour (277 kilometers per hour). The company produced 1,014 plus an additional 227 RS Club Sport models.

245

1995–1998

1997 Turbo
With enough patience, ideas, and resources, a buyer can get almost whatever they wish from Porsche Exclusiv, the custom order/special wishes department. The list of options and special features on this car are longer than the lines on a page of this book.

produce a car for one series or another. Barth raised the issue with two colleagues, Patrick Peter, who organized the Tour de France, and Stéfane Ratel, owner of the Venturi company, a firm with serious racing ambitions. Together these three men created the BPR series, using the first initials of their last names as the acronym. They established rules that appealed to competitors.

Porsche produced cars to meet these criteria starting with the 1993 Carrera RS 3.8, based on the 964 rear-wheel-drive platform. These engines developed 300 brake horsepower. Adjustable roll bars let competitors tune chassis for each venue. Weissach fitted aluminum doors and front deck lids, and formed the rear deck lid and spoiler in fiberglass. Porsche charged DM 225,000 for the cars, roughly $140,625

at the time, and buyers in Europe could run them on the streets with optional radios and air bags, or compete with an available roll cage and fire extinguisher system. This homologation package helped legalize the real racer, the 3.8 RSR, a car welcomed in BPR's GT3 and GT4 categories. The all-out machine, with no air bag or radio options, sold for DM 270,000, about $160,450, and offered center lock wheels, built-in pneumatic jacks, and supplemental brake cooling. The 3.8 engine produced 325 brake horsepower. In 1993 and 1994 the RSRs took overall victories in Spain, Belgium, and Japan, and a class win at Le Mans in 1993 as well as more class titles throughout 1994. They did not break.

For street racers seeking staggering performance, Porsche waited until mid–model

Carbon fiber, brushed aluminum, and leather upholstery dyed to match color samples set off the interior. Between 1995 and 1998, Porsche produced 5,978 of the 993 Turbo coupes, but to the best of this owner's knowledge there is only one like this.

The 993 Turbo was no slouch to begin with, offering 408 brake horsepower and four-wheel drive with a viscous clutch, a modern update of the 959 with nearly the power. The yellow color is not from Porsche's palette, but from Ferrari's.

1995–1998

year 1995 to introduce the 993 Turbo. With the 959, Porsche set a precedent, later loosely enforced, that any series production model providing more than 400 horsepower would be all-wheel drive. With 408 brake horsepower coupled to front-driven wheels as well as the adapted Weissach rear axle suspension, these 3.6-liter automobiles provided memorable performance and handling. Magazine testers typically reached 62.5 miles per hour (100 kilometers per hour) in 4.4 seconds, and the Turbos topped out at 180 miles (290 kilometers) per hour. Porsche manufactured 2,457 during 1995 (not including 9 early production cars done before the Christmas holidays in 1994). These sold for DM 212,040, $151,000, in Germany but only $99,000 in the United States.

Porsche tried its Speedster look one more time with a single prototype assembled on a 993C2 wide-body platform in 1995. As with prior 911 versions, this two-seater provided the manual roof and expected plastic hatch covering the rear luggage platform. Porsche never put the 993 Speedster into series production and never set a price.

To reset its road-going standards, Porsche introduced a stronger Turbo S in 1997. With 430 brake horsepower advertised, the company quoted a top speed of 188 miles per hours (300 kilometers per hour). In Germany, the S sold for DM 235,000, $137,000 in equivalent dollars. But when U.S. buyers got them in 1998, Porsche reversed its previous practice. and Americans paid $155,000 for the exclusive model despite a nearly identical exchange rate from 1997 to 1998. Porsche manufactured only 199.

Series production 993 models for 1996 provided buyers 285 brake horsepower. The increase from 272 the previous year came from Porsche's Varioram intake system that first appeared on 1995 European-market-only Carrera RS and Club Sport 911 models. This system utilized two intake pipes for each cylinder. The longer one, tuned for maximum mid-range torque, fed fuel and air up to around 4400 rpm when the shorter one opened. Exposed by a sliding sleeve, this pipe affected horsepower developed at medium and high engine speeds. The system opened again at around 5800 rpm to provide a large cross tube for the highest engine ranges. This sophisticated system not only evened out horsepower and torque bands, it also added to the driver's listening pleasure as engine tones changed with each new induction path.

Tony Hatter and Harm Lagaay created a new Targa using an innovative sliding glass roof that opened a large section of the cabin

1996 Typ 993 Targa

Porsche introduced its updated Targa system with the 1996 model year. Starting with a modified cabriolet body, Zuffenhausen assemblers bolted and bonded the preassembled glass roof system onto the car body. The glass roof consisted of three pieces comprising a front wind deflector, center electric sliding panel, and rear window.

Understanding human nature, Porsche installed a high-capacity air-conditioning system in the Targas. With the wind deflector raised—or the roof closed—an electric shade could cover the passenger compartment to shield against bright sun or cold winds.

to the skies for 1996. Lagaay had conceived this idea in 1977 as another idea for his 924. The 993 version followed Wiedeking's practice in which outside suppliers delivered complete subassemblies ready for installation. Zuffenhausen assemblers fitted the roof system onto reinforced cabriolet bodies and welded side rails and front and rear mounts into place. The glass roof and its mechanisms added a mere 66 pounds (30 kilograms) to the curb weight of the Carrera 2.

Porsche's financial health enabled it to introduce more special bodies. Porsche had brought wide-body styling to the 964, offering Turbo-look cabriolets and coupes. Now with the return of the Turbo, Tony Hatter's gently exaggerated shapes found strong appeal among the company's product planners. They mated the Turbo body, its brakes and larger wheels to the C4 chassis with its normally aspirated engine as a new C4S for 1996. Rest-of-world cars used Turbo springs and shock absorbers though Weissach's engineers recognized the poorer condition of U.S. roads and fitted softer suspensions for American buyers. For 1997 Porsche offered a C2 in the Turbo-look body, designated the Carrera S.

As welcomed as they were, and as exciting to drive and to admire, the 993 wide bodies marked the end of their own era. A new car with a new sound and a new shape was ready. It represented the culmination of decades of ideas, developments, and concepts. Born in Porsche's hard times, it would take the company into its best times. ∎

CHAPTER FIFTEEN

TWO CARS ONE FACE

who had earned an industrial design degree in Rome and an automobile design degree at the Royal College of Art in London. Larson split his time finishing the show car and working with Lai on the new production cars. In the end, Lagaay chose their concepts, and both men began working on the two cars with one face. But they are, as Lagaay put it, "two different characters."

"So I am no longer just mediator," he recalled, "I am a preacher, a divorce lawyer, a marriage counselor, anything, everything, to keep these two fellows working together. And it didn't work.

"It didn't work in terms of design. It wasn't good enough because what we had in our heads was so difficult to put under one hat that we were in trouble. Because, in the meanwhile, in the background, we had this fairy tale, this futuristic concept car, going on at the same time. And it was different from what the teams

1993 Boxster Concept Car

Larson's lovely little car was impossibly small. Vehicle regulations throughout the world enlarged the Boxster to fit safety bumpers, emissions-reduction equipment, audio systems, air bags, cooling radiators, and much more.

1993 North American International Automobile Show, Detroit, Michigan

Anticipating the worst during the worst of times, Porsche management had prepared for a variety of hard questions from journalists who might ask, "What are you going to do now that you almost are out of business?" Instead the first question was "What's under the cover?" Wendelin Wiedeking, center, leaning against the car, and Harm Lagaay, red tie, unveiled the Boxster, and suddenly nobody cared about business.

were doing, what we had selected of Grant and Pinky."

Porsche took Grant's concept to the North American International Auto Show in Detroit. In those days, the organizers allocated space based on U.S. sales. Porsche got the smallest, darkest corner. "Porsche was finished," Lagaay recalled. "Detroit didn't want us. They ignored us.

"The night before the Detroit Motor Show, management was very nervous. The U.S. distributor Fred Schwab sat down with all of us from Germany and we had a so-called 'crisis meeting.' We wrote down all the difficult questions we anticipated would come from the journalists the next day: 'What will Porsche do when it goes bankrupt? What

1997 Boxster

From concept in 1992 to show car in 1993 to production in late 1996, the Boxster captivated everyone involved. It represented a survival strategy for Porsche; to many buyers it represented the first time they ever owned a Porsche.

CHAPTER FIFTEEN

happens to American customers when you are finished and gone?'"

The next day, at their press conference, the area was packed. Porsche could not get extra lights for their unveiling. The union refused to cooperate, fearing it might not get paid. Every journalist attending the previews knew they had to witness what might be Porsche's last auto show in North America as an independent company or as an automaker at all.

"There were hundreds of journalists," Lagaay continued the tale. "All our people had prepared their answers to all these terrible questions. And when Fred Schwab finished his remarks, he asked if anyone had questions.

"'What's under the cover?'" Wendelin Wiedeking waved Lagaay to pull off the silver cloth.

The "Boxster," named in a marathon brainstorming session by designer Steve Murkett by combining the Boxer nickname for the flat-six engine with the word "Speedster," was an instant and huge hit. Journalists loved it. Newspapers, magazines, and television featured it. Through the week, Detroit area dealers manned the stand and recorded deposits from people who demanded they be first on a waiting list even though no one could promise them the car would even reach production.

Hours after the press left the stand, Lagaay phoned the Weissach studio. The car rekindled interest in Porsche. The company was not dead; Porsche had this great Boxster.

While Larson was thrilled, it didn't ease the challenge he and Lai faced back home. They

With its mid-engine, the Boxster gave couples a great escape vehicle with storage trunks of equal size—4.6 cubic feet (130 liters)—on either end. The power top disappeared beneath a lid that opened and closed automatically.

could not get their styling themes to work on the 986 and 996. Worse, the Boxster concept was a tiny car while 986 was midsize and 996 was a full-size 911. Lai and Larson were days away from scrapping their concepts and starting fresh. Not only was the appearance troubling them, aerodynamic concerns on the new 911/996 were impossible.

"We were not allowed to even think of a moving spoiler by the platform team," Pinky Lai remembered. "They had a very tough bean counter at the time in their department. He showed up every day.

"You can only design a *body* that will meet the aerodynamic target. That's how the whole thing started. One day in the wind tunnel, we cut one of the grille louver panels and put it on backward. Suddenly the aerodynamic changed.

"We came up with the argument that it wasn't a moving spoiler, it was a moving grille! They started to buy it. Maybe it's not as expensive as a moving spoiler. We just gave them a moving 'finger,' and it became a whole arm.

1999 911 Typ 996 Cabrio

The engine designer's directive to switch to water cooling added to the challenge of developing two cars using a shared structure. These cars were difficult to design and engineer but vitally important to the survival of the company.

CHAPTER FIFTEEN

"It was really late. Almost too late. We were just about to scrap the whole Nine-Nine-Six clay model with a fixed spoiler, about to start a new program."

Lagaay's call from Detroit energized and inspired the Larson/Lai team. Lagaay suggested that the two men take the Boxster design and enlarge all the proportions 20 percent to make the new 986. Share the front end treatment with 996. With the popularity of the Boxster and the good feelings management had after Detroit, Lagaay argued he might find some money for a "moving finger."

"Give me another few days in the wind tunnel," Lai recalled telling Lagaay. "Let me see what else we can do. Sometimes a stubborn head can help a lot. It wasn't even about designing a beautiful car," he continued. "It was only about survival. We didn't have the time to fix the aesthetic problems. We spent all our time to meet all these requirements but still maintain a Nine-Eleven appearance.

"The Nine-Eight-Six/Nine-Nine-Six programs, that was a new chapter for Porsche," he went on." It was the most crucial turnaround. Toyota and whoever else was queuing up to buy us. We had three CEOs in two years. It was really about just survival."

These new cars were no less challenging for the engine and chassis engineers. Porsche engineers looked to the future and saw increasingly tight standards for noise and noxious emissions competing always with the challenge to provide a stronger, faster, and more fuel-efficient engine than its previous model.

1997 Boxster

While the Boxster grew in every dimension, its performance potential grew as well. Introduced with a 2,480cc water-cooled flat-six with bore and stroke of 85.5x72mm, the engine developed 204 brake horsepower and provided 0-to-62-mile-per-hour acceleration in 6.9 seconds.

For the 986, Porsche's Project Manager for the Boxster line powertrain and Supervisory Board Member Jürgen Kapfer devised one of the company's most innovative flat-sixes. There were some who believed that no more improvement was possible for the 911 engine. To improve performance, they wanted to adopt four-valve technology. In experiments with aluminum four-valve cylinder heads, "we almost melted the aluminum at three thousand five hundred revolutions. This led to the radical discussion to have water-cooling," he explained. "Our philosophy was to take what was good from the old and determine what to make better. The only thing that survived was the flat-six

Designer Matthias Kulla embraced the challenge every Porsche designer faces: make each new Porsche evolutionary so that customers immediately recognize that it is "the next new Porsche." Kulla's interior is at once familiar, comfortable, and new.

configuration and the one hundred eighteen millimeter cylinder bore centers!" That led to "lots of tests on lots of materials."

Kapfer's engineers conceived a block cast in two pieces that split vertically and bolted together to form the block. They used forged-steel "cracked" connecting rods. A laser beam scored a point midway down the circle on the rod's big end. Freezing this end made it brittle. A machine pulled it, cracking the end roughly along the laser-scored line. The resulting irregular surfaces mated together around the forged-steel crankshaft more securely than traditional machined surfaces and worked almost as if they still were one piece. Kapfer selected aluminum main bearings because the first cast-iron ones were too heavy.

The engine's integrated dry sump lubrication was another Kapfer innovation. Unlike a true dry sump with a separate tank, this system used a tank integrated into the engine block but separated from the crankshaft. "The target," Kapfer explained, "was to not have a separate oil tank, to facilitate meeting emission and noise standards. Still, the car had to be drivable like a classic Nine-Eleven on a racetrack." To do that, Kapfer's engineers devised "oil flaps," baffles within the tank that restrained the sloshing that occurred during high-speed cornering.

Another clever concept was the truly interchangeable cylinder heads, identical for both three-cylinder banks. These four-valve/single-plug heads with cam-drive chains at one end were completely interchangeable, saving time in design and assembly, and money in needing to mold and manufacture just one head. Cup tappets opened the valves and conical springs closed them. Kapfer's engine used automatic hydraulic valve adjustment and had automatic chain tensioners. His target was no maintenance.

Cooling a centrally placed fully enclosed engine presented substantial obstacles. Kapfer's engineers adopted a racer-style cross-flow system sending coolant from the exhaust side to the intake side around the cylinders in an open-deck design. Keeping temperatures even around each cylinder ensured complete and consistent combustion, important to minimize emissions. The resulting new engine displaced 2,480cc with bore of 85.5mm and stroke of 72mm. The engine, with its cast-aluminum cylinder block, developed 201 brake horsepower.

For Weissach's engineers tasked with developing the new 991/996 engine, water-cooling that power source was the only reasonable reply to the questions facing the company.

"Water-cooling," Stefan Knirsch explained, "allowed us to get higher performance because of the better cooling of the cylinder head." Knirsch had joined Porsche in 1996 as these new engines reached preproduction phases. He was the troubleshooter for the start of production for both Boxster and 996 engines. "The robustness of these heads against knocking is much better. So our ignition angle is earlier. This helps in fuel economy, and it helped in power output.

"The only drawback," he went on, "was additional mass, the twenty liters of water and all the parts. But it made sense for a sports car with a high power putout and good fuel consumption. You need low temperatures of the components, of the cylinder head, and of the block to get a high output and good fuel economy." Pinky Lai's 996 body concepts, in his efforts to meet aerodynamic and anti-lift targets, had elevated the tail. This height allowed engineers additional space to accommodate a somewhat physically larger engine.

The new engine displaced 3,387cc with bore and stroke of 96mm and 78mm. Four-valve cylinder heads fit easily since the head no longer needed cooling fins. Design engineers reverted to a single spark plug ignition. Horst Marchardt was gratified that the new engine no longer needed a large dry sump for cooling because that rid the cars of troublesome oil leak points. Porsche rated the new engine at 296 brake horsepower. Engineers tuned intake and exhaust manifolds not only for flow efficiency but also for the sound they produced. Water-cooling further reduced engine mechanical noises and improved heating and defrosting capabilities. Porsche and Getrag designed a new six-speed transmission to handle not only the additional power, but to accommodate much more as they contemplated variations they knew would follow introduction. The Tiptronic S transmission offered five speeds.

1994 Prototype 996

Where to put the water-cooling apparatus? This first running prototype for the 996 evolved from a 993 body that had morphed, stretched, and swollen a bit behind the rear window. The water radiators ended up in this rear wing.

1996 Prototype 996

Tatchun Centre is on the banks of the Yukon River in Carmacks, Yukon Territory, Canada. It is a full-service hotel/restaurant and service facility used to seeing automotive engineers in town to test new cars. The average winter temperature is -29 degrees F (-34 degrees C), falling as low as -59 degrees F (-51 degrees C).

As the cars raced toward production start, the similarity of the front of the two cars troubled Larson. "We hoped that all the carryover parts between the Boxster and the 911 would be invisible. But the fact was that it was just the whole front of the car. Look at them and you can tell that they had the same front fascia and exactly the same bumper for several months during development. The only thing that you could see that was different on the front of the cars was that the windscreen was shorter on the Boxster.

"We had this funny little late night discussion with Harm Lagaay," Larson continued. "'Harm, we've got a big problem here. The cars are identical.' It's okay for the Boxster to do something like this, but I thought a year later when we introduced the Nine-Eleven, we would have had a hard time selling the new Nine-Eleven with the mask of the Boxster on it.

"He said, 'Yeah, you're right. But not on the Nine-Eleven. We'll change the Boxster.' It was just weeks before the final cutoff point when we're supposed to deliver data. And basically we convinced him in that fifteen-minute meeting. That was the turning point in the Boxster that it would at least get its own front bumper.

"We were very thankful for that because as the Nine-Eleven came out, it had a different face. Same headlamps, but that was all cost-and-investment driven."

Porsche took a big gamble with its Boxster and 996. Giving the two cars front end styling so nearly identical validated Horst Marchardt's engineering, design, and financial estimates. Yet the timing of introductions sent a confusing message to enthusiasts and journalists. The 996, introduced as a 1998 model in Europe was the company flagship, yet it appeared too much like the entry-level product introduced a year earlier. Butzi Porsche, the creator of the 911's form language, its *formsprache*, declared the shape of those "same headlamps" as incomprehensible. Harm Lagaay recalled their origin.

"The overall sculpture of the car [was] much more an identity than just a couple of headlamps, and having the module was a typical Porsche decision," he explained. "They said, 'We need to be able to mount the headlamp in twenty seconds. Push it in, fix it in place. Twenty seconds.' So we came up with these five functions in one piece: main beam, dipped beam, fog lamp, turn signal, light washer. It was a typical business decision."

In terms of performance, handling, interior comfort, and sophistication, few people had any complaint. Acceleration to 62.5 miles per hour came in 4.6 seconds.

1997–2005

1999 911 Typ 996

Weissach's director of research and development Horst Marchardt came up with the idea of "two cars, one face," in which both the entry-level 986 Boxster and flagship 996 shared major components from the windshield forward. The process challenged engineers and vexed designers, who tried to keep both cars from looking exactly alike while beneath their skin, they were mostly alike.

Porsche quoted a top speed of 174 miles per hour (280 kilometers per hour). Cabriolets appeared in mid-April 1998, the same time Porsche Cars North America introduced the full line to U.S. buyers.

All-wheel-drive C4 models had accounted for more than 20 percent of 964 purchases and 30 percent of the series 993s. All-wheel-drive C4 996 models appeared in Europe in October 1998 and the following spring in the United States. Buyers could order the C4 with the Tiptronic transmission.

Porsche's Stability Management system, PSM, distinguished C4 models from rear-drive Carreras. Bosch developed the system, and Weissach engineers adapted it to the 996. It expanded the capabilities of anti-lock braking, ABS, by applying brakes electronically to an individual wheel if conditions of excessive under- or oversteer affected cornering stability.

Pinky Lai's refined 996 forms swelled seductively with the Turbos when they appeared in 2000. Georg Wahl's chassis engineers put all-wheel drive underfoot to keep the Turbo's 420 brake horsepower most efficiently on the ground. The same transmission engineers who had beefed up the Tiptronic to handle C4 purposes reinforced it enough to accommodate Turbo power for the first time. Magazine reviewers proclaimed their delight with 0-to-62.5-mile-per-hour accelerations in less than four seconds and top speeds in excess of 190 miles per hour (305 kilometers per hour).

Second-generation headlights that appeared initially on the Turbos spread to the full 996 line in its second generation with the 2002 models. The C4S with its Turbo-look wider rear-body form betrayed a performance upgrade across the line. Engineers lengthened piston stroke from 76mm to 82.8, enlarging displacement to 3,596cc. The new VarioCam Plus valve timing technology helped boost output to 320 brake horsepower.

Porsche revised the Targa for 2002. Reliability problems and warranty claims against jammed glass roofs led engineers to rethink the system. Sustained high-speed driving caused lift that had stressed the welds of roof members mounted on top of the reinforced 993 cabriolet bodies. Body engineers devised a new system for the 996. An assembly-line robot inserted the new roof through the windshield opening of a strengthened, modified, and decapitated coupe body before welding it in place from the inside. Any lift characteristics helped seal the seams more tightly.

The Boxster gained improvements as well. For 2000, Porsche increased displacement

2001 911 Turbo

With its three large air intakes covered with black grilles, the front of the Turbo differed from normally aspirated cars. The first cars into the United States ran afoul of U.S. Department of Transportation bumper height regulations. Rather than fighting for months, Porsche Cars North America quickly shipped small black bumper guards with mounting instructions.

The articulated splitter wing rose at speeds above 75 miles per hour (120 kilometers per hour). The turbocharged and intercooled 3.6-liter engine developed 420 brake horsepower, transferred to the ground through four-wheel drive with a viscous clutch.

2004 Turbo Cabriolet

Porsche specifications suggested it was possible to drive 190 miles per hour (305 kilometers per hour) in the 996 Turbo Cabriolet. Acceleration to 62 miles per hour took 4.3 seconds in these 420-brake-horsepower, four-wheel-drive 3,652-pound (1,660-kilogram) open cars.

Another product of Porsche Exclusiv, the buyer ordered this 2004 Turbo Cabriolet with sport seat backs, interior trim panels, and brake calipers painted to match the yellow body color.

of its base engine from 2.5 to 2.7 liters. With 220 brake horsepower available, the car accelerated from 0 to 62.5 miles per hour in 6.6 seconds and reached a top speed of 155 miles per hour (240 kilometers per hour). An S version also arrived. This 3.2-liter engine developed 252 brake horsepower and propelled the car to 62.5 in 5.9 seconds and to a top speed of 162 miles (or 260 kilometers) per hour. The S version came with a tighter suspension mounted on 17-inch wheels.

CHAPTER FIFTEEN

2002 996 Targa
Introduced in December 2001, the new Targa differed from 993 versions because its original basis was a coupe with its roof removed. Robots inserted the roof structure through the windshield and welded it from the inside.

A year later, in 2001, technology took another leap with the Boxsters as electronic throttle linkages reached the car line. "Fly-by-wire throttle linkage," engineering chief Jürgen Kapfer explained, "offers no friction, and they don't break. All signals go directly to the motor management system which instantly calculates timing, fuel flow, and all other factors." The "system," Motorola's Motronic ME 7.2, accompanied the 911's PSM to the Boxster lineup.

For 2003, the entire Boxster lineup experienced a face-lift. Grant Larson supervised a new nose and tail and reconfigured the side air inlets. New engine management from the Motronic ME 7.8 system boosted base model

2004 Boxster S

In 2002, Porsche revised the base engine to 2,687cc with 220 horsepower. It also introduced a Boxster S model equipped with a 3.2-liter engine that developed 252 horsepower. In 2003 the 2.7-liter engine gained another 8 horsepower, and a year later the 3.2 added 6 more to reach 266. Top speed for the 3.2 Boxster S was 165 miles per hour (266 kilometers per hour), and acceleration to 62 miles per hour took just 5.7 seconds.

2002 Typ 996 Turbo

One of the many options packages that Porsche Exclusiv offered was to replace countless interior panels with teak, burl, walnut, or mahogany woods. Wood softened the high-tech look of the Turbos.

Despite the luxury, performance was the point of the Turbo, and the 996 four-wheel-drive version set its own standards. With 420 brake horsepower, acceleration from 0 to 62 miles per hour required 4.2 seconds. Another 5 seconds got the car to 100 miles per hour (160 kilometers per hour). The top speed was 190 miles per hour (305 kilometers per hour).

output to 228 brake horsepower and the S up to 266.

Porsche produced a commemorative 50th anniversary Boxster honoring its roots to the 1953 550 Spyder and limiting production to 1,953 copies. Painted GT Silver Metallic, the cars got a special dark brown "Cocoa" interior. Equipped with the S engine and chassis package, the cars were capable of 165-miles-per-hour (266 kilometer-per-hour) top speeds.

Automakers do not work in a vacuum. What goes on around them—the shifts in economies and in currencies, the strategies to combat global climate change, or the politics of oil-producing nations—affects them. But the impact of these influences works in two separate time frames, the present day and the future. Automobile designers and engineers work in a time warp, conceiving, developing, and testing cars years before the public sees them. By the time any criticism of the 996, its headlights, its appearance, or its similarity to the successful Boxster, reached Weissach, project managers such as Bernd Kahnau and August Achleitner and design chief Harm Lagaay already had resolved those issues in "face-lifts" that were advancing through development processes as new products and next-generation models moved across drawing boards.

"Porsche is recognized," Harm Lagaay theorized in an interview several years ago, "apart from the fact that by now everybody knows the Nine-Eleven which makes it easier, by its own form language. This is shaped in a different way from other cars. There is a lot of time spent to achieve this visual identity, a lot

2004 911 GT3

A very high percentage of GT3 owners spend time with their cars on a track, "practicing their hobby," as GT3 development director Andreas Preuninger puts it. These cars bring back an "old days" function in which owners drove their cars to the track, competed, and drove the car home at night.

Because of its competition basis, Porsche used the earlier Hans Mezger–designed 3.6-liter flat-six with dry sump lubrication for Turbos, GT2, and GT3 models. This version developed 381 horsepower.

of modeling experience and expertise to have these soft shaped structures. This is the most difficult. You can make a soft shape with larger radii or softer transitions. But if it is chaotic, if it is not structured well, then it looks like a mess. At Porsche, you have to be in total command of that shape which is recognizable as Porsche. Another step forward, it moves its boundaries again."

Through the six years from introduction in 1998 to the final 996 Turbo coupes and cabriolets issued in 2005, the car evolved. It became the best-selling 911 model of all as Porsche delivered more than 170,000. It easily engaged first-time Porsche buyers and turned them into Porsche enthusiasts and loyalists. The 996 moved the company from barely surviving to fully thriving. It allowed them to move their boundaries again, embracing and introducing products that would befuddle and bedazzle loyalists and observers alike. ∎

CHAPTER SIXTEEN

REMINDING *LE MANS* OF PORSCHE'S CAPABILITY

1998 911GT1

At the 500-kilometer race at Silverstone, England, Porsche's factory entry driven by Uwe Alzen and Joerg Mueller could do no better than second behind the new Mercedes CLK-GTR. At Le Mans a month later, everyone at Porsche was happier.

For decades, Weissach's Customer Sports department produced cars that won races for its clients. The 1994 911S LM evolved into the GT2 to fit within BPR rules. This category required that manufacturers sell 25 identical cars each year they planned to compete. Customer Sports sold 45 GT2s before introduction, 43 in 1995, and 14 in 1996. Weissach fitted 21 of these for road use.

The gutted race cars weighed 2,447 pounds (1,112 kilograms), while road customers got a 2,850-pound (1,295-kilogram) version and 430 brake horsepower for their outlay of DM 276,000 (about $193,000). Racers invested DM 248,500, $174,000, on a no-frills model and got 480 brake horsepower.

Fully optioned race-equipped GT2s priced out nearer DM 335,000, about $234,000.

Roland Kussmaul and Customer Sports raised the bar for 1998, producing 25 GT2s with electronics adapted from Porsche's Formula One effort with Techniques Avant Garde, TAG. This nudged engine output up to 450 brake horsepower. Customers could order air bags, electric windows, and air conditioning, but no all-wheel drive, since Porsche had not used it for homologation.

As its name implied, GT2 was not BPR's premier category. That was GT1. In this group, Porsche found daunting challenges from its former F1 ally, McLaren, and designer Gordon Murray's carbon-fiber F1-GTR, which had won Le Mans in June 1995. Perpetual competitor Ferrari had its own new V-12-engined 333SP prototypes. While Porsche held a solid hold on GT2 and GT3 classes, those who had been around during Peter Schutz's early days remembered his speech in 1980: "We won't go anywhere that we do not intend to win outright."

Rules for BPR's GT1 category required that manufacturers offer road versions for sale. To shrewd BPR rule readers, it appeared that one single car would suffice. Norbert Singer already knew the 911GT2 needed better aerodynamics, greater downforce, and more horsepower to compete for overall wins. GT1 cars had to have a flat bottom from the nose to the rear axle. From there back, the undercarriage could rise to form one or more venturi to help hold the car down, but these could not run full-length to provide vacuum cleaner–like suction. Singer and Ampferer believed this could work if they mounted the engine backward, ahead of the rear axle. The cars could use longer wheelbases, and Singer stretched that of the GT2 from 89.4 inches (2270mm) to 98.4 inches (2499mm) for the GT1.

Engineer Horst Reitter worked with Singer to develop package specifications that included the necessary mechanicals. Reitter incorporated the production car's front end; it had passed both U.S. and German crash tests, necessary for the single road car's homologation. Using the production front end let Weissach fit the 993 instrument panel as well. The supervisory board already had given this racing project a provisional okay, but one condition for final approval was clear: The car had to be "identifiable as a Nine-Eleven at first glance."

"Initially, my job was to keep the cars looking like Nine-Eleven Porsches," Tony Hatter recalled. "Norbert Singer soon found out we worked with the newest technology in the automotive world which the racing department didn't have. We could build cars digitally. We offered him a system where he could create shapes and forms and cars, and mill them out in zero-time.

1996 911GT1

The FIA rules for the GT1 category required manufacturers produce a minimum of one road-going version of the prototype they wished to enter. To be safe, Porsche manufactured two.

With only wide side mirrors for rear visibility, driving in street traffic might have been challenging. The GT1 stood only 46.1 inches (1,173mm) tall, but its twin-turbocharged, twin-intercooled, water-cooled flat-six 3,163cc engine provided its drivers with 544 brake horsepower in a 2,464-pound (1,120-kilogram) package.

1996 911GT1/96

Following McLaren's win at Le Mans in 1995, Porsche's racing customers needed a better tool to fight the competition than overweight, underpowered GT2 Evolution models. Racing manager Norbert Singer, engine chief Herbert Ampferer, and designer Tony Hatter responded with the GT1 derived from production 993 models.

"He was very skeptical at first. He's a man with a lot of hands-on experience, and he couldn't touch anything. He'd walk away. I'd do something on the screen while he was gone."

Hatter lengthened the 993 and widened it to accommodate racing tires. Computer aided systems accomplished this faster and more easily than Singer's collaboration with Dick Soderberg had been on the 1978 935/78 "Moby Dick." The board gave the go-ahead in late July 1995.

Between then and January 1996, work progressed feverishly. To mount a production nose over a racing suspension forced Horst Reitter to modify his concept. Herbert Ampferer revised the engines that had propelled the 962 coupes to victories throughout 1994. He retained their 95mm bore (shared with the 959) with 74.4mm stroke for a 3,164cc engine. But he water-cooled the entire engine, taking it beyond both 959s and 962s, which had only water-cooled heads. Porsche completed a road-going version for homologation requirements with a tame 3.3-liter Carrera engine tuned to develop 300 brake horsepower.

Barth drove the race car prototype on March 14. Through the rest of the month,

CHAPTER SIXTEEN

Porsche took first and second in the GT1 class (second and third overall) at Le Mans in June 1996 with the factory-entered cars. This quickly prompted 30 private teams to order their own cars.

the pace turned frantic. That was when Tony Hatter got a phone call.

"It was the roll-out of the GT-One car," he explained. "I think it was Roland Kussmaul. We pushed the car out at about eleven o'clock one cold night. We were getting the car ready for [the April trials at] Le Mans. It was the first time out of the workshops, it had just been put together. Kussmaul started it up and drove it out. Everybody ran out behind. It was freezing cold. Kussmaul drove it off into the distance. You could hear it moving around the track. He came back in.

"They had gotten some lights ready for it. Kussmaul turned the engine off and smoke came from everywhere. It was absolutely surreal. They took off the front and rear, checked everything out. They put it all back together again and sent him out.

"The next time he came past, the car made this really unearthly 'woooouuuuuum' sound. I stood there thinking, Jesus Christ! I had something to do with this car. It was utterly unreal, like a close encounter of the third kind."

In Singer's typical manner, he and his staff tested the new car exhaustively. They ran

CHAPTER SIXTEEN

1997 911GT1

In 1997 Porsche began delivering customer race cars and a few road-going versions at $891,000 (about DM 1.5 million) apiece. Le Mans was populated with them in 1997, but Mercedes-Benz had joined McLaren in the category, and Porsches had a frustrating time.

more than 1,200 miles in one five-day test alone. When chassis 001 and 002 reached Le Mans in June, they were ready. At the checkered flag, chassis 002, with Bob Wollek, Thierry Boutsen, and Hans Stuck driving, had finished second overall and first in GT1 class, behind Reinhold Jöst, driving a Porsche-engined open sports racer.

"Less than forty-eight hours after Le Mans," Jürgen Barth recalled, "we got ten calls, orders for street cars. By Friday, we had close to forty orders and they only slowed down when we told them they got a car with three-hundred horsepower, not the Le Mans engine!"

Weighing just 2,328 pounds (1,058 kilograms) and running with 600 brake horsepower, the race car's acceleration was astonishing. From a standstill it reached 130 miles per hour (210 kilometers per hour) in 9.8 seconds, using gearing for a top speed of 174 miles per hour (280 kilometers per hour). Longer Le Mans ratios allowed top speeds near 235 miles per hour (375 kilometers per hour).

In each of the remaining three BPR events, at Brands Hatch, Spa, and in China at Zuhaï, one or the other car won outright. By year end, Weissach began to fill nearly 30 solid orders for road and racing versions of the car known as GT1/96. Road cars ultimately got 544 brake horsepower engines, not the Carrera engines. They sold for DM 1.4 million, or about $930,000.

In the rarified stratosphere in which Porsche GT1 road cars and racers operated, the company found itself in an unexpected crossfire. McLaren had improved its F1-GTR as well as its own million-dollar three-seater road car. Now, however, neighboring Mercedes-Benz made Kussmaul's and Singer's successful GT1s their own target for the 1997 racing season. M-B announced plans to compete in the GT series now annexed by the FIA as an eleven-race event under its sanction and incorporated onto its calendar. Mercedes unveiled its V-12 6-liter CLK-GTR. Whatever Wendelin Wiedeking's earlier plans had been for the company's GT1 prior to Mercedes' announcement, he supported Norbert Singer and Horst Marchardt now. Having sold 30 race cars to customers, Porsche could not abandon them. Singer sought to develop a competitive evolution; he and Tony Hatter made enough changes that they had to create a new road car as well. This picked up styling cues of the new production models nearing completion in the design department. Porsche committed to the full eleven-race FIA series.

The GT1s did not distinguish themselves through 1997 against the Mercedes-Benz. Singer, Kussmaul, and their customers knew what it would take to get back into the

1998 911 Typ 996GT1/98

The hard work that Norbert Singer, Herbert Ampferer, Tony Hatter, and their teams of co-workers endured paid off in 1998 with first- and second-place finishes overall. Running at an average speed of 123.9 miles per hour (199.2 kilometers per hour), the winners covered 352 laps for a total distance of 2,975.8 miles (4,761.3 kilometers).

game. A new chassis of carbon fiber that would save the extra 200 pounds (90 kilograms) that everyone felt the car had to shed. Wiedeking's cost-saving efforts in Zuffenhausen had coalesced successfully, trimming losses and production time. This benefited the final run of series production 993s that captured customers' imaginations. The company and its chief executive now were in a position to renew Porsche's commitment to customer racers.

There would be a GT1/98. With support from the company's highest officials, Norbert Singer, Tony Hatter, Horst Reitter, Herbert Ampferer, and dozens of other engineers and mechanics had a new assignment.

"While all the guys were working through all the new production car challenges," Tony Hatter explained with a laugh, "I got lost in the racing department with various hybrids based on the Nine-Nine-Three. First, this was based on the Nine-Nine-Three, and then, still based on the Nine-Nine-Three, but with the new headlights. And in the end, of course, we made one car without anything to do with a Nine-Eleven, and we still stuck the new headlights on it. Strange when you think about it."

The *formsprache*, or form language, that Pinky Lai and modeler Eberhard Brose created for the 996 made adaptation easier for Hatter as he designed a successor. He had to fit a 26.4-gallon fuel bladder behind the cockpit. This forced him, Singer, and Reitter to lengthen the wheelbase from 98.4 inches (2499mm) to 113 inches (2870mm). At that point it was a new car.

Hatter and the racing engineers started from scratch. They developed the body and

1998 996GT3 Cup

Patrick Huisman, 1998 season champion, led a crowd out of the pits at Monza for the Porsche Supercup race. Roland Kussmaul produced 30 cars for 26 teams. The cars weighed 2,515 pounds (1,143 kilograms), and their engines developed 360 brake horsepower.

carbon-fiber tub entirely on computer screens. They never produced a full-scale studio model. Hatter's computer design mirrored work he and racing engineers did with scale models in the wind tunnel.

Singer and Reitter moved the driver to the right side to better suit most of the world's racing circuits. Hatter slightly enlarged the new 996 headlamps to accommodate extra bulbs. A family resemblance preserved Porsche's form language, but this definitely was a race car. Revisions to the engine left it with 95.5mm bore and 74.4mm stroke for 3,198cc total displacement. It developed 550 brake horsepower. The 1988 season, however, was frustrating for Porsche, as their latest GT1 perpetually finished behind new 1998 Mercedes-Benz CLKs except at Le Mans.

Toyota, Nissan, Ferrari, McLaren, and of course Mercedes-Benz each supported teams and presented new cars to challenge Porsche's three GT1/98s in France. When the 24-hour race ended Sunday, June 7, Porsche finished first and second. On Monday, Motorsports and Customer Sports learned of a new project at Porsche, but it was one that left them out.

Wendelin Wiedeking announced a Porsche-Volkswagen collaboration. Porsche's DM 1 billion commitment expanded the company's product line in a direction few immediately understood. It added a new factory and fueled a firestorm of criticism that took years to extinguish. Journalists and

2002 911 Typ 996GT3RS

Roland Kussmaul began to develop GT3R models in late 1998 when Porsche approved GT3 production. RS models used carbon fiber for doors, roof, front and rear deck lids, fenders, and the adjustable rear wing.

loyalists did not know what went on far behind the scenes and could not imagine the questions yet to be posed. The size of this investment on a new type of Porsche vehicle apparently left no money for motorsports beyond commitments for production-based 911s.

The GT1 life had ended anyway. The FIA discontinued the GT1 category for 2000. Two new Le Mans Prototype, LMP, categories arose instead. Word soon spread that Porsche had begun to develop an open spyder, the LMP1-98, for Le Mans in 1999. Months after Wiedeking's Le Mans decision, Porsche announced it would wait for another year, until Le Mans 2000. As the rules changed for 2000, this decision made sense. Wiedeking had authorized the engineers to develop the new racer. This car, known as LMP2000, also was an open-cockpit prototype. Original plans called for racing the car with the turbocharged flat-six. However, Herbert Ampferer had developed a normally aspirated 3.5-liter V-12 and then a similar 3.5-liter V-10 for the Footwork Arrows Formula One effort. This Typ 3512 engine had been a frustrating project, and Footwork and Porsche ended their relationship during the 1991. Porsche shelved the V-10. As Le Mans rules dictated, a normally aspirated engine fit the bill, and Ampferer and fellow engineer Thomas Ludenbach expanded its displacement to 5.5 liters. It developed 680 brake horsepower.

Lola Composites of Britain fabricated a carbon-fiber tub beginning in the summer of 1999. Singer and his racing engineers borrowed and upgraded suspension from the LMP1-98 and developed a carbon-fiber body in the wind tunnel.

Soon after Porsche and Lola finished the first chassis, Singer's engineers completed assembly and ran a two-day test on the car at Weissach in late November 1999. Within days, Porsche announced it was abandoning the project. Kussmaul retired the car to storage. He and Le Mans winners Allan McNish and Bob Wollek drove the car. Magazines later quoted Wollek as saying "It was good." Kussmaul said recently, "Good! It set a new lap record at Weissach." The release that Porsche Press Department issued at the time said ending the project was a business decision so Porsche could concentrate engineering resources on the development of new products. People assumed that meant the coming SUV.

Porsche already had made a strong commitment to racing its 911s. In February 1997, Roland Kussmaul began developing a new series of 996 Supercup GT3 models. Porsche had contracted with FIA to run these 50-mile (80-kilometer) match races at all European Formula One grand prix events through 1999. The cars, selling for DM 185,000 ($103,000) at the factory, ran engines that blended dry-sump cast-aluminum blocks with full-water-cooling and four-valve heads. They developed 360 brake horsepower. Since the first days in 1993, this series had run with unleaded gasoline to demonstrate Porsche's ecological responsibility. Catalytic converters remained on the equipment list for the 996GT3 Cup cars. The 1998 models used understated rear wings that performed well but provided insufficient adjustment. The specification and series continued through 1999 when civilians could buy a road version of the GT3 for DM 179,000 ($102,500). Those who lamented that the 996s looked tame compared to the wilder 993C4S variations fell silent on seeing and then driving the 360-brake-horsepower road-going GT3. If they attended races, they had cars to cheer as they watched the new GT3R models. These commanded almost double the prices of the street versions, at DM 359,200, nearly $200,000. These were 2,760-pound (1,255-kilogram) 420-brake-horsepower no-compromise race cars. The 2001 GT3RS gained another 30 horsepower. For Cup contestants, 2001 models provided a larger adjustable wing and 370 brake horsepower.

With constant upgrades, Porsche campaigned 996-based GT3 racers to great success through 2005, winning the category at Le Mans seven times in succession. In addition, privately entered GT3RSR models took first overall in 24-hour races at Daytona and at Spa in 2003. ∎

The normally aspirated engine developed nearly 450 brake horsepower. But with no turbochargers to muffle engine noise, Kussmaul called this one of the loudest race cars Porsche ever had built.

CHAPTER SEVENTEEN

CHANGING PERCEPTIONS AND THE *BOTTOM LINE*

2003 Cayenne S

Porsche planned a base level, the Cayenne S, and the Turbo model with usual Porsche line expansions to follow. Porsche introduced the $55,900 Cayenne S with an all-new 4,511cc water-cooled V-8 that developed 340 brake horsepower.

THE EARLY 1990S WERE A CHALLENGING PERIOD OF TIME FOR PORSCHE. Designers and engineers had embarked on a complicated dual-vehicle project that they and management hoped would save the company from extinction and rekindle excitement from customers and journalists. While 986 and 996 development moved forward, Wendelin Wiedeking convinced the supervisory board to embark on a strategy of growth. But growth in which direction was the question they asked in return for their conditional approval. Wiedeking already was aware of vehicle market potential in areas of the world whose infrastructure was beginning to awaken and whose citizens had growing resources.

The United States covered 3.7 million square miles (9.6 million square kilometers). In 1993, it still was one of Porsche's largest markets, and it boasted 1.63 million miles of paved roads. Of these, 45,800 were interstate highways (73,740 kilometers). Germany had 398,000 miles (636,000 kilometers) of roads of which 313,000 miles were paved (501,000 kilometers) and 6846 miles (10,955 kilometers) were autobahn.

China is nearly the same size as the United States. In 1993 that nation had nearly 643,000 miles (1.03 million kilometers) of roads. Of these, just 715 miles (1,145 kilometers) were freeways. However, 513,000 miles of that total (821,000 kilometers) were "class 4" and "substandard" roads, basically dirt paths. Russia, roughly 1.8 times the area of the United States with 6.22 million miles of roads (9.95 million kilometers) had only 210,000 miles (336,000 kilometers) of "conventionally paved" and 260,000 miles (416,000 kilometers) of "all-weather gravel surfaces." The rest were not paved. To the south, India, slightly larger than the United States, had about 670,000 miles (1.05 million kilometers) of roads, of which some 112,500 miles were paved. Saudi Arabia had 79,000 miles of roads, of which 21,500 were paved.

Wiedeking assigned Horst Marchardt to determine suitable products and to select the one that the company should pursue. Marchardt tapped an engineer named Klaus-Gerhard Wolpert to work with a few others to investigate the options. Wolpert joined Porsche in 1984 and worked mostly for outside clients such as Volkswagen, Ford, Chrysler, Mercedes-Benz, and Audi. For Volkswagen he did the Passat and Golf Synchro prototypes. He worked routinely on electronically controlled chassis systems, anti-lock brakes, four-wheel steering, and air-suspension control systems. He worked with Helmuth Bott and with his team as they engineered the 959 and the Paris-Dakar rally entries. By the end of the 1980s he was responsible for every electronically controlled chassis system at Porsche.

"We did research for the corporation at the mid-nineteen nineties," Wolpert explained. "We were looking at brand segments, the small sports car segment, the small convertibles, the sport utility segment. We did seven or eight segments to determine which was best for Porsche.

"Together with my colleague [financial officer Dr. Wolfgang] Lindheim, we worked nearly a year under cover. We did a lot of consumer tests, marketing tests, and in the end, we decided to invest into the SUV segment. If you look back in Porsche history, the first Porsche was in a four-wheel drive. Through the war, we did many special models in four-wheel drive. The SUV segment is, worldwide,

286

CHAPTER SEVENTEEN

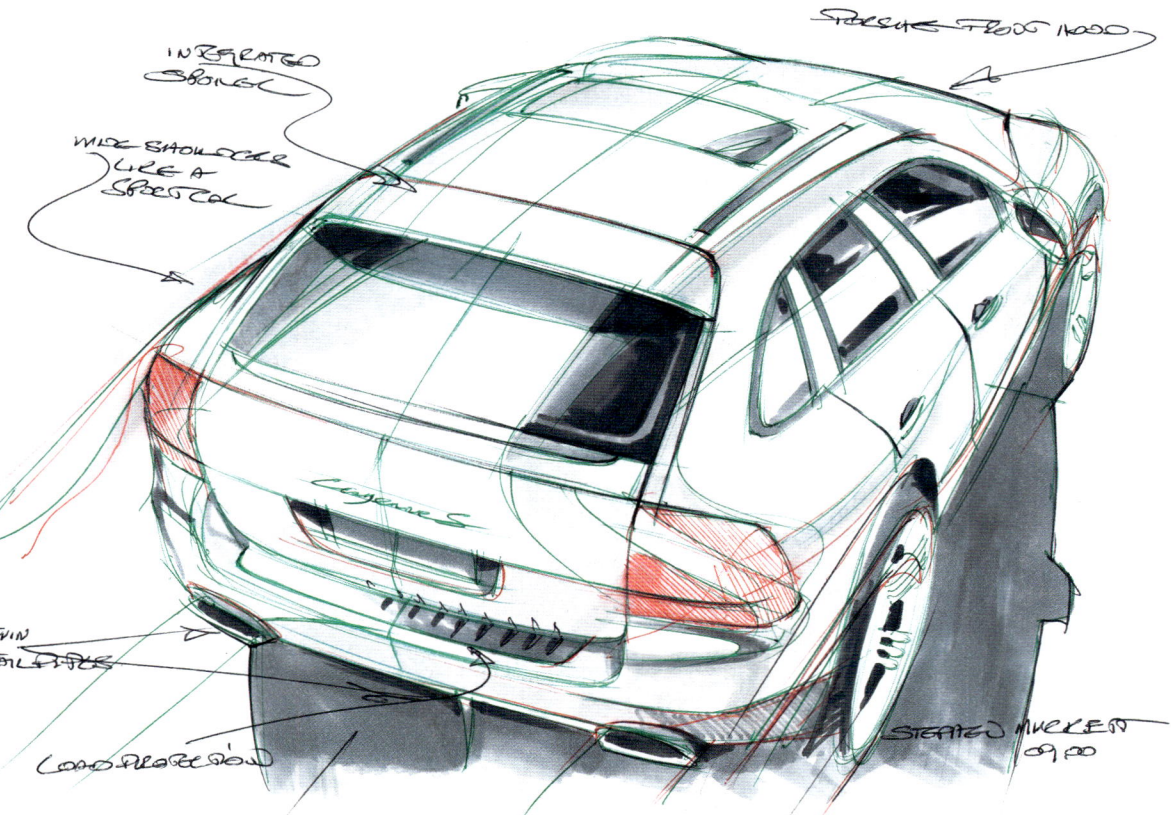

2000 Concept Drawing

In the late 1990s, Klaus-Gerhard Wolpert headed a small study group at Weissach to determine suitable products for future production. When they determined the SUV was the best target, team member Steve Murkett began creating some sketches of what the vehicle could look like.

By late 2000, Murkett had devised one of the new vehicle's "signature" features, its "head-on-shoulders" appearance, with a narrower greenhouse or window area on top of a typically Porsche "wide-shoulders" lower body.

still the area with the most growth. In the early nineteen nineties, especially in the exclusive upper end, there was no real competition."

For Porsche, the next move was to find a cooperating partner with whom they could forge a strategic alliance to share research and development costs so each partner could produce a similar but different vehicle. Mercedes-Benz had sold a boxy utilitarian Austrian-made Gelandewagen mostly for European customers with a few sneaking across the Atlantic to U.S. customers. But this was not the vehicle Wolpert's and Lindheim's research had indicated customers wanted.

With their research and concepts in mind, Wiedeking approached Dieter Zetsche. Daimler already had announced plans to construct a $300 million plant in Alabama to assemble a sport utility vehicle. While executives crafted licensing and other legal details, engineers and designers began sharing ideas, concepts, sketches, and data. The proposal was to develop jointly vehicles based on a next-generation G-wagen platform. But a problem lurked around the corner.

As negotiations neared completion, a member of Daimler-Chrysler's board sitting

2003 Cayenne Turbo
The Turbo Cayenne sold for $88,900 in the United States, and Porsche used the same four-valve 4.5-liter V-8 but added two turbochargers and intercooling to increase brake horsepower to 450. The Cayenne, named for the hot red pepper, provided full-time four-wheel drive and great off-road capability as well as typical Porsche highway ride and handling.

across the table from Wiedeking said that in exchange for what D-C was bringing to the end product, Daimler felt it fair to ask for a small percentage of Porsche stock—sources say it was around 5 percent—in compensation. Wiedeking had worked Porsche's management and manufacturing staffs hard on the turnaround that would begin with the production Boxster. He would not give up their future, and he refused the demand. The meeting ended within minutes and the collaboration stopped that day.

"That was not negotiable for the Porsche and Piëch families," Wolpert explained. "It was a mistake from Daimler at that time." Porsche's supervisory board gave thought to continuing on their own, but the development costs appeared too great. Porsche then took the idea to Volkswagen. And they agreed. Porsche would produce a Cayenne, VW its Toureg.

"Volkswagen was a very self-confident company," designer Steven Murkett said. "They knew exactly how to design cars. They knew what they wanted. Porsche in late nineteen ninety-seven was not there. We had just gotten the Nine-Nine-Six on the market. The Boxster had been out a year. We were still seen as the sports car company that was struggling to save itself."

Murkett had joined Porsche in September 1983. During the slow times that followed, he busied himself sketching, creating, inventing. He had won two international design competitions, first with a six-passenger hybrid and then with a Smart-Car-sized urban vehicle. He had done the production version of the 959 and then the 964.

1989 911 Panamericana Show Car

Porsche designer Steve Murkett designed a concept car that promoted Porsche's all-wheel-drive technology. After several auto shows, countless magazine stories, and minor revisions, Porsche Styling donated the car to Ferry Porsche (center in maroon jacket) for his 80th birthday gift.

2004 Cayenne V-6

For 2004, the company introduced a new base model with a 3,189cc water-cooled V-6 with four valves per cylinder. As with the Cayenne S and Cayenne Turbo, the transmission for the 247 brake horsepower V-6 was the six-speed Tiptronic S.

2005 Cayenne Turbo

Steve Murkett faced many challenges designing the Cayenne. Not least of them was making the interior look and feel Porsche-like. Five-instrument clusters, left-hand key ignition, and Porsche seats were just the obvious cues.

and reportedly it was one of Ferry Porsche's least favorite birthday gifts from the Styling Department. But that car developed form languages that defined later 993s, 996s, and current 997s.

Murkett was called on to translate "Porsche-Ness," the form languages all enthusiasts and customers knew and love, into a utility vehicle.

"The Cayenne was a very controversial car to work on back then," he said. "Many of my colleagues were quite happy to not work on it. 'Who wants an SUV Porsche anyway?' The discussions we heard in the press were that people were against the sheer principle of doing that car. So [I] had to argue for that car in the first place. It was easier for the Volkswagen people because the step from a Passat Combi to a Toureg was not as big a step. But the step from a 911 to a Cayenne was a big step."

Defining that big step, delineating its boundaries, was the job Klaus-Gerhard Wolpert tackled. "From the technical . . . the

Instead, Bez left and Harm Lagaay asked him to create a concept for the 1989 Frankfurt Motor Show based on the new 964 all-wheel-drive platform. Murkett's first version lifted the car up on its tires and resembled a hyper-stylish Baja Buggy. When Chairman Arno Bohn saw it, he reminded Lagaay and Murkett that "Porsche doesn't produce an off-road car. What we have is a four-wheel-drive sports car." Murkett recalled the chief executive saying, "And we're trying to promote the idea that you need four-wheel drive on the road." The resulting Panamericana was one of Porsche's most controversial show cars,

2006 Cayenne Turbo S

By revising the engine-control system, installing larger intercoolers, and increasing turbo boost from 23.2 to 27.5 psi (1.65 bar to 1.95 bar), Porsche boosted the 4.5-liter V-8 output to 520 brake horsepower. Adding 14.9-inch brake rotors up front to stop the car moved off-road brake performance to a new level.

product point of view, we wanted to make a sporty SUV for daily use as every Porsche is," he explained. "Today you can drive with a 911 for shopping as well as on a racetrack. That was a target for this new vehicle. It had to be a sporty vehicle, not a Land Rover, not a car for going through a field or on a rocky mountain.

"We never had a discussion to build a very small SUV or a very large nine-seater. Our marketing research told us that we had a lot of *potential* customers—and today I can say they are actual customers—that have a family with two or three kids. They want to have the Porsche brand, they want the power, they want the size of the Carrera but they have no need for a people mover."

Wolpert told Wiedeking that he needed for all his project managers to sample all the competitors in daily use. "It's different to drive a car for an hour," he said, "You get feedback. But if you drive a car in every situation, winter, summer, to the opera or carrying kids . . . you know it. We bought them all. Jeep Grand Cherokee, Range Rover, M-B, later the BMW. We exchanged the cars every three to four months.

"If you drive it and use it, you can see a lot of small details. Seating position, seat comfort, how you fold the seat. How you use a switch, what is the position of the switch? After three, six months, you have a good overview of what is best in this category. Then you can think about what you can do better than your competitors or what you can make different? What is *not* Porsche?

For engines the questions were similar. Porsche routinely established targets in performance and among its competitors. Acceleration times, tops speeds, fuel economy, and CO2 emissions all got specific attention. Dr. Heinz-Jacob Neusser directed the engine project, and he and his colleagues concluded that they had to start with both a normally aspirated V8 and the same engine with a turbocharger. Eighteen months into the development process they added a V-6.

"It's easy to explain," Neusser explained. "We started with the V-Eight in a competitive area where nearly none of the other cars had this performance level. The normally aspirated one you found at BMW and there were performance versions of the Range Rover. But the Turbo was outstanding. There was nothing to compare to that. High performance versions from Daimler came later, done at AMG. Then we found that we already were at a high enough performance level that it made sense to have something below this.

"Not all customers in this very broad market range were interested in having such high performance. There were some customers interested in driving a Cayenne off road. The V-Six just positioned into this starting segment.

"Due to the fact that Volkswagen has a lot of V-Six engines, we decided to do our own with special characteristics, with a different induction system, combustion improvements, and the exhaust system gas exchange so we have a significant power difference from what Volkswagen offers."

Engineers broke new ground to develop a chassis capable of the performance Porsche enthusiasts and longtime customers expected of any vehicle from the company. The question that took longer to resolve was the looks of this new model.

"We had design models that looked like a Hummer with a fastback," Steve Murkett said, laughing. "We had cars that looked like Nine-Elevens with four doors that were up on their toes, with high ground clearance and huge wheels. We had some cars that were really racy-looking with very low roofs. These were influenced by Paris-Dakar, by the Baja buggies.

"Then we got additional help from F. A. Porsche, Butzi," Murkett recalled. "Butzi had always been an SUV enthusiast. It was his—and his brothers'—enthusiasm that helped convince the family when Wiedeking decided that the company needed this car. It was *their* enthusiasm that made the deal go through.

"And F. A. said, 'If you guys are going to design that car, I want to be involved.' Suddenly he was coming here every month, looking at the models. Then he said, 'We're going to do our own model.'

"That was a moment. We've got this design department and we've been working for months and years on this, and now F. A. Porsche is going to come along with the family advantage and he's going to design the damned thing for us!

"I took this very seriously. I was very diplomatic. But at the same time, I was thinking: 'He may have this name, it may be his name on the company. He did the original Nine-Eleven.

It takes great wheels like these 20-inch Sport Techno wheels and a lot of rubber (277/40R20) to take advantage of the performance offered by the 2006 Cayenne Turbo S. The cost of this level of performance? $111,600.

His products are successful. . . .' Nevertheless, Harm, I, we, the studio felt that we have brought this company out of troubled times. We did the Boxster, we did the Nine-Eleven. We turned the whole product pallet around. We're going to do this one as well!"

As part of Wolpert's original project team, Murkett drove every vehicle as well. When the time came and the evaluation vehicles left Porsche, Murkett bought the Land Rover Defender.

"It has absolutely nothing to do with what a Cayenne is. But it is an icon," Murkett explained. "It has character and to me every car, every thing that has potential for success is not just attractive. It's not just pretty. It has to have a character that remains in your mind.

"I developed a pretty good relationship with Butzi Porsche probably because he had a Defender as well. He was nuts about his, and his cars always were green. Now I had a nice olive green Defender with a big winch on the front and massive tires. It's got a snorkel on the side. And it was always covered in mud and parked here when Butzi would arrive.

"Anytime we got into a stalemate situation where we couldn't agree about anything anymore, we'd start talking about tires on our Defenders. Harm would get out of the way."

Butzi's staff at Porsche Design in Zell am See worked on his concept for the new car. His took, as Murkett characterized it, a product design approach.

"He wanted the car to have really simple shapes, like straight-radius-straight-radius. His

2007 Cayenne Turbo S

Production of the Turbo S ended in 2007 at around 1,500 copies, but not before establishing all-time off-road (and a few on-road) vehicle credentials. Acceleration from 0 to 62 miles per hour took 4.8 seconds, and the Turbo S reached a top speed of 167 miles per hour (267 kilometers per hour).

car would quite possibly have been the most radical approach to the motorcar that the industry ever had. But quite possibly it would have scared the daylights out of half the industry and most of the public!

"We ended up doing a clinic in the studio, marketing and the board of directors invited in. They had to give their marks and comments on Model A and Model B. Rate side, rear, front, details, everything. No one told them whose car was whose.

"We won. Flat out. But there is no doubt of his contribution to the simplicity of the Cayenne, which was something that made it a little bit difficult for some people to accept at the beginning. It doesn't have all the little muscles and edges, the functional-looking edges that BMW's X-Five or a Mercedes ML has. That was Butzi's thing: Keep it simple. Don't put unnecessary lines or details on the car."

Porsche introduced the Cayenne in the fall of 2002 as the 2003 normally aspirated Cayenne S and the Cayenne Turbo. The shapely vehicle had undergone extreme testing, the most rigorous of any Porsche vehicle ever, because once the Cayenne excelled at its on-road capabilities, the engineers felt challenged to make it an excellent off-roader.

"We had one test," Heinz-Jakob Neusser explained, "our testers drove into a small river. They shut off the engine, waited two minutes, then restarted the engine and drove out. We realize people drive into water and panic and do the wrong thing.

"We needed to test these and other things in challenging conditions you don't find in central Europe. We did the Trans-Siberia roads. We did Mongolia. We put in more than one-and-a-half million kilometers [nearly 940,000 miles] testing. It wasn't only the distances, the point was the big differences in testing. We did tests for road driving then go onto a racetrack for two thousand kilometers, then back on the road, then the track, then the road."

The six-speed Tiptronic S easily handled the 520 brake horsepower of the Turbo S. The large dials behind the shifter controlled locking front, center, and, optionally, rear differentials. Ride height is adjustable from inside the cabin or adjusts automatically with vehicle speed.

The Cayenne shared common parts below the cockpit with Volkswagen's Toureg, including the heating box and air conditioning, seat structure—but only structure, some of the suspension body controllers, and some of the engine controllers. But the cars had different "B" and "C" pillars (the center and rear pillars), different roofs, and cockpits. The gearboxes were the same, but the Cayenne

2008 Cayenne Turbo

The expected styling "face-lift" reached the Cayenne range with the 2008 model year. The strip of lights below the new headlights is a band of high-intensity LED fixtures.

used different software from the Toureg. There was a Porsche drivetrain.

The first-generation 4.5-liter V-8s developed 340 brake horsepower with the normally aspirated engine and 450 brake horsepower with the turbocharged version. Permanent all-wheel drive split traction 62 percent to the rear and 38 percent up front. The six-speed Tiptronic transmission coupled to an electronically controlled locking differential, a low-range gearbox, and an automatic braking differential (ABD). The Porsche Stability Management System (PSM) controlled vehicle stability. An optional air-suspension system offered six settings with ground clearance on road from as low as 6.2 inches (157mm) for loading to as much as 10.7 inches (273mm) off-road.

Six-piston fixed calipers grabbed hold of 350mm front discs and 330mm rears to stop the car. The Cayenne S reached a top speed of 150 miles per hour (242 kilometers per hour) and accelerated from 0 to 62.5 miles per hour (100 kilometers per hour) in 7.2 seconds. The turbocharged model reached 62.5 miles per hour in 5.6 seconds and topped out at 165 miles per hour (266 kilometers).

An entry-level V-6 appeared in 2004, using a 24-valve 3,289cc engine that developed 250 brake horsepower. Later that model

2008 Cayenne GTS

The new GTS fits in between the Turbo and the S models with engine modifications that increased displacement to 4.8 liters from the previous 4.5. With 405 brake horsepower, the biggest news is a six-speed manual transmission that is standard, offering Cayenne buyers the first chance in the model's history in the United States to shift for themselves.

year, Porsche offered the S model with a six-speed manual transmission (though not in the United States).

The success of the Cayenne surprised critics. It sold well in the United States and did better its second year in 2004. Porsche's original plan was to assemble 20,000 each year. In 2005, its third year, Cayenne was Porsche's largest-selling car line with 42,000 vehicles manufactured compared with 40,000 Boxsters and 911s combined. The market for Cayenne continued to grow, and it has redefined the company in some parts of the world.

"Today," Klaus-Gerhard Wolpert said, "in the emerging markets, China, Russia, India, Cayenne stands for Porsche." In the Middle East in 2001 and 2002, Porsche sold 400 units. In 2007, sales reached 5,000 cars. Porsche's largest-volume dealer in the world is in Dubai. This dealership sold 1,200 Porsches, 85 percent of which were Cayenne.

"In the Arabic states, normally you go somewhere together with friends or a group. You never go out alone. It's not in the culture of the Arabs. If you own a Boxster, it is impossible. You need two Boxsters, and there aren't so many roads.

"In China, while everyone is equal, it is a sign of status if you are driven. To ride in a Nine-Eleven looks as if you go with a friend. And there aren't so many paved roads."

To answer the environmentalists in lands with tens of thousands of miles of paved

Porsche's highly intelligent active stability management system (PASM) joins the Cayenne line first with the GTS, which is aided in handling by the addition of 21-inch wheels and tires, with 295/35R21 rubber all around. The GTS sells for $69,300.

interstate highways, Porsche announced a Hybrid Cayenne available at the end of the first decade of the 2000s. This innovative system was Dr. Neusser's work for several years. Unlike systems from Ford and Toyota, which used a "dual-mode" configuration requiring two electric motors and an electric gearbox, Porsche's technology incorporated a conventional gearbox with the electric motor and the internal combustion engine operating through it. Electric motors run through electric gearboxes were inefficient systems.

The biggest challenge with any hybrid was restarting the engine seamlessly. While Toyota's and Ford's large electric motor moved the car, a second motor restarted the engine. A torque converter blended conventional engine power to drive the car. Porsche's system involved not a "black-white" clutch, simply in or out. Theirs was more like black-grey-white. This "grey" function eliminated the need for a second starter motor, yet allowed Porsche's Hybrid to run up to 75 miles per hour (120 kilometers per hour) on electric motor/battery drive. Those were autobahn speeds in speed-limited areas and national limits throughout much of Europe.

Porsche didn't reveal just how this "grey" area works. That was technology they hope to sell to other manufacturers. But, as was typical of Porsche, they set their target high.

"We did a lot of tests with a Lexus RX Four-Hundred-H," Neusser said. "That was our target, to achieve this comfort-level in transition from electric to gasoline engine drive. This was now the tenth birthday [in 2007] for initial automotive hybrids. We had it a bit easier than Toyota did in those days. Electronics are much better in the last ten years."

In 2007, China highway planning had brought the length of paved highways up to 81,250. This was an increase of 1,100 percent. The country planned a new 34,000-mile (55,000-kilometer) interprovincial expressway system by 2020. In Saudi Arabia at the end of 2007, the government said the Kingdom had increased its paved roads to 33,750 miles (54,000 kilometers). This was a jump of 60 percent.

In each of those countries, the name Cayenne still meant Porsche. ■

CHAPTER EIGHTEEN

HEARING A *NEW* DRUMBEAT

2004
2005

2005 Carrera GT
Translating the show car to the street required big changes, including an increase in wheelbase to accommodate radiators and a useful fuel tank. Tony Hatter did the production design work to turn Grant Larson's dream car into a street racer.

THE CARRERA GT WAS AS MUCH A PROCESS AS IT WAS A NEW FLAGSHIP AUTOMOBILE. That process started in Formula One; it moved through Le Mans and dealt with problems in cornering, lost engines, broken contracts, and commitments with time limits, and then it hinged on the answers to two significant questions. This started in 1991. Porsche was in Formula One with its V-12 engine in Footwork Arrows cars. Herbert Ampferer was in charge of all engine development at Weissach.

Horst Marchardt was working as number two for Ulrich Bez, who was the head of all research and development at Weissach. Marchardt approached Ampferer and asked him to help out with a racing problem.

It was Ampferer's first contact with the racing department. Marchardt handed him the responsibility for solving the problems the Formula One V-12s were suffering.

"We were in real shit with that engine," Ampferer explained. "It had a problem with cornering. The engine was not getting enough oil for lubrication under heavy cornering. Especially Monza. When the car went through Parabolica Curve, we lost an engine. Next engine, through Parabolica, lost. Next engine, quick warm-up lap. Into Parabolica. Lost."

Ampferer stopped the project. Porsche would return in October for the Japanese Grand Prix at Suzuka. That gave him three months. His engineers struggled to find out what the problems were. They found solutions and manufactured new engines. Then Marchardt and Bez came back to him.

"'Is this a good engine?' They asked me, 'Can we do something with these, go ahead with racing?'

"This one was a little bit too heavy. Too long. Too weak. My recommendation as a technically experienced guy, not with Formula One but with the knowledge I had, was 'I think you need a new engine.'

"Management decided. We dropped out of Formula One. We didn't go to Suzuka."

Porsche met great success in Formula One earlier with a twin-turbocharged V-6 engine that Hans Mezger designed for the McLaren

1991 Footwork Arrows FA12 Porsche

Running Porsche's ill-fated Typ 3512 engine, the 3.5-liter V-12, the Footwork's Formula One effort was a great idea whose time never came. The overweight and underpowered engine frustrated Porsche engineers, Footwork's drivers, and the car's designers.

CHAPTER EIGHTEEN

In October 1991, the sun set on Porsche's Formula One efforts, leaving the company defeated and embarrassed. Herbert Ampferer, called in to help solve engine problems, looked far to the future and conceived a V-10 engine for Formula One efforts for 1994, but it would find other purposes.

effort. He mated two of his V-6 engines with a central drive to comply with this new 3.5-liter normally aspirated formula.

By this time, Porsche's board had not renewed Bez's contract. Instead it promoted Horst Marchardt to run Weissach. He called Ampferer and asked him more questions.

"'What kind of problems do we have in this motorsport?' he asked me. 'Do we have the skills to do Formula One?'" Ampferer said he didn't know but he did think so. He knew Porsche had good engineers.

"Then Mr. Marchardt asked me, 'What do you need to prove that we are able to do Formula One?'

Porsche's stylists created the eye-catching graphics while Arrows' designer Alan Jenkins designed the low-front-wing/tall-nose configuration. The Porsche V-12 provided about 650 brake horsepower, but oiling problems killed many engines.

2000 Carrera GT Show Car

While Walter Röhrl looked cool and comfortable driving the prototype for these photos and for presentations videos, Porsche's striking background landscape was the desert of Nevada in mid-August 2000 where daytime temperatures averaged 105 degrees F (40 degrees C).

"Big question. To an engine designer as I was in those days, that was *the* big question.

"I need a little bit of money and a little bit of time. I will try to find out if we are able to do it. But I will not promise . . . ," he recalled.

Marchardt gave him time and a little money. The time stretched to three years. The funds did not. From 1991 into 1994 they worked on the V-12. Having already withdrawn from Formula One (and settled with Footwork over Porsche's breach of contract), Weissach engineers redesigned the V-12 without changing its basic elements. They developed new camshafts, new connecting rods, and new pistons. Ampferer hoped to determine if the V-12 could produce suitable power if they developed it further.

"We improved the performance, the power of that engine, to a level that we were convinced we would be competitive in Formula One. This was a real step forward in power. Formula One in those days was somewhere around seven hundred horsepower. The V-Twelve in the unmodified engine had something like six hundred twenty to six thirty horsepower. After doing our improvements we had seven hundred-plus with pump fuel. We understood how the fuel burning process worked. How the rest had to be handled. And we told Marchardt, 'Look, we think we can do it.'

"He said, 'But the engine still is too heavy. It's the wrong engine.'" Ampferer issued a challenge to Marchardt:

"If you need to prove to the management that we can do it, we will make you a new engine if you give us a little bit more time."

"What kind of money do you need?" Marchardt asked him.

"A little bit," he recalled with a laugh. Marchardt gave him funds that allowed his team to develop a new Formula One engine. It was "a handful of engineers, but not with the target to go to Formula One. Just to prove that Porsche engineers were able to do something like a Formula One engine."

In addition to determining if they could develop a successful engine, they had another question: What did the modern Formula One engine (in 1993/1994) have to provide in terms of "package requirements" given by the car?

"Having an engine on the dyno is an easy story. But making the engine suitable to a modern Formula One car? This is a different story.

"So we contacted a Formula One team. We told them the story and asked if they would supply us with their actual car's package data. And they did!" The team's identity remains undisclosed to this day. Marchardt had very good contacts with Formula One from his work with TAG and McLaren from 1984 to 1988.

Porsche's Southern California design studio translated Grant Larson's concept drawings into scale and full-size models. The project returned to Weissach to fabricate two show cars, one to push around and this one for Walter Röhrl to drive for photos, videos, and demonstrations.

"I got an extra fax machine at my home, not here in the company. I exchanged data with the team. We worked as if we were making them an engine. But this team was dealing with another manufacturer, this was clear. But they helped us."

At the end of 1994, Ampferer had the engine configured to the mystery team's specifications on a Weissach dynamometer revving to 14,800 rpm. It could not go higher only because Porsche's dynos peaked at 15,000 rpm. "But our engine was on the limit, to be honest.

"This was a V-Ten engine," he explained, "with pneumatic valve systems, with variable intake valves, variable exhaust valves, with variable trumpets. All our variables were on that engine."

CHAPTER EIGHTEEN

2000 Carrera GT Concept

Just when people thought Porsche had gone permanently SUV, the company showed a new supercar. The concept was the response to Wendelin Wiedeking's question after Le Mans in 1998: How many times do we need to win Le Mans?

He ran the cylinder heads in 1994 in a 20-hour durability test at 20,000 rpm. This effectively covered the distance of ten Formula One races in one day of testing. "Then we had the entire engine on the dyno and ran it for two hours supplying seven hundred sixty horsepower with pump fuel. This was an engine we could use." Marchardt was convinced: Weissach had engineers who could produce an F-1 engine. Ampferer believed this accomplishment gave them approval for Le Mans. He pushed ahead with the GT1 for 1996, 1997, and 1998.

"And we still had this V-Ten engine," Ampferer went on. "What do we do with that V-Ten engine? Nothing. It was just to prove our engineering capability. We put it into storage." Then one day, he had to talk to Wiedeking after Le Mans 1998. "What's now?" the chairman asked. Ampferer knew that between July and the following April trials gave them only seven months to design and produce a new racer.

"'I said, 'Ninety-nine is too short and tight of a budget. But two thousand . . . that would be something. New car, new engine.'" Wiedeking told him to go ahead with design and testing, but he would decide later about entering the race.

"So what was the logical step in terms of engine? The V-Ten Formula One? The carbon chassis from ninety-eight?" He took that new V-10. But 3.5 liters was not enough for Le Mans. An engine designed for two or three hours was not good for 24. He needed something new.

Ampferer's engineers redesigned it, enlarging displacement from 3.5 to 5 liters. They replaced pneumatic valves with standard spring valves. Other considerations of a modern V-10 engine—the 65 degree V-angle, torsional vibration of the crankshaft, of cam drive, gearing systems of cam drive, the cams themselves—remained unchanged.

He believed if it worked for an F1 engine at 15,000 rpm for two hours, it should serve as well for Le Mans where engines ran 8,000. "So we took it as it was. Increased the displacement. Same length because the cylinder bores were the same, the camshaft was the same, but different deck heights because we increased displacement."

Formula One engines of that time ran a stroke of 40mm and bore of around 95mm. Ampferer estimated that increasing stroke to 70mm would enlarge a 3.5-liter engine to about 5. The different connecting rod length required a different deck height.

"But the rest of the engine . . . if you see this Formula One engine and you see this Le Mans engine, they look very much the same. You can see it.

"But we did not go to Le Mans. The car was ready but we did not go.

"We talked with Wiedeking. He said, 'Nice car, this race car.'" But then he posed questions that would change Porsche's history.

"He asked me something. 'How many times has Porsche won Le Mans?' We told him sixteen.

"'What difference does it make if Porsche goes to Le Mans and wins seventeen times instead of sixteen times? It's another Le Mans win? Who is next to us? Ferrari. How much do they have?' 'Eight,' I said.

"Then he asked me another question: 'What do you think we are as Porsche? Are we *the* sports car manufacturer in the world?'"

In early 1999, rumors and stories from other automakers about future products filled the automobile world. The supercar genre that Porsche had invented with its 959 had fathered many challengers. Ferrari talked about an Enzo. McLaren and Mercedes leaked hints about an SLR. The name Bugatti had resurfaced.

"'We are the sports car manufacturer,' Wiedeking told me, 'and these are sports cars they are talking about. So we need a sports car like that. What do you think? Doesn't it make more sense than to go once again to Le Mans?'

"And I had to agree with him. Yes, yes sir."

2005 Carrera GT Assembly, Leipzig, Germany
Porsche selected its exceptional facility at Leipzig in eastern Germany to assemble the Carrera GT. The highly skilled assembly staff separated in two teams, one in white that manufactured the Carrera GT, and the other in red that assembled Cayenne models.

But rumors slipped out that Porsche had a car, a Le Mans Prototype category 1 entry for 2000, LMP2000. Insiders had heard that it was fast but Wiedeking had killed it. Voices hinted that the SUV project needed money.

"Wiedeking did not change his mind," Ampferer said emphatically. "We got the approval for a Le Mans two thousand car. But he stated from the first minute that we discussed this issue with him. He said, 'Do the car, do the concept. Go to a certain level of the development. But this is no confirmation that you will go to Le Mans in two thousand.' Clear commitment."

Ampferer, Roland Kussmaul, Norbert Singer, and dozens of others at Weissach hoped that when they had the car, Wiedeking would let them proceed. Had he let them develop it simply for morale purposes? Had he already in mind doing a supercar from the LMP2000? From the beginning, he had been very clear: Go to this point and we'll talk again.

"It was hard, because it was a really good race car," Ampferer said. "We ran the car. We got a new lap record at Weissach. But we never got the approval. On the other hand, having something as a vision in front of me which was a super sports car was good too.

"Then we had a long consideration phase. What car? What engine? What concept? And, and, and . . ."

"And one day I got a call from August Achleitner," Grant Larson picked up the story.

While a team of workers in the background assemble the engine support framework, one waits to attach it to the tub where another technician secures seat mounts. At front a fifth worker threads the wiring harness through the steel compressible structures that make up the car's crash safety.

Porsche staff at Leipzig built the Carrera GT entirely by hand. Preformed carbon-fiber assemblies arrived with partial wiring harnesses already threaded; however the finish work on this engine cradle at left and all other assemblies was done with a human touch.

The complex racing suspensions—more Le Mans racer and Formula One car than typical street exotic—bolted on to the carbon-fiber tub. Hand-assembled suspensions were monitored by alignment equipment at every turn of the wrench.

Achleitner was packaging manager for the new 911 whose department made sure every element necessary for an automobile fit within the confines of designers' concepts. Larson was designing the next 911, the Typ 997, in Porsche's satellite design studio in Huntington Beach, California. The Samsung Group, who manufactured electronics, built ships, and operated one of the world's largest construction firms, wanted to try the auto industry. It built a state-of-the-art design facility to bring an American West Coast flavor to its products and to develop auto trends for a future vehicle line. A talented designer, Roland Heiler, directed the operation. Ultimately Samsung changed its mind, and Porsche acquired the facility and its staff. Porsche, too, would design products there but also isolate its car designers from prying eyes and corporate politics.

"Achleitner needed some sketches for an all-new car, a mid-engine supercar." A sleek racer was to become a stylish road car. "I put down a few things on paper as a kind of teaser sketch. What always helps with deciding these projects is to have a rendering for them to visualize."

Larson created several ideas through February and March 1999. By May, Horst Marchardt had approved one of his concepts, and Grant divided his time between the 997 and the new supercar. He spent seven months on tuning the design. Near the end, Wiedeking and Lagaay commuted to California every other week to review Larson's model. In early 2000, Marchardt forwarded Wiedeking's approval to move forward.

"We had been standing around hoping to get the go ahead and wondering how we were going to get the thing finished by Paris in late September two thousand. Then we got a double go ahead: Make two!"

One show car had to run so Walter Röhrl could drive it for a video and its live presentation at the Paris show. The second was strictly a "push-around" for times when two shows coincided, such as Los Angeles and Detroit around New Year's 2001. A year later in Detroit, on January 8, 2002, Wiedeking announced that Porsche would produce the car called the Carrera GT.

"The Carrera GT was a continuation of everything we had learned in the GT-One chain of cars," designer Tony Hatter explained. Lagaay brought him into the project early. "The decision to make the car was based on, 'Okay, we have this LMP-One entry . . .' which I was involved with, an open prototype carbon-fiber monocoque with a V-Eight engine in the back. The decision was, 'Let's make a sports car out of this for the road.'"

Porsche show cars were rooted in reality. They had to be manufacturable and return a profit in production. But a direct translation from auto show turntable to the street was not always realistic.

"When you see these two cars, you think they are the same car," Hatter explained. "But

Appearance is everything, especially in a supercar. Here, an assembly technician aligns gaps on front quarter panels, trusting his eye before using a gauge to verify separations.

Final assembly inspection details included front trunk panel installations, and workers reviewed a long document itemizing the way each car was specified. Roof panels, mated to each body, were test fit, then test "stored" in the front trunk before any car was released.

every single millimeter was completely new and different from the show car to the production model. This one didn't have the machinery behind it. Once the guys in Weissach started to work with it, it became clear that we had to change everything whether it was safety or packaging or snow chain clearances or cooling the engine which was a major thing. And the thing had to have a roof which our boys hadn't exactly thought about.

"When we started to make a production car out of it, we made a digital model of the exterior and interior. We milled it. That was the basis for the wind tunnel tests. But because of the shortened period of work,

Final inspection included verification of engine performance. If the engine did not meet limits, inspectors could replace it. Here an inspector waited as his supervisor, center, phoned in the order for another engine.

they took this data set that we made here in the studio and made the first series of prototypes. They assembled ten or twelve running cars from data. We didn't have a full-size clay model of the car at that time. We used the same computer data as the basis of our clay models. We carried on refining the shapes of the car at the same time the engineers were developing running prototypes.

"Creating a car digitally is what people think happens. But the clay model is there for the visual subtleties." Hatter continued. "A digital model is on a screen. But when the presentation is over, you switch it off and it's

"The concept was clear for this car," Michael Hölscher, Carrera GT project manager, explained. "Mr. Wiedeking said we take this race car technology to the road for our customers."

gone. A clay model is always there. The chief can walk around it at night or the next day or a week later. This allows you to get a bit of distance from it and come back."

Hatter and Norbert Singer took one of the show cars into the wind tunnel. "What came out of the wind tunnel was horrible," Tony recalled. "Air blowing down the side of the car does not automatically turn ninety degrees and go into air scoops. To get the car to cool, those openings at the back had to be so big that the car would look nowhere near like the

314

CHAPTER EIGHTEEN

show car. Cooling had to go to the front. The radiators on the Carrera GT are at the front, two in the side and the big one in the middle. The air openings behind the doors on the side are for induction air, air conditioning, and air circulating around the engine compartment. When you look at the car, it was just a plumbing exercise."

Cooling the engine became more critical than just for driving. It was a challenge for the material Porsche chose to build nearly the entire car: carbon fiber. Michael Hölscher was project manager for the car. He was a veteran mechanical engineer with experience in entire car development and manufacture. Now he learned a great deal about working with a material previously limited to the motorsports world. Cooling air easily surrounded racing engines running at full throttle. The Carrera GT had to crawl through traffic.

Engine compartments baked. Carbon fiber typically did not survive more than 130 degrees Celsius, about 266 degrees Fahrenheit, the temperature at which most of it was created. The fibers were fine, but resins failed and the part collapsed. The challenge was to create something that resisted 180 degrees Celsius, about 356 degrees Fahrenheit, by using different resin. To help, engineers isolated exhaust pipes and mounted engine-temperature-controlled fans in the compartment to cool the engine, gearbox oil, and air conditioner condenser.

"The concept was clear for this car," Hölscher continued. "Mr. Wiedeking said we take this race car technology to the road for our customers. That meant we stay with carbon fiber. This is a material with very special characteristics. You have to orient the fibers. Steel has the same characteristics in every dimension, but with carbon fiber you can make an orientation and have different characteristics in one way or the other. You can easily make sandwiches, two very thin layers with a core between them of paper, or aluminum. You have a piece this has great bending stiffness but weighs nothing." Porsche's sandwiches used aluminum honeycomb.

The car was mostly carbon fiber, but not its front crash structure. Porsche had ample experience with crash structures in steel. Hölscher and his growing team of engineers (it started out at 15 and by the time production began it had grown to 200) reasoned they would make no "experiments" with crash structure. Their suppliers developed a new high-energy-absorption stainless steel that saved some weight.

Working with carbon fiber for series production threw Weissach engineers countless first-time challenges. In addition to engine compartment heat management, another was the engine cradle. In an actual race car, designers bolted the engine and transmission directly to the chassis as "stressed members." They mounted rear axles directly to the gearbox, making the rear of the car a large, stiff compound.

"The problem," Michael Hölscher explained, "was you had no noise isolation at all. Race drivers are hard people, and they have a helmet and ear plugs. In our GT-One, I made a test. I drove the car. It was so noisy. If you drove at one hundred kilometers you cannot talk with your passenger. The noise was not a nice noise, not exhaust, not intake. It was all mechanical, gears and chains. We knew we needed to isolate the engine. That meant we needed a support frame on which to mount it."

While developing their high-heat-resistant carbon fiber, they planned a steel-tube framework (dismissed as "too 1960s") and then an aluminum frame as backup plans. The ATR Group in Colonnella, Italy, met their challenges, "baking" the nearly 1,000 pieces that made up the Carrera GT in an autoclave at 180 degrees Celsius at 85 psi, 6 bar, of pressure for four hours. After Weissach confirmed this material through its own tests, engineers tackled the next challenge. That was the engine and clutch.

Herbert Ampferer had warned the development team, "If we want to do a super sports car, you need a modern racing engine in that. A high-revving V-Ten with this typical sound, WooWooWoo, we needed something like that.

"The alternative would have been making something from the Cayenne, a V-Eight turbo or something like that. Strong, but not really what enthusiasts love to hear, love to see. So we decided to take the V-Ten from that race car that was not used at Le Mans two thousand. This already had five-liters displacement. Cylinder arrangement, everything, had been checked and tested. Development time was short. Budget was short."

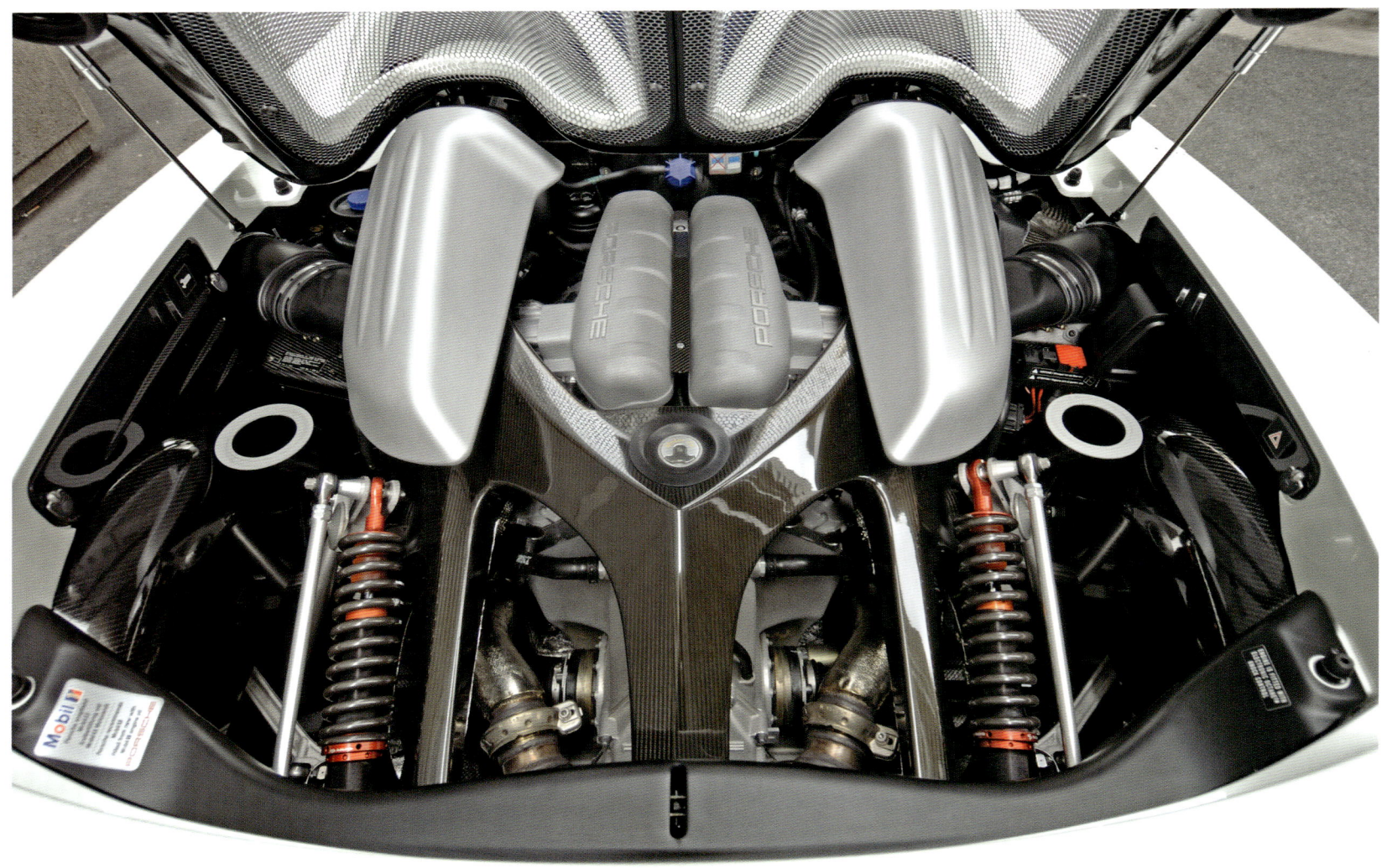

Herbert Ampferer warned the development team: "If we want to do a super sports car, you need a modern racing engine, a high-revving V-ten with this typical sound: WooWooWoo."

Ampferer's engineers took a race car engine suitable for 24 hours and made it durable for 24,000 and more. Still, they had to contend with air-conditioning condensers, a big alternator, and a hydraulic pump.

"Our engine in this car was a real race engine," Michael Hölscher said. "It was designed for this Le Mans car and the most important point in the design of a race car engine was to have a low center of gravity." Flat Boxer engines had exhausts below the cylinders which consumed space, elevating the engine position in the car. V-configurations allowed a lower center of gravity because exhausts sometimes were higher than oil pans.

"But if you had the V and a conventional engine, you had a clutch like a pizza plate," he continued. "This also caused the need to raise the engine. So race cars all had nice small carbon-fiber clutches, some not more than 100mm in diameter [4 inches]. Racing teams threw them away after one race or two."

Porsche worked with Fichtel & Sachs. Even if Weissach had invested heavily in developing carbon-fiber clutches, Sachs could not guarantee more than 12,500 miles (20,000 kilometers) and perhaps only half that depending on driver skill. Porsche would not accept having its customers change clutches as often as motor oil.

Hölscher and Ampferer remembered Porsche's success with carbon-reinforced ceramic brakes. They tested prototype composite clutches. At high revs, they burst. In their ceramic brakes, Porsche's suppliers used resin with very short carbon fibers and pressed this into the form. Porsche went the opposite direction. Using preimpregnated woven carbon-fiber sheets, Sachs pressed these preform composites with reinforcements of the woven materials into ceramic discs during a 12-week process. Ampferer's engineers had set the V-10's engine rev limiter at 8,400 rpm. Porsche typically demanded their clutches survive nearly double that speed for safety reasons, nearly 15,000 in this case. The new ceramic clutches withstood 20,000 rpm. Exceptional wear-resistance and a working diameter of 6.3 inches (160mm) proved to be two additional bonuses. With this small diameter, Porsche installed the engine so low it set a world record for crankshaft height above the pavement of 4 inches (102mm) at its lowest rotating point.

This, however, put the engine output below the centerline of the driving wheels. Mezger's original design took care of this by using a rotating countershaft above the drive shaft to transfer engine output to a gearbox. The low position, however, enabled Hölscher, Hatter, and Singer to incorporate air tunnels beneath the car. "This entire composition," Hölscher

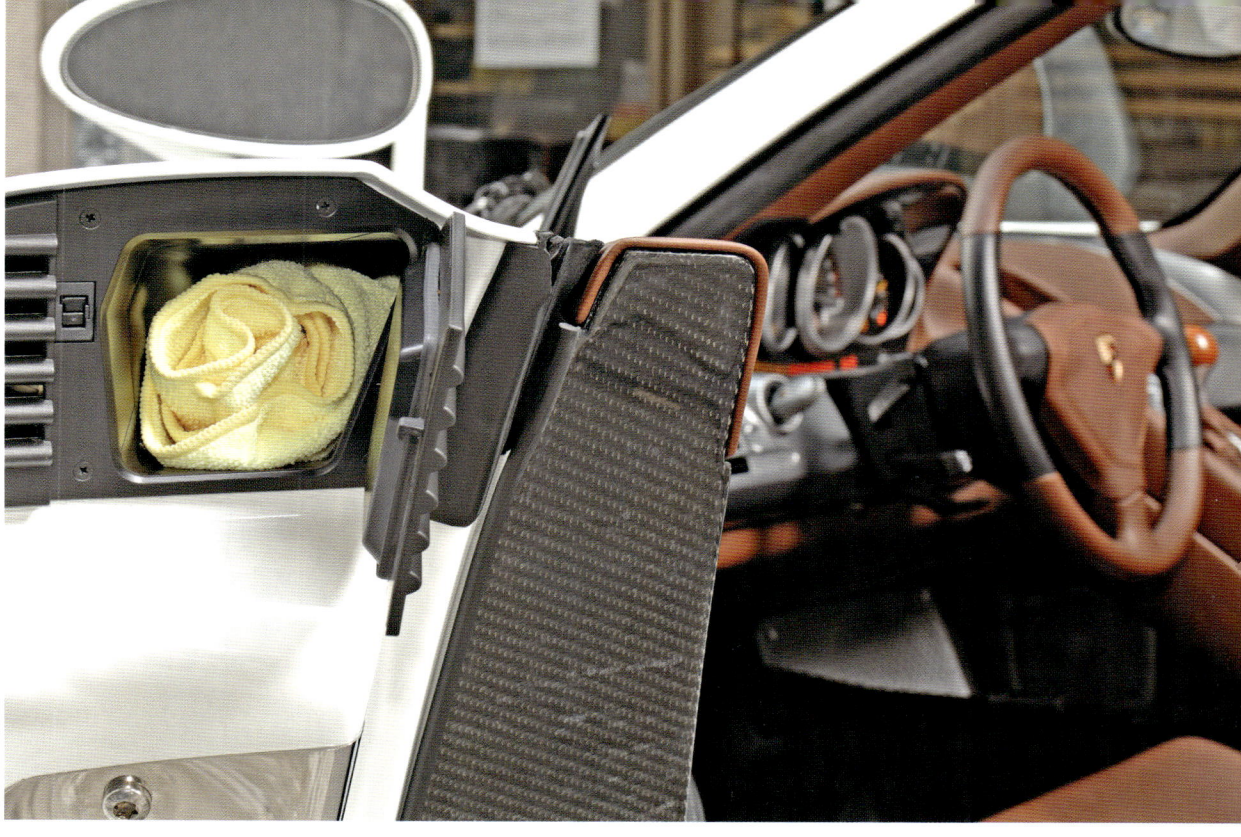

The story went that as Wendelin Wiedeking looked over preproduction versions of the car, he expressed concern over storage space. "What about the doors?" he supposedly asked, "What goes in the extra space there?"

One of many features styling chief Harm Lagaay appreciated was the raised gear shift lever and the mount on a center console that formed a bridge. In the car, two of the lowest technology materials were the leather seats and the wooden shift knob.

When assembly ended, Porsche had manufactured 1,270 production models. It made money for Porsche, and, as importantly, the car startled everyone.

CHAPTER EIGHTEEN

explained, "allowed us to have a diffuser over the whole width of the rear of the car. That brought us tremendous downforce. At top speed, we have about four hundred kilograms [880 pounds] of downforce."

The car offered racing-world performance to street-car customers. It reached a top speed of 205 miles per hour (330 kilometers per hour) with acceleration to 62.5 miles per hour in 3.9 seconds. The final 5.7-liter version of the V-10 developed 612 brake horsepower. Hölscher's engineers installed 15-inch (380mm) brake rotors inside 19- and 20-inch front and rear wheels in the 3,043-pound (1,380-kilogram) two-seater. It sold for $444,400, or about DM 390,000 at the time. But none of this would have satisfied Wendelin Wiedeking had not other considerations been met. First the car had to be usable; it had to be the Porsche among the supercars. Second the car had to have a Porsche feeling and a Porsche look.

"Usability was a question," Michael Hölscher recalled. "We had big coolers in front for the six hundred horsepower. We could not sacrifice performance for trunk space. To be the Porsche among the supercars meant that it was really close to the racetrack. It was not only for driving fast on the autobahn which can bring you fun. Its real purpose was to be fast on a racetrack.

"It was not easy to modify a real racing engine to meet the requirements of everyday driving. You must also be able to drive in a traffic jam with it. You must know that you don't have a flywheel but only a little clutch that has a tenth of the inertia of the big flywheel. Electronics bring the effect that the flywheel normally provides.

"The electronics sensed the revs. If rpms lowered a bit, electronics increased injection fuel volume. In former days you had the throttle with a damping element. If you dropped the throttle very fast, the throttle ran against the damper and moved back slowly. Now it was a function in the Motronics called the 'dashpot function.' It was almost as if there was a control driver between you and the engine. But it was important that the driver did not feel there was somebody who controlled him!"

Usability of the car generated a huge challenge to production car designer Tony Hatter. He had to make sure a roof would fit on a car that still had to be open some of the time.

"It had to stay on at two hundred miles per hour. We had to have wind-up windows and the top of the windows at the B-pillar had to meet the roof. The show car had these lovely styled rollover bars that were a long way from the top of any window. It was a compromise of getting the roll bars as small as possible while still remaining functional, getting the tapering of the side glass so small. Then we came up with the idea of these two removable panels. But the question was where to put them? In the boot! The packaging guys worked wonders and managed to put the two panels on top of each other in different directions. There was a special leather overnight bag that fits in the area below so you did have a bit of room in there for a bit of luggage."

Production began for the 2004 model year. Advanced orders and customer interest suggested that Porsche might produce as many as 1,500. Hand-assembled at Porsche's new factory in Leipzig, a small crew of 110 workers turned out three cars per day. As with any of its models, Porsche invited custom exterior and interior colors, though these did not get assembled till the end of the run in 2005. When assembly ended, Porsche had manufactured 1,270 production models. It made money for Porsche, Wiedeking's other primary consideration, unlike the company's earlier supercar, the 959. It generated countless magazine, newspaper, and television stories, just as the 959 had done. More importantly, the car startled everyone. Loyalists and cynics alike, who feared Porsche had become an SUV maker, were stunned and thrilled.

"I think we learned," Michael Hölscher summed up, "that it is possible to bring a really special product to the market but one that has very different demands from our big production numbers. How do you deal with it? You must do things differently. With suppliers you must have a different approach.

"But you cannot make such a project one after another. You have to learn how the customers think. They do not buy such a car every year. You must know when the time is right to bring a new drumbeat to the market." ∎

CHAPTER NINETEEN

BACK TO THE **FUTURE**

2005–2008

2005 Carrera S Cabriolet

Based on 996 sales, Porsche planners knew that about 40 percent of 997 sales would be cabriolets. Traditionally half of those have gone to the United States.

"THE LEAD MODEL OF THE 997 SERIES WAS THE CONVERTIBLE," August Achleitner said, "and not the coupe." Achleitner was Porsche's Director of Product Line Management for the Carrera. Before this he managed new vehicle concepts and packaging for all Porsche vehicles from 1989 through 2000. The 997 was largely his creation. "This strategy came from the engineers' point of view," he explained. "The convertible is more difficult because of the stiffness that is necessary. Your work is easier when you consider the reinforcements from the beginning." Before the 997, Porsche had developed coupes first, and after they were finished, engineers started on open cars. With the 997, Achleitner's team developed both simultaneously.

Wolfgang Dürheimer, Porsche's vice president for research and development, explained the advantages the 997 derived from Achleitner's simultaneous effort. Starting with the cabrios provided Weissach's engineers some unexpected benefits as they worked through target conflicts. These were the good-new-bad-news dilemmas arising when one decision revealed two or three more choices.

"It was clear for us right from the beginning that we will have a coupe and a convertible. That was more or less the same with the Nine-Nine-Six. But this time we did it in a very concentrated fashion. All the derivatives that the Nine-Nine-Seven will see, the Targa, the all-wheel drives, the various GT models and others, we took into consideration from the beginning."

This forced engineers to plan these models from the start. Weissach spent more time thinking about the car before designing it and welding the first parts. But improvements to the cabriolet strengthened the coupe as well. Making a coupe stiff is not difficult because the closed car has a structural roof. To stiffen the cabriolet body, engineers devised a so-called third load path for passive safety. This transferred forces of an impact through the top of the door to the back of the car.

A strong beam inside the sheet metal extended across the top of each door starting at the base of the A-pillar at the instrument panel. When occupants opened their doors, they saw a three-corner aluminum piece in the B-pillar at the rear of the door. This was the point at which the door beam connected, making a very rigid torsional-, bending-, and stiffness-load passage from the front fenders to the rear of the car. This also fortified the passenger compartment in a front, side, or rear end crash. It kept the compartment from folding in on itself as may happen in other open cars in high-speed accidents. It provided the new 997 cabriolet with 5 percent greater torsional stiffness and 9 percent more flexing stiffness than the 996 cabrio.

The 911 heritage offered as many challenges to engineers and designers as it provided guidelines. Its characteristic front fenders still retained a form that, as Ferry Porsche first dictated to Erwin Komenda, allowed the driver to see where the front wheels were located. The 911 carried on Butzi Porsche's iconic angled-down roofline. It still defined itself with the rear engine that has dictated the car's shape, its form, its handling, its sound, and its appeal.

"Designing to fit the Nine-Eleven heritage is a big challenge," Grant Larson said. Working with Matthias Kulla, they made 997 coupes, cabriolets, and Targas seem so Porsche-like. "My goal was to make the car look more technical, more precise, more agile." The work

Porsche so far has not embraced the folding metal top concept. It would be difficult to house the bulky structure, and its added weight resting over the engine would adversely affect handling.

An entirely new convertible roof structure allowed drivers to raise or lower the roof while driving as fast as 31 miles per hour (50 kilometers per hour). Using a lot of magnesium in the structure reduced weight, a consideration when the top was raised or lowered and set at the rear over the engine.

he and Kulla did defined the car. While their later tweaks with engineering also enhanced aerodynamics, reducing the drag coefficient from 0.30 for the 996 to 0.28 for the new coupe, the original concept was more revolutionary.

"Grant Larson made his first sketches with taller, wider tires," August Achleitner explained. "This choice had wide-ranging ramifications." The tires intensified loads under cornering, acceleration, and braking so greatly they literally destroyed the first running prototypes in 2001. It forced body, chassis, and suspension engineers to redesign much more of the car than they anticipated. Starting with the unibody of the 996, they developed techniques to weld and glue components. These methods increased body rigidity by 8 percent. Additional reinforcement and adhesives resulted in a 40 percent improvement in chassis stiffness.

Achleitner was one of several engineers boasting that the new 997 was 80 percent

323

2005–2008

2005 911 Typ 997 Coupe

Body engineers began developing the 997 with a cabrio platform, devising a strong beam system through the top of the door that transferred load forces from the front to the rear. While essential for open cars, it benefited the coupe as well, providing even greater rigidity, which improved ride and handling.

changed from the 996. More than half of that was beneath the surface. Not a single suspension piece was interchangeable. This conflicted with Wendelin Wiedeking's often-repeated goal of commonality of parts, but many of the new pieces were simpler to manufacture and easier to install. The 20 percent that remained unchanged included expensive elements such as the roof panel, the interior rear seats, and the 3.6-liter engine block, crankshaft, and pistons.

Nineteen-inch wheels forced powertrain engineers to rework gearboxes. Larger rolling circumferences required shorter final drive gears to best use engine torque and horsepower. Weissach engineers then addressed other concerns in the manual and Tiptronic transmissions. They developed a new six-speed manual gearbox with torque

Except for seldom-used back seats, the interior of the 997 was nearly entirely new. Interior designer Anke Wilhelm and interior chief Franz-Josef Siegert, an import from Daimler-Benz, took an already comfortable and user-friendly 996 interior and refined and upgraded it with new fabrics and even greater attention to details.

A new active electronic suspension system, Porsche Active Stability Management (PASM), allowed the new car to be two cars in one. "We can make our 'top guns' very happy," Wolfgang Dürheimer explained, "and still bring them on a long distance trip from A to B and get them out of the car relaxed and ready for their next appointment."

and horsepower capacity to spare. Engineers raised gearshift pressure and increased stall speed on the five-speed Tiptronic. This gave drivers faster starts from a standstill, more powerful and spontaneous acceleration, and quicker shifts especially in lower gears.

"This is a passion we follow," Wolfgang Dürheimer said. "If you get the chance to work on the Nine-Eleven, on the one hand this is a very big opportunity and on the other hand, it's an obligation. The health of the company is affected. Many jobs are at stake. Many engineers at Weissach make their application to Porsche after they finish their university degree. They get hired and stay at Porsche all during their career. They are deeply into their subjects, aerodynamics, acoustics, basic engine work, and they constantly ask themselves, 'What can I improve?'"

Engineers and designers often filled notebooks and desk drawers with ideas so that when they got the next chance, they were ready. They pulled out their wish lists. Dürheimer chided them: "Don't stop making new suggestions. If you are not successful in bringing it into the present project, bring it next time. Do not abandon it." One idea that engineers brought back to the tables for the 997 was the Porsche Active Suspension Management, PASM, the automatic stability system.

"We tried PASM for the Nine-Nine-Six," Bernd Kahnau said. Kahnau was project manager for 997 and served the same role for 996 and 993. He grew up inside Porsche. His father was production manager in the 1950s, and Kahnau's earliest technical education came in the back seats of 356s. "The technology wasn't ready for what we wanted the Nine-Nine-Six to be able to do."

2007 911 Typ 997C4 Targa
Porsche carefully researched Targa buyers before formalizing plans for the 997 version. Desiring distinctive design, even exclusivity, Targa owners also were more safety conscious than they were desirous of uncompromising performance.

Achleitner's commitment to 19-inch wheels and tires on the Carrera S motivated Porsche to raise the technology to meet its standards.

Ambitions grew bold. The standard suspension always presented a compromise to Achleitner, even under its best of conditions. When conceptual work on the 997 started in late 1998, he assembled a team of 20 engineers, designers, and staffers from the predevelopment group and sales. They decided what the car looked like, how it was equipped, how much horsepower it had, and made dozens of other choices. They relied not only on their own instincts, but they also queried 993 and 996 owners as well as some individuals they located who had test-driven a 996 or a 993 but not bought one.

"For some people the Nine-Nine-Six was a little too soft at that time," Achleitner said. There was no 996GT3, Turbo, or C4S yet. "*We knew what was coming but we took this feedback and decided that the Nine-Nine-Seven should be a little more muscular, a little bit sportier.*" This required a balance. Porsche didn't want to lose customers it had won from Mercedes-Benz and BMW. These were buyers who never would have bought a Porsche before. The Nine-Nine-Three had been too harsh, loud, or uncomfortable for them.

How would they achieve this balance? What makes a car faster? How do you make the car smoother and more comfortable without sacrificing sportiness? The PASM system met many of these challenges. Aside from the 959, which many still considered a large run of prototype cars, this 997 was the first time Porsche offered an electronic spring and damper system. In the cabrio, this was an industry first.

Early in the development, Achleitner explained, "meeting the target to make the car comfortable wasn't so hard because we didn't see a chance to make the car better than the Nine-Nine-Six. But we learned a lot about what was possible with software. We could make tiny changes, even to accommodating a single bump in a smooth road."

What PASM and laptop computers allowed the engineers to do was fine tune characteristics that transformed each Carrera S model (on which this suspension system was standard equipment) into any of a variety of cars. As Wolfgang Dürheimer characterized it, "We have made it possible that two demands which could not be fulfilled in one car in the past could be covered with one new suspension system. It's very sporty on one side. We can make our 'top guns' very happy and still bring them on a long distance trip from A to B and get them out of the car relaxed and ready for their next appointment."

This capability recalibrated open car handling. Achleitner's engineers substituted the coupe's front springs with coils 10 percent softer for the cabrio and substituted the coupe's rear suspension bushings with some much harder for the open car. They compressed the PASM's range of variability to fit the cabriolet's slightly diminished stiffness and the anticipated character of cabrio drivers. Its stiffest "sport" settings were roughly 15 percent softer than calibrations for the coupe, while the softest point was slightly gentler than the coupe.

For 997 coupes, Porsche offered a full Sport Suspension, but for European customers only. This lowered ride height by 0.79 inches (20mm), leaving it too low for U.S. federal ride height standards. Engineers provided a mechanical differential lock on the rear axle of 22 percent under acceleration and 27 percent under deceleration or braking to enhance directional stability. Buyers could order it through Porsche *Exclusiv* as an option on the Carrera or in place of the PASM on the Carrera S. The ride was much harsher because Porsche conceived it "for the ambitious driver not so much interested in comfort but rather in super performance and agility," Achleitner explained.

Bringing these mannerisms to the road was a daunting task. Powertrain manager Stefan Knirsch was part of the 20-member group making concept studies outlining their goals.

"You always want more power in the next generation of any Porsche," he said. He and his staff came up with intake and exhaust modifications to the familiar 3.6-liter 996 engine that added 5 horsepower to reach 325 brake horsepower for the "base" Carrera. This engine carried over the VarioCam Plus valve management system comprising two

Using the C4 and C4S platform gave engineers 1.7 inches (44mm) more width at the rear. While this improved cornering, it also gave designer Matthias Kulla a more aggressive, dynamic, and distinctive body form to work with.

interacting switching cup tappets on the intake side of the engine, driven by two cams of varying size on the intake camshaft.

Enlarging cylinder bore from 96mm to 99 but retaining stroke at 82.8mm brought the new S engine displacement to 3,823cc, 3.8 liters. It developed 355 brake horsepower. The new Carrera coupes reached 60 miles per hour in 4.8 seconds (5.2 for the cabriolet) and 4.6 seconds for the S (but 4.9 seconds for the S cabriolet). Porsche quoted top speeds of 177 miles per hour (283 kilometers per hour) and 182 miles per hour (291 kilometers per hour), respectively. This was the first time since 1977 with 2.7-liter and 3.0-liter engines that Porsche offered two normally aspirated engines simultaneously.

Porsche introduced the 997 Carrera and Carrera S coupes in Europe and the United States as 2004 models. Through the 2005 model year, it continued manufacturing and selling 996 Turbo S and Turbo S cabriolets. Cabriolet versions of the 997 Carrera and Carrera S reached dealers worldwide in April 2005. The first all-wheel-drive models reached dealers in midsummer, with Targas, Turbos, GT3s and GT2s, and other models following into 2006, 2007, and 2008.

Except for its back seats, the 997 interior was nearly all new, the work of interior designer Anke Wilhelm and interior chief Franz-Josef Siegert. In the late 1990s, Harm Lagaay hired Siegert away from Mercedes-Benz, and he brought in a staff of designers only to do interiors and still others to attend to the details, the jewelers, as he called them. Wilhelm and Siegert's instrument pod seemed familiar to Porsche owners and Uli Sauter's graphics were quickly comprehensible to those driving one for the first time. The 996 interior was the most comfortable and user friendly of any previous model. Porsche would not shy away from its new enthusiast base. The 997 offered four seat options, satisfying most backs and body shapes. All were comfortable and supportive with headrests two inches higher and angled closer for better support. There was much more metal and less plastic in this new interior than ever before.

For Larson and Kulla, the legacy of the Porsche Cabriolet went back generations. Butzi Porsche designed a version in the early 1960s that barely left the design studio. When the production version appeared in 1983, Peter Schutz and Helmuth Bott used it to proclaim that despite reports of its death,

2007 997GT3RSR Nürburgring 24 Hours

Timo Bernhard, on his way to victory for a second year in a row, flew his GT3 at the Nürburgring 24 Hours. The RSRs use Porsche's normally aspirated 3.8-liter water-cooled engine that develops 485 brake horsepower.

Even as 2007 GT3 Cup cars took to the tracks, the competition remained heavy and diverse. Campaigned now in 18 countries, the cars weigh just 2,470 pounds (1,120 kilograms) with ceramic brakes.

the 911 was alive and well. The 1983 cabrio was lively, but none of Porsche's design staff thought it looked very well.

Porsche had carried over the same convertible roof from the 911SC and 3.2 Carreras through the 964 series. "The first ones were more functional," Grant Larson explained. "I think that's the best way to describe it." From Tony Hatter's efforts to improve the 993 cabrio roof came Lai's forms with the 996 and then Larson's with the 997.

"From generation to generation," Larson said, "they've gained so much experience. We have a lot of magnesium in the new roof to make it lighter. We have a new 'Z' folding mechanism that made a whole lot more sense for the Nine-Nine-Six and Nine-Nine-Seven versions. Those early cabriolet roofs took a whole lot of weight and pushed it back further where it shouldn't be on the car."

According to Dürheimer and 997 project manager Bernd Kahnau, 40 percent of all 997s for 2005 were cabriolets, and customers tended to steer about 50 percent of those to the United States. The solid, fixed-glass back window with an electric defogger was one of many selling points, something introduced at the 996 face-lift in 2002 and slightly enlarged with the 997. Unlike any 996, at speeds up to 31 miles per hour (50 kilometers per hour) the 997 driver could raise or lower the roof. That process, including dropping and raising side windows, took 20 seconds in either direction.

2007 911 Typ 997GT3RSR

Wide wheel arches stretched the car by 1.97 inches (50mm, per side), which allowed extra-wide Michelin 27/65-18 slicks on the front and 31/71-18 slicks on the rear. The cars weighed 2,701 pounds (1,225 kilograms).

Roland Kussmaul's engineers reinforced the body shell. The business-like interior was laced with 98 feet (30 meters) of high-strength steel tubing to make up its roll cage, stiffening the car another 10 percent over the 996GT3RSR models.

Porsche's wholly owned subsidiary CTS, Car Top Systems, developed the mechanism for the 997's top and manufactured the complete system with bows, hinges, motors, inner lining, glass, and outer material. These arrived from CTS fully assembled and, as did everything else on the Zuffenhausen assembly line, just in time for two men to lift it and set it onto the painted car body. Porsche offered it in black, grey, cocoa, and blue. The entire assembly weighed 93 pounds, 42 kilograms. But weight always was an enemy to Porsche engineers. While the cabriolet gained a total of 297 pounds (135 kilograms) over the coupe, diligent management of every system kept the net weight increase to 187 pounds (85 kilograms).

Because the roofline could not exactly mimic the coupes, August Achleitner's engineers tweaked rear spoiler performance. It rose 20mm higher on the cabriolet than on the coupe to provide more aerodynamic effect.

The subtly higher wing was not the only effect that top-down Porsche drivers noticed. "The exhaust sound was even more aggressive with the cabrio," Bernd Kahnau explained with a broad grin. "Because of the open cabin, we wanted our customers to really be able to hear the engine." It reminded some drivers of the 993 more than a water-cooled 996. Because of America's relaxed exhaust-noise standards, U.S. buyers got the loudest exhausts of any 997 purchaser. Bernd Kahnau knew the sound and explained the reason. "Our exhaust engineers? They are our Mozarts."

For 60 years Porsche has listened to its engineers and designers as they have worked to deliver Ferry Porsche's dream car to an ever-changing world. Dr. Erhard Mössle, who was the four-wheel drive manager for the 997 Turbo gave an example.

His team had identified "characteristics of the Targa buyer," he explained. "They desire exclusivity, distinctive design. They primarily are cruisers, you know, connoisseurs of automobiles rather than racers. And traditionally, they are safety conscious." So Porsche "repositioned" the Targa to differentiate it from those that came before and from the cabriolet and coupe.

For Mössle, whose title is Product Manager Four Wheel Drive, and his team, their decision to start with the C4 and C4S platforms immediately addressed and resolved questions about what the new Targa would be. The 1.7-inch (44mm) wider rear end provided the aggressive and dynamic form that engineers and stylist Mathias Kulla had in mind. This single decision gave them the distinctive appearance as well as safety and stability controls they believed appealed to potential Targa buyers. Porsche's engineers and marketers understood that these owners routinely use their cars year round in climates with snow, so the C4 drive system made further sense. Its 0.4-inch (10mm) lower ride height didn't hurt its overall visual appeal, either. But each of these factors combined to preclude any possibility of a Targa 2 or Targa 2S.

To further appeal to this audience, Mössle and his engineers recalibrated the actual suspension and the virtual electronic one. By increasing anti-roll-bar diameters, they limited body roll in cornering. Lowering the spring rates kept the ride suitably compliant

Intense attention to airflow over the car and into and out of radiators, brakes, and engine improved aerodynamic efficiency by 7 percent over the 996 version. Porsche assembled 35 of the cars for the 2007 season.

2006 911 Typ 997GT3RS

In the calm before doors opened to the public, a VIP visitor to the Paris Mondial de l'Automobile admired the GT3RS, which Porsche introduced at the show. Based on the C4 platform (but strictly rear-wheel drive), the GT3RS was 1.73 inches (44mm) wider than previous generations, allowing Porsche to take full advantage of car width regulations to improve handling.

for those whose attendance at track days was limited to the spectator side of the fence. They also shifted PASM calibration slightly toward the moderate-to-softer end of its calibration range of sport-to-soft.

"The glass roof," Tomas Christiansen, manager of body engineering, explained, "is two kilograms lighter than the glass in the Nine-Nine-Six. This makes a very big difference so high above the center of gravity. It is two kilograms less [4.4 pounds], even with the hatchback mechanism."

"We started the entire development process on Nine-Nine-Seven models with the cabriolet," Christiansen said. "By fixing the basic structure in the cabriolet, this allowed us to develop everything else. The adjustments to PASM, to roll bars, and springs," Christiansen went on, "give a comfortable driving experience that is more important to the Targa owner than sport or performance handling."

The Targa glass roof comprised two layers of glass—each green and each just 0.1 inch (2.6mm)—and a third plastic interface 0.04 inches (1.1mm) that was gray. This combination reduced sunlight transmission through the roof by 31 percent. It cut heat transmission to only 17 percent. A single rocker switch on the center console operated both the glass roof and an interior semitranslucent black cloth sunblind in seven seconds at any speed.

The C4S, in its own right and as the basis for the Targa, has been so thoroughly tamed beyond even its 996 predecessor that anticipated heavy front-end sensations never appeared. Porsche derived and developed the C4 964, introduced in 1989, with an increasing U.S. market in mind. It tended to understeer when drivers pushed it too hard. This was a comfortable response for most Americans, and Porsche engineers—dealing also with a heavy load of equipment up front—settled for this reaction. In the 993 they compensated; some would say they overcompensated. This car produced handling characteristics that were more rear-dominant, reminiscent of earlier two-wheel-drive 911s. With the 996 and 997 C4 and C4S, turn in was crisp, precise, predictable, and dependable.

At the time Porsche introduced the Targa to journalists, Dr. Erhard Mössle had a Turbo and a new Targa as his "company" cars, understandable in his role as product manager for four-wheel-drive vehicles. He said that "each car dictated my driving style. When I was in my Turbo, I always pushed it. But, you know, I noticed the scenery and the weather when I drove my Targa."

Porsche began shipping its all-wheel-drive 997 C4 and C4S models to the United States in November 2005. Mössle's driving style observations were enough to make purists run for their checkbook and order the Turbo, shown first at Geneva in February 2006 along with the GT3, the other model guaranteed to quicken the purist's pulse. The 3.6-liter Mezger engine stretched to 480 brake horsepower in the Turbo. Acceleration to 62.5 miles per hour took 3.9 seconds, and Porsche quoted its top speed as 193 miles per hour (311 kilometers per hour).

In a testimony to Weissach's engineering, the Tiptronic version of the all-wheel-drive Turbo was quicker reaching 62.5 miles per hour, taking just 3.7 seconds. The Turbo cabriolet arrived in September 2007 boasting nearly identical performance figures, a long-time goal for Weissach's engineers. Marketing's tendencies for greater luxury that first plagued Herbert Ampferer with the 930 in 1975, continued with the latest generation. Fully optioned Turbos, especially if buyers optioned "paint-to-match" exterior color schemes and interior leather and

2007 911GT3

On the high-bank circuit at CERAN outside Paris, the GT3 reached terminal velocity: 193 miles per hour (311 kilometers per hour). While centrifugal force on the banking churned occupants inside, the car handled it easily, and driver and passenger comfort remained high with air conditioning cooling the cabin.

Andreas Preuninger and Roland Kussmaul created the GT2 model to satisfy FIA regulations for American Le Mans Series and European Le Mans Series racing in the GT2 category. As a result, the car is rear drive only, since no paved racing organization accepts four-wheel-drive chassis.

2008 911GT2

The 530-brake-horsepower coupe offered top speed capability of 204 miles per hour, the first time Porsche had provided such potential in a production, street-legal 911. The large horsepower jump over the previous 996GT2 resulted from using twin turbochargers and a newly designed expansion intake manifold.

other appointments from Porsche *Exclusiv*, elevated high performance to performance art.

The GT3 appeared alongside the Turbo in Geneva in 2006. This normally aspirated version of the Mezger 3.6-liter flat-six achieved 415 horsepower in this incarnation, giving owners acceleration to 60 miles per hour in 4.1 seconds and a top speed of 193 miles per hour (311 kilometers per hour). Still a homologation "special," project leader Andreas Preuninger explained the genesis and evolution of the car.

"It's a close as you can get to a race car with a license plate on it. We wanted to translate the feeling a race car gives you, the emotion, the wish to drive to your destination in a circle, not in a straight line, because you don't want to get out of the car!

"This car still gives you something left that you can try," Preuninger explained. "The normal driver takes a long time to handle this car perfectly. It's not because you have to be a good driver. It's easy to drive. But if you really want to drive very fast, you have to develop some special senses for the car. That's what you can do best on a track.

"Seventy percent of all our customers, of GT-Three owners, take their car from time to time to a racetrack to perform their hobby! Seventy percent. It was quite astonishing to us as well. Club sport series, even just track days. That's quite a lot. Compared to the Turbo which is twenty percent, and the Turbo is the next high. The Carrera S is below ten."

In 2007, Porsche offered its GT2, Preuninger's rear-drive 530 horsepower 911 that reached 204 miles per hour (328 kilometers

2007 911GT3RS

Traction control off, the GT3RS was a very entertaining drive on a tight-handling circuit set up for journalists to meet the car before its Paris auto show debut. With 415 brake horsepower in a 3,032-pound (1,375-kilogram) automobile, the power-to-weight ratio offered opportunities for enthusiastic cornering.

per hour), the company's first production street-legal 911 to exceed 200 miles per hour. This large horsepower jump came about by using twin turbochargers and a newly designed expansion intake manifold. The "distributor" pipe was longer than that used on the Turbo while the intake manifolds were shorter. Weighing 3,175 pounds (1,440 kilograms), the car reached 62.5 miles per hour in 3.6 seconds. Ironically, because the GT2 is another Porsche homologation model and the category is rear-wheel drive only, acceleration to 62.5 miles per hour was faster in the all-wheel drive Tiptronic Turbo than the rear-wheel drive GT2.

With 45 years of accomplishment behind it, from the 901 through the latest 997, owners know best what the car is about: It's the driving experience. Andreas Preuninger, a mechanical engineer with years of experience driving other cars for Germany's automotive magazine of record, *AutoMotor und Sport*, now is Porsche's Project Manager, High Performance Cars. He has what many would consider a dream job. His philosophy echoes what Ferry Porsche told Peter Schutz 25 years ago. His advice would bring a smile to both men:

"I think we are producing and developing these cars for ourselves.

"In our own experience, the harder you drive a GT-Three, as long as the oil is warmed up properly, the better it goes. It needs it. Drive yours as if you stole it!

"Just give it five minutes to warm the oil up properly. And then floor it!" ∎

CHAPTER TWENTY

THREATENING TRADITION

As designer Pinky Lai worked through his concepts of what a Boxster Coupe could look like, a variety of "greenhouse" treatments—the roof and window glass portions of the car—worked their way across his drawing board.

"THE CAYMAN WAS REALLY A WONDERFUL EXPERIENCE," Pinky Lai said. "None of the projects are identical. Each one is such a different journey." Lai joined Porsche in 1989, the first member of the design team that Harm Lagaay brought in from BMW when Ulrich Bez (also from BMW) hired Lagaay. Lai was born in Hong Kong but moved to Rome where he earned an industrial design degree in 1978. A scholarship from Ford in Cologne sent him to London's Royal College of Art where he earned a second degree in 1982 in car design. After two years at Ford, he joined BMW and met Lagaay. His first assignment at Porsche was the exterior and interior of Bez's passion, the four-door Typ 989. While he now chiefly designs projects for outside clients, his most recent Porsche was the Typ 987 Cayman. It evolved from the 986 Boxster.

Grant Larson designed the first generation Boxster. Once it entered production, Lagaay asked him to think of "something more than just a Boxster but based on a Boxster." With a small budget Larson built a full-scale "see-through" prototype with windows and a mock-up interior. Essentially it was a Boxster with a coupe top.

"It was pushed back and forgotten," Pinky Lai explained. "By the time I took over the Boxster second generation I was asked to pick it up again, to get some ideas about what we could think of as a closed Boxster."

Not yet an official program, this idea had emerged during product discussions on Boxster's second generation. Marketing feared the Boxster alone would not survive the competition by the time it reached the market. They compared the 986 to the 911, which had ten or more variations to offer customers from C2 to Turbo to GT2 to open cars. They worried that even a second generation Boxster was too weak to compete against strong competition Porsche expected from other German carmakers, the Japanese, and the Americans.

"We started putting up a lot of variations," Lai said, "very conservative ones. Grant's proposal was considered very conservative. Basically it was the "three-box" sports car. That represented one end of the spectrum. The other end was a stretched greenhouse. We called it the "Snow White Coffin." BMW had designed Z1 and Z2 concepts with long greenhouses. Lai remembered a Volvo in the mid-1970s with two doors and a long greenhouse (the P1800ES). Lai's design group covered that approach and everything in between.

"Marketing really supported the idea. During the initial stage, they were pushing. They needed volume and variety to satisfy the customers. They were around all the time. Every time we had discussions, showed our stuff, they were very supportive. They picked ideas from what they saw and made comments. This was a combination of studio, marketing, and platform, the first time in our history at such an early stage.

"We had a lot of ideas. But we couldn't overexaggerate it with nineteen-inch wheels or twenty-inch wheels on a totally different wheelbase. We were dealing with the reality that the lower body of the car would be within the Boxster periphery. We could only play around with the greenhouse area and proportions. We knew after a few reviews we had to decide how we would convince the board of directors. They didn't know about what we were doing. They only knew the platform team was responsible to take care of the Boxster long term. They had to do something instead of just leaving Boxster on its own.

A collection of ideas reflected the look of 22-inch wheels supporting an American "chopped and channeled" hot rod. At this stage, the concept remained "Boxster with a hardtop."

A more finished concept illustration not only showed the Cayman as it became, but displayed its historic roots in the 1953 Typ 550/01.

"Christmas was coming up. We put two final selections together, a short roof and a long roof version."

Marketing staffers worried that it was unwise to have only Photoshop concepts to show the board. They found some money and funded two see-through models. One was the original short-greenhouse idea of Larson's.

A stylized illustration for Porsche's annual styling calendar showed a treatment proposal for the Cayman front end with the inspiration from many Porsche racers in the background.

The other was the longer-greenhouse fastback. Both were called the Boxster Coupe. (The "Cayman" name came much later.) Timing was crucial because Porsche closed for its winter holiday. Lai contacted several high-quality shops he knew for cost estimates for these models. He passed on the numbers to the platform team.

"It was a bit more than they expected to spend but I knew from my experience that the Board of Directors . . . if you show them a really super painting or drawings, they will look at it and make some comments. But if you are asking them to sign a paycheck to initiate the development program, then they expect to look at something more than pictures. Ideally you show them a real model, something that looks like a real car, and then they will sign the check."

The only way this shop could meet Lai's deadline was to work from data, the x-y-z-coordinates marking the thousands of points on the car that defined its shape. Time was too short to follow conventional procedures with two-dimensional section drawings to develop a surface to start the three-dimensional model. Lai had advanced this digital process when he did the 996 Turbo program, developing many of its forms on computer.

Porsche's supervisory board had an important meeting scheduled for the spring of 2000. They were deciding long-term development schedules over a decade span. Had the platform team balked at the expenditure, funding for see-through models would have slipped six months, delaying the car two years or longer. The platform team delivered two first-generation Boxsters in raw-body form to the model shop. They

Pinky Lai's proposals began to stretch out the roofline, turning the hardtop configuration into the fastback that it became.

2006 Cayman S

Going from an open car to a closed one, enclosing the Boxster as a coupe was an unusual practice for Porsche or any carmaker. As this transition took place, the Cayman became its own car.

sliced off each upper body, packed the lower bodies with modeling material, and began milling the two body versions. The project was essentially Lai's. Harm Lagaay and Horst Marchardt appeared rarely and offered only minor suggestions.

Just before Porsche's Easter Holiday in 2000, the company hosted a dealer and importer meeting for U.S., Australian, and European markets. Under Lagaay's direction, all presentations had become sophisticated, even dramatic events. This "internal clinic"

The stainless steel rear body panel extends from the door front pillar, or A pillar, up along the roof seam and down to the seam above the rear lights. The complex and compound curves that come down from the roof and then rise again over the wheels presented huge challenges to body engineers.

took place in the wind tunnel. No one knew what they were going to see. It was a top secret visit. They were told it was going to be an in-house clinic; they were expecting something new.

As Pinky Lai worked with his modelers to compromise with body engineers who had to stamp those shapes from one piece of steel, he watched the white highlights as they started to "squeeze together, to bubble up." Beyond this point he would not compromise.

The see-throughs that came from the model maker were body shells with crude interiors. They needed extensive sanding but only minor changes. Lai's team upgraded everything for the importers show and the board review. They had carried over passenger compartments from the Boxsters. They improved the interior and cut the lift gate. The luggage area had been just a sketch, but they opened up front and rear trunks so viewers could see them. Lai got a couple of guys from the trim area to finish them to look convincing.

"So they came to the wind tunnel by motor coach and when they walked in, it was so quiet. It was just like the sound was sucked in," Lai recalled. "We only had the two cars," Lai recalled, "so it wasn't a pure clinic but more a case of them picking one model out of these two and telling us why they chose one over the other and making some indication about how many pieces they could sell in a year. They were asked to do something for the first time in our history." This show took place before the board meeting. When the directors convened, they had feedback from the dealers.

"Going from an open car to a closed car, this also was new in the company. Normally you have a closed car and you chop it and fix it. You always can expect a higher price for the open car. In this case, we were doing the reverse. We were basing the coupe on an open car which was supposed to be more expensive than the coupe. But it was not going to be cheaper than the Boxster because it was a new body! The whole rear fender, the whole rear end was new.

"I can recall the first directors' show," Lai said. "It was really impressive. With all the background data from the dealers, they had initial calculations of the whole project into production. Dr. Wiedeking was there and he said, 'We have to be profitable. Doing something beautiful is not enough. We have to survive!'

"He mentioned a figure, how many percent, the margin of profitability. 'Give me that margin and I will do it. It's too pretty to kill it.' And that was more or less the end of the presentation. He was walking across our courtyard toward the exit on the opposite corner. He turned back and he was looking at the long roof.

"'It would be a shame to kill it,' he said, and he left. Then the financial guys did their tricks. It is their 'art' to create workable figures, and we got the program—finally. We started the official production.

"All the ingredients were there. It was a mid-engine car. We had the opportunity to play around with the greenhouse. The location of the backlight is determined by the transition of the greenhouse to the rear fender. We call it the Mountain and Valley, the ups and downs. That was the sexiest part of the car. If you look through the outside rear view mirror over the rear shoulder, you can see what I mean.

"This was another thing. It was the first time in the history of stamping technology that they made one piece out of that. They had a heart attack over at body engineering. They said it can't be feasible—we spent a lot of time, extra weeks working that shape."

Lai was willing to work at it, to make some compromise from a styling point of view. But when body engineering's suppliers asked him for "some room to play with," he refused to let them "play" with the rear fender transition into the greenhouse. Lai's team worked it out themselves. Each week they sent new data for stamping simulations.

"When they pull, or draw, that big piece of sheet metal out of the stamp, they might grind the metal over the stamp. That is bad for painting. You would never get a good paint job if you had those marks. So we kept moving and moving. Half a millimeter each time. At the end, they had to rework an angle on the rocker sill area in order to get a more favorable draw angle on the entire piece. Because we insisted, 'That's the end. We are at the end of our compromise.' Anything more than that and we lose the sexiness. We came up about one centimeter [0.4 inch] in the valley. Anything more than that, you just ruin the flow of the highlight through the canyon area."

The "one-piece body side" started with the rocker panel at the A-pillar behind the front door where assemblers fixed hinges to the door bolt. The front fender screwed onto the body side. Front fenders were never considered body-side in manufacturing. From there, the A-pillar went up to the roof. That was the reason for two channels. These were the welding points of the body side and roof panel. This incorporated the whole rear fender, up the C-pillar and all the way down to the rocker. On the Cayman this was one piece of stainless steel.

"It's like a monument, a huge sculpture in stainless steel. A lot of those insider bits of knowledge are hidden. Once you see a

Porsche introduced the base Cayman with a five-speed manual transmission while the Cayman S got a six-speed. The Tiptronic S also was available.

beautiful car on the road, it's just beautiful. It's taken for granted. But all the hardship behind it, all the blood, sweat, and tears go along with that. They're just not visible."

There was just one operation to stamp it. The workers lifted it without rubbing or scratching it. The most difficult area for the stamping was the valley and mountain, called a "negative draw." The draw angle was sideways. The sheet metal had to wrap up to the roof frame and end with a flange. The rocker sill had flanges that turned in and up. The mold makers had to work a certain draw angle that did not create any rubbing of the mold.

"As we worked to resolve this draw angle, we kept constantly moving the highlight up and down. We are moving half a millimeter of material. Then the highlights, that white line, they start creating 'bubbles' up and down, we work a light stick up and down. You see a highlight can start to squeeze together, to bubble up. That is not good. We are designing cars but we are also designing highlights."

However aerodynamics, Lai recalled, were "a nightmare. It was a less-favorable greenhouse aerodynamically than the Nine-Eleven." They carried over the Boxster's rear trunk so they could use its spoiler mechanism. Lai had anticipated

The Cayman S uses the 3.4-liter flat-six that develops 295 brake horsepower, good enough to push the car to 62 miles per hour in 5.4 seconds and to a top speed of 171 miles per hour (275 kilometers per hour).

unacceptable figures on the first measurement. It helped clarify the group's decision on what type of moving spoiler they would choose.

"We didn't think the Boxster type-telescoping wall-type of spoiler would be very appealing on this car," he explained. "What about the double-plane spoiler of the Turbo? Everybody agreed and we went from there. If it worked on the Turbo, it should work there as well, maybe not as efficiently as the Turbo because that one was longer. The space we had to work with was half the size of the Turbo. We spent a few weeks in the wind tunnel and got our goal [0.29]. We got lucky.

"The front end was really tight in terms of budget and creativity. We were only allowed the front bumper to play with. So we thought of the most obvious. On the Boxster we had a rectangular light unit for fog lights and turn indicators in the bumper. We wanted something different so a circular lamp was the best choice at that time.

"And that was it. It was a very different experience from the Nine-Nine-Six. Very different. The Nine-Nine-Six was about survival. The Cayman was about giving support to the Boxster as a model line." Porsche's Boxster already had set a benchmark for competitors.

They could approach the Boxster on paper but on a fast track, the Boxster ran away. Porsche did not want to see potential customers go elsewhere because they wanted a closed sports car, a car with a proper coupe body. Porsche did not have it, and they already had lost customers. This no longer was about survival; it was about keeping customers satisfied.

From the beginning Porsche offered the Cayman with a more powerful and larger engine displacement S sibling. The base Cayman used a 2.7-liter flat-six that developed 245 brake horsepower. With this engine, the car reached a top speed of 160 miles per hour

(258 kilometers per hour). Acceleration to 62.5 miles per hour took 6.1 seconds. The S used Porsche's 3.4-liter flat-six and achieved 295 brake horsepower and a top speed of 171 miles per hour (275 kilometers per hour). The S needed just 5.4 seconds to reach 62.5 miles per hour (100 kilometers per hours). Jürgen Kapfer's innovative "integrated dry sump lubrication" from his Boxster engines carried over to his Cayman versions as well. The base Cayman used Porsche's five-speed manual gearbox while the S took advantage of the six-speed unit. The five-speed Tiptronic S was available for either model. Both manual transmissions incorporated short-throw shift action and connected to the engine through dual-mass flywheels and hydraulic clutches.

Front and rear MacPherson struts made best use of space in the platform and ensured exceptional handling. Porsche's Stability Management, PSM, system was standard while the PASM active suspension management system was optional on both models. Base models rode on 17-inch wheels and tires, but the S fitted 18-inch rubber. Four-piston monobloc aluminum brake calipers grasped 11.7-inch (298mm) front rotors on the base Cayman, and 12.5-inch (318mm) discs on the S. Both models shared 299mm rotors at the rear. Porsche's ceramic composite brake system, PCCB, was available as an option and provided 350mm diameter front rotors and six-piston monoblocs. Pinky Lai's rear wing rose from the body rear deck at 75 miles per hour (120 kilometers per hour). As with every other vehicle in Porsche's lineup, countless options were available through Porsche *Exclusiv* to personalize the car to any taste.

The subtle rear lip past the end of the hatchback is an aerodynamic wing that rises from the body at speeds above 75 miles per hour (120 kilometers per hour). Drivers also can manually control it from inside the car.

"We've been around a few years in the philosophy and design of the Porsche car," Pinky Lai said. "The customers never expect any revolution from us. We are not supposed to offer them a revolution in design. That is rule number one. What they expect is something new, and appealing. But it has to say—without looking at the badge—that this is the New Porsche or in the Porsche family. So that is intuitive.

"What is good in doing this Cayman this way is that we have opened up a very long potential of continuing to do things for it, and for a next generation. It's a really good car. And it's a really great car to drive!" ■

INDEX

911 in the Wind Tunnel

In a company serious about its work and its products, long days and nights in engineering labs, design studios, and wind tunnels have always led to ideas, new experiments, and the need to blow off steam. No one recorded the coefficient of drag of this 911 Turbo pillow.

Aachen, Germany, 62
Abarth Carrera, 61, 63-64, 66, 69, 91
Abarth, Carlo, 61-63
Abate, Carlo Mario, 65
Achleitner, August, 270, 309-310, 322-323, 326-327
Ahrens, Kurt, 133, 136
air shock absorbers, 55
air-cooled engine, 11, 130, 140, 169, 178, 194, 205, 241, 252
air-suspension control system, 286
Alfa Romeo, 62, 130, 162
　Tipo 33/2, 130
Allison, Bobby, 151
all-wheel drive, 208, 210, 221-222, 224, 226-227, 240, 242, 244, 247-248, 264-266, 269, 274, 286, 288-290, 297, 322, 328, 331, 333-335
Alpina, 146
Alzen, Uwe, 242, 273
AMAG, *Auto und Motore, AG*, 23
American Sunroof Corporation (ASC), 234
AMG, 292
Ampferer, Herbert, 171-172, 242, 274, 276, 280-282, 302-303, 305-309, 315-317, 333
Andial, 226
Andretti, John, 194
anti-lock brake system (ABS), 152, 221, 234, 264, 286
anti-theft lock, 56
Arkus-Duntov, Zora, 36-37, 48-49, 55, 150
Armco safety barrier, 138
ATE, Alfred Teves, 58
ATR Group, 315
Attwood, Richard, 113, 132
Audi, 121, 172-173, 176, 234, 286
　100, 176
　Quattro, 207
Audi-NSU, 121, 176
audio systems, 232-234, 255
Austro-Daimler, 11
Auto für Jedermann, 11
Auto Union, 10, 12, 41, 71
Autodelta racing organization, 130
Autodromo di Vallelunga, 154
Automobil-Revue, 20
AutoMotor und Sport, 335
Baja Buggy, 290, 292
Bantle, Manfred, 209, 221-222
Barcelona, Spain, 115
Barnard, John, 196-197
Barth, Edgar, 70
Barth, Jürgen, 113, 115, 143, 145, 150, 161, 163, 178, 189, 191-193, 207, 227-228, 230-231, 244, 246, 276, 279
BASF, 75
Beckley, Jack, 187
Behra, Jean, 184
Beierbach, Walter, 84, 89
Bell, Derek, 190, 193-194, 201, 204
Berger, Wolfgang, 146, 151-152, 154-155, 159
Berlin, Germany, 9, 10, 12, 30
Bernhard, Timo, 328
Bertone, Nuccio, 91-92
Beutler, Ernst and Fritz, 16, 18, 20, 22, 24, 55, 63, 89
Bez, Ulrich, 226, 228, 238, 240-242, 244, 252, 290, 302-303, 338
Bezner, Fritz, 221-222, 224, 226

Bilstein, 200
Biral, 59, 97, 152
Blank, Bernhard, 15, 20, 22-23
BMW, 119, 146, 148, 154-155, 162, 195, 226, 292, 326, 338
　CSL, 146, 162
　X5, 295
　Z1, 338
　Z2, 338
Boge, 95, 98
Bohn, Arno, 242, 252-254, 290
Böhringer, Eugen, 101
Bonnier, Jo, 43, 65, 72, 77
Borgward, 32
Bosch, 97, 133, 170-171, 200, 203, 264
　K-Jetronic, 159, 167, 170-171
　K-Jetronic, 203
　LH-Jetronic fuel injection, 233
　L-Jetronic, 203, 206
　mechanical fuel injection, 95, 97, 147
Bott, Helmuth, 37-38, 48-49, 53, 55, 71, 83, 85, 87, 89-90, 92, 102, 146, 148, 150-151, 168, 172, 191, 196, 200-201, 203, 205, 207-210, 220-222, 224, 226, 233, 240, 242, 252, 286, 328
Boutsen, Thierry, 279
BPR, 245-246, 274, 279
braking system, 57-58, 66, 75, 92-93, 108, 112, 123, 141, 146, 159, 181, 214, 238, 240, 247, 290, 297, 317, 319, 329, 345
Brands Hatch, 107, 115, 141, 194, 196, 279
Branitzki, Heinz, 168, 224, 226, 238
Braumbart, Martin, 146
Braunschweig, Robert, 20
Bremgarten circuit, 20
Brodbeck, Tilman, 98-99, 145, 148-150, 153, 155
Brose, Eberhard, 280
Brussels, Belgium, 23, 52, 55
Buenos Aires, 40
Bugatti, 308
Bursch, 169
bürzel (ducktail), 145, 150, 153
Buzzetta, Joe, 113
C.H. Wiedenhausen Karosserie, 30-33
Cahier, Bernhard, 84
Canadian-American Challenge Series (Can-Am), 122, 127, 138-140, 142-143, 152, 165, 170
Car and Driver, 98
Car Top Systems (CTS), 330
Cassell, Chuck, 77
catalytic converter, 96, 181, 207, 213, 283
CERAN, 333
Cerda, Sicily, 65, 66
Champ Car racing, 184, 186-187
Championship Auto Racing Teams (CART), 186-187
Chandler, Otis, 136
Chaparral, 184
Chapman, Colin, 102
chassis system, electronically controlled, 286
Chevrolet, 49, 94-95
　Corvair, 90
　Corvette, 49, 94-95, 170
Christiansen, Tomas, 332
chronometric tachometer, 63
Cisitalia, 16, 41
Clean Air Act, 96
Cleare, Richard, 153

Cobra, 78
Cologne, Germany, 146, 194, 338
Colonnella, Italy, 315
Comfort package, 235
Commission Sportive Internationale (CSI), 115
Competition Motors, 35
Connaught Engineering, 23
Cooper, 71
Coppa D'Oro Delle Dolomiti, 13
Cosworth engine, 184-186, 189, 195
Courrèges, André, 103
Cunningham, Briggs, 77
Cuoghi, Ermanno, 138
D'Ieteren Frères, 52, 55
DAF (German National Labor Front), 11-13
Daimler-Benz, 10, 71, 324
Daimler-Chrysler, 286, 288-289, 292
Dakar, Senegal, 209
Dauer, Jochen, 195
Davies, Peter, 138
Davis, Colin, 77, 102, 104
Davis, Grady, 136
Daytona, 66, 75, 77, 102, 104-105, 107-108, 113, 136, 140, 184, 194, 283
de Beaufort, Carel Godin, 40, 184
Dean, James, 45
Dechent, Hans-Dieter, 140
Dennis, Ron, 195-197
DeTomaso
　Mangusta, 120
　Pantera, 146
Detroit, Michigan, 120, 256-257, 259
die Ahnherr, 14
Digital Motor Electronics (DME) unit, 203, 206, 241
Dijon, France, 16
Donahue, Mark, 139, 141-143, 152
DOT (U.S. Department of Transportation), 206, 210, 230, 265
Drauz Karosserie, 25-26, 52, 55
Dreikantschaber (DKS), 65, 67, 69-70, 75, 78
Dresden, Germany, 24
Dron, Tony, 153
Dunlop tires, 171, 200
Dürheimer, Wolfgang, 322, 325, 327, 329
Dusio, Piero, 16, 41
Dutch Grand Prix, 197
Eagle, 184
Earl, Harley, 95
Earl's Court auto show, 23
East African Safari Rally, 148-149, 156-157
Ehra-Lessien, Germany, 150
Eifelrennen, 32, 34
electronic throttle linkage, 267
Elford, Vic, 109, 132-133
EMW, 32
engine management system, 203, 206, 233, 267, 290
Enna-Pergusa, 165
Environmental Protection Agency (EPA), 92, 210, 230
Enzo, 308
E-Type Jaguar, 62
European Grand Prix, 196
European Hill Climb Championship, 102
European Interserie, 140-142, 172
European Rally Series, 158
Evolution package, 245
Exclusiv options, 206, 231, 246, 266, 268, 327,

335, 345
exhaust system, 71, 82, 92, 96-97, 113, 121, 123, 127, 133, 157, 169-171, 181, 206-207, 224, 228, 241-242, 255, 259-261, 292, 306, 315-316, 327, 331
Falk, Peter, 101, 134, 136, 138, 146, 152, 192, 200, 238
Farina, Battista "Pinin," 14, 84
Farouk, King, 20
F-Wagen, 12
Fédération Internationale de l'Automobile (FIA), 61-62, 68-69, 71, 74, 87-88, 103, 109, 115, 127, 130-131, 134, 140, 143, 146, 152, 157-161, 165, 177, 186, 194-195, 197, 207-208, 227, 245, 275, 279, 282-283, 334
Fédération Internationale du Sport Automobile (FISA), 194
Fellersleben, Germany, 13
Ferrari, 62, 65, 78, 102, 120-121, 130, 195, 197, 245, 247, 274, 281, 308
　Ferrari 206, 120-121
　Ferrari 246 Dino, 120-121
　Ferrari 250LM, 120
　Ferrari 330P, 130
　Ferrari 330-P4, 186
　Ferrari 333SP, 274
　Ferrari 365GTB/4 Daytona, 146
　Ferrari 512, 112
Fiat, 118
　850 GT, 149
Fichtel & Sachs, 316, 317
Field, Ted, 184-186, 189
fire extinguisher system, 246
Fittipaldi, Emerson, 151
Flegl, Helmut, 134-136, 138, 141, 146, 152, 164-165, 169-170, 178-179, 181, 228, 230
Flunder, 115, 136
Follmer, George, 138-139, 142
Footworks Arrows, 282, 302-303, 305
Ford, 94, 118, 120, 130, 146, 155, 195, 286, 299, 338
　Capri, 146, 148
　GT, 135, 143
　GT40, 113, 120
　Mirage, 136
　Mk IV GT40, 130
　Mk IV, 186
　Mustang, 146
　Taunus, 33, 118
　Thunderbird, 94
Ford of Germany, 146
Ford Zakspeed, 146
Ford, Henry II, 130
Formula One, 59, 68-69, 71-72, 74, 85, 87, 115, 136, 140-141, 146, 184, 192, 195-197, 232, 244, 274, 282-283, 302-303, 305, 307-308, 310
Formula Two, 40, 71
Foyt, A. J., 186-187, 189
Frankfurt auto show, 30, 47, 54, 81, 84-85, 87, 88, 90, 171, 177, 203, 210, 232, 290
Frankfurt, Germany, 29-30
Freiberg hillclimb, 30
French Alpine Renault, 162
Frère, Paul, 34, 36, 190
Fröhlich, Karl, 11
Fuchs wheel, 92, 123, 154, 206
fuel system, 83, 85, 92, 95, 97-98, 104, 121, 123, 127, 132-133, 139, 141, 143, 147, 157, 159, 167, 170-171, 190, 191, 193-194, 203,

224, 231, 233, 241, 248, 259-260, 267, 280, 292, 301, 305, 319
Fuhrmann four-cam engine, 25, 51, 56, 66, 68-69, 71
Fuhrmann, Ernst, 38-41, 51, 56, 66, 68-69, 71, 96, 132, 145-146, 148, 151-155, 157-159, 162, 164, 168-170, 172, 177-181, 184, 189, 195, 200, 203, 238, 252
F-Wagen, 12
G50 gearbox, 244
General Motors, 36-37, 48, 90, 95, 170, 179
Geneva Auto Salon, 20-23, 30, 59, 81, 84
Geneva International Auto Show, 92, 134, 231, 333, 335
German National Labor Front (DAF), 11-12
Getrag, 261
Ghia Carrosserie, 118
Gilbert, Howard, 187
Ginther, Richie, 45
Girling braking system, 57
glass roof system, 248-249, 264, 332
Glöckler,
　Helmut "Helm," 30, 32, 34
　Otto, 29-33
　Walter, 30, 32, 34
Gmünd, Austria, 13, 15-16, 18, 20-22, 82, 89
Goldinger, Josef, 13
Gordini, 32
Gorrison, Wolfhelm, 179
Gran Turismo (GT) series, 61, 245, 279
Grand Prix races and cars, 10, 12, 41, 70-71, 197
　France, 72-73
　Holland, 40
Grand Sport (GS), 51
Great Britain race, 40
Grossmütter, 75, 78
Group 3, 146, 157, 159
Group 4, 146, 153-154, 159, 165, 176-177, 207
Group 5, 153-154, 160-162, 165, 207
Group 6, 162, 190, 207
Group 7, 207
Group B, 158-159, 207-210, 212
Group C, 165, 190, 192-195, 245
GS-GT package, 25, 42, 48
GT1, 245, 273-275, 279, 282, 311
GT2, 245, 271, 274, 334, 338
GT3, 246, 270-271, 274, 329, 333
GT4, 246
Gugelot Design, 120
Gugelot, Hans, 119-120
Gulf Ford, 136, 140
Gulf Oil, 132, 135-136
Gurney, Dan, 43, 72-73, 184, 186
Hahn, Carl, 78
Hall, Jim, 184
Hamburg, Germany, 130
Hanomag automobiles, 30
Hatter, Tony, 226, 238, 241-242, 248-249, 274, 276-277, 279-281, 301, 311, 313-314, 317, 319, 329
Hawkins, Paul, 108
Haywood, Hurley, 184, 201
Heilbronn, Germany, 25-26, 52
Heiler, Roland, 310
Heinkel-Flugzeugwerke, 75
Heinrich Gläser Karosserie, 24
Hensler, Paul, 92, 95, 97, 171, 210, 213, 224, 226, 235
Herrarte, José, 36

346
INDEX

Herrmann, Hans, 34, 36, 39, 104-105, 108, 132
Heuer, Erich, 24
Hild, Wilhelm, 18, 32, 34, 39, 68-69, 71, 82
Hill, Graham, 45
Hirth crankshaft, 52
Hirz, Ernst-Joachim, 36
Hitler, Adolf, 10, 12, 15, 118
Höchschule für Gestaltung, 120
Hockenheimring, 43, 91, 104, 146, 148
Hoffman, Max, 23, 25, 27, 38, 91
Holbert, Al, 194
Holbert, Bob, 43
Hollywood, California, 35
Hölscher, Michael, 314-317, 319
Hönick, Hans, 72
Hoppen, Jo, 184, 186-187, 189
Horsman, John, 135-136, 138, 140
Hühnlein, Major Adolph, 12-13
Huisman, Patrick, 281
Hummer, 292
Huntington Beach, California, 310
Ickx, Jacky, 154, 163, 165, 192-193, 201, 204, 209
ignition system, 97, 124, 203, 231, 233, 260-261, 290
Imola, 165
IMSA, 127, 184, 194, 195
Index of Performance, 34, 79, 104
Indianapolis, 136, 141, 151, 183-184, 187, 189-191, 200, 226, 242
Innsbruck, 102
intake system, 71, 86, 97, 231, 233, 260-261, 265, 292, 306, 315, 327-328, 334-335
intercooling, 154, 174, 177, 190-191, 217, 223, 265, 275, 288, 290
International Race of Champions (IROC), 151
Interscope Racing Panasonic, 183-185, 187, 189
Jaguar, 195
Jantke, Manfred, 192
Japanese Grand Prix, 302
Jeep Grand Cherokee, 292
Jenkins, Alan, 303
John Wyer Racing, 132, 135-136, 140
Johncock, Gordon, 151
Jones, Richard, 153
Jöst, Reinhold, 115, 194, 279
Jowett, 32
Juhan, Jaroslav, 36
Kaes, Ghislane, 18
Kahnau, Bernd, 270, 325, 329, 331
Kangaruh, 102
Kapfer, Jürgen, 259-260, 267, 345
Karmann G.m.b.H, 55-56, 58, 87-89, 118, 121-122
Karmann Ghia, 118
Karouse, 154
Kauhser, Willi, 134, 140
Kern, Hans, 16
King, Richard, 185
Kinnunen, Leo, 135-136
Klett, Lord Mayor Arnulf, 21
Klie, Heinrich, 120
Knirsch, Stefan, 260, 327
Koblenz, Germany, 62
Koinigg, Helmuth, 152
Kolb, Eugen, 104, 115, 129, 190, 193
Komenca, Erwin, 9, 12, 14, 16, 18, 21, 23-24, 27, 39, 55, 62, 67-68, 76, 82-84, 87, 90, 179, 322
Koni shock absorber, 92, 98
König, Willy, 195
Konstruction Rennfahrzeuge, 102
Kraft durch Freude (KdF), 11-12
Kranefuss, Michael, 146
Kremer, Erwin and Manfred, 194-195
Kugelfischer fuel injection, 85, 191
Kühnle, Kopp & Kausch (KKK), 171, 190-191, 213, 235
Kulla, Matthias, 260, 322-323, 327-328, 331
Kunstle, Jean-Pierre, 45
Kussmaul, Roland, 192-193, 228, 230, 245, 274, 277, 279, 281-282, 309, 330, 334
Lafferentz, Bodo, 13
Lagaay, Harm, 172-173, 175, 177, 226, 238, 241, 248-249, 252-257, 259, 262, 270, 290, 293-294, 310-311, 317, 328, 338, 341
Lai, Pinky, 254-260, 264, 280, 329, 337-338, 340-343, 345
Lamborghini Miura, 120
Lancia, 62, 192-193
Flavia 2+2, 84

LC-1 Spyder, 192
Land Rover, 292
Defender, 293-294
Langheck body, 129, 132-134
Lapine, Tony, 95, 99, 133-134, 136, 150, 154-155, 169-170, 172, 176, 178-179, 202, 205, 212, 226
Larrouse, Gerard, 134
Larson, Grant, 253-259, 262, 267, 301, 305, 309-310, 322-323, 328-329, 338-339
Lastenheft, 221
Lauda, Niki, 196-197
Le Mans Coupé, 70
Le Mans movie, 114, 136
Le Mans Prototype (LMP), 282, 309
Le Mans, 32, 34, 36, 39-40, 49, 66, 69-70, 79, 102, 104, 107-112, 114-115, 127, 129-130, 132, 134-136, 140, 150, 153, 158, 165, 177-178, 184, 186, 188, 190, 193-195, 200-201, 204, 208-209, 231, 244-245, 247, 273-274, 276-277, 279, 281-283, 302, 307-309, 310, 315-316, 334
Leiding, Rudolf, 140, 168, 172-173, 175
Leipzig, Germany, 308, 310, 319
Leuze, Helmut, 102
Lexus RX400H, 299
Liggett and Myers Tobacco Company (L&M), 139, 141-142
Lindheim, Dr. Wolfgang, 286, 288
Linge, Herbert, 36, 39, 48, 65, 70-71, 91, 101, 104, 110, 114
Lohner, Jakob, 11
Lola Composites, 283
London, England, 255
Loos, Georg, 150
Lotus, 71, 102-103, 115
Europa, 120
Lotus-Porsche, 102
Lotz, Kurt, 121-122, 140, 168-169
lubrication system,
dry sump, 86, 98-99, 260-261, 271, 283, 345
wet sump, 86
Lucas braking system, 57
Lucerne, Switzerland, 20
Ludenbach, Thomas, 282
Ludwigsberg, Germany, 121, 157, 203
Ludwigshafen, Germany, 75
M471 package, 147, 155, 157
M472 package, 147, 155
M491 option, 155
M506 option, 210
MacPherson strut front suspension, 83, 85, 345
Malcher, Jean-Pierre, 242
Malmsheim airport, 37, 49, 71
Marathon de la Route, 110, 125, 127
Marchardt, Horst, 242, 252-253, 261-262, 264, 279, 286, 302-303, 305, 307, 310, 341
Martini-Rossi team, 132, 140, 164-165
Mass, Jochen, 154
Mathé, Otto, 13-14
Matra, 120
M530, 120
Mayer, Teddy, 195, 197
McAfee, Jack, 25, 27
McLaren International, 192, 195-197, 245, 274, 276, 279, 281, 302, 305, 308
F1-GTR, 279
MP4, 197
MP4/2, 197
McNish, Allan, 283
McQueen, Steve, 114, 136
mechanical systems, 95
Meisl, Charles, 23
Mercedes-Benz, 10, 82, 140, 195, 209, 240, 279, 281, 286, 288, 292, 326, 328
CLK-GTR, 273, 279, 281
ML, 295
SLR, 308
SSK racer, 10
SSKL racer, 10
280GE Gelandewagen, 209, 228
methanol, 183, 185, 190
Mezger, Hans, 59, 71-72, 79, 85-86, 92, 102, 104, 109, 115, 132-134, 141-142, 146, 152, 158, 161, 171-172, 186-187, 194, 196-197, 271, 302, 317, 333, 335
Michelin tires, 330

Mickl, Josef, 16, 83
Milan, Italy, 62
Mille Miglia, 39
Mimler, Hubert, 68-69
Mitchell, Bill, 95, 170
Mitter, Gerhard, 77, 102, 107
Möbius, Wolfgang, 178-179, 209, 212, 221-222
Modena, Italy, 62
Moneim, Prince Mohammed Abdel, 20
Monte Carlo Rally, 101, 115, 127, 153
Monthléry circuit, 22, 78
Montjuïc Park, 115
Monza, 102, 107, 165, 194, 281, 302
Morse, Kerry, 228
Moss, Stirling, 45
Mössle, Dr. Erhard, 331, 333
Motorola Motronic ME, 267, 319
Mueller, Joerg, 273
Müller, Herbert, 141, 152, 159
Mulsanne Straight, 108, 162, 177, 193
multilink axle, 240-241
Munich, Germany, 12
Murkett, Steven, 257, 287, 289-290, 292-294
Murray, Gordon, 274
Mussolini, 12
Nader, Ralph, 90
NASCAR, 151
National Socialist Motors Corps (NSKK), 12
Neckarsulm, Germany, 176, 234
Neerpasch, Jochen, 111, 113, 146
Neusser, Dr. Heinz-Jacob, 292, 295, 299
Nikasil, 152
Nissan, 195, 281
Nordhoff, Heinz, 118, 120-122
Nordschleife, 110
Norisring, 224
North American International Automobile Show, 256, 311
Nürburgring, 30, 32, 38, 63, 65-66, 70, 75, 79, 102, 109-110, 115, 124-125, 127, 152, 154, 164, 226, 328
Nuremberg, Germany, 11, 24
O.S.C.A., 32
Offenhauser engine (Offy), 186-187
Ojjeh, Mansour, 197
Olivier, Gustave, 49
Olley, Maurice, 37, 48-49, 55
Ollon-Villars hillclimb, 102
Ongais, Danny, 184
Ontario Motor Speedway, 187
Opel Kadett, 118
Opel, 95, 118
Organization of Petroleum Exporting Countries (OPEC), 143, 175-176
Osnabrück, Germany, 55-56, 118, 121
Österreichring circuit, 136, 153
Pabst, Augie, 77
Parabolica Curve, 302
Paris auto show, 197, 311, 335
Paris Mondial de l'Automobile, 332
Paris Salon de l'Automobile, 18, 23, 84, 87, 123, 157
Paris, France, 11, 22, 51, 112, 130, 134, 209, 333
Paris-Dakar Rally, 207-209, 227, 286, 292
Parnelli, 184-185, 189
Patrick, Pat, 184, 186
Pearson, David, 151
Penske, Roger, 141-143, 151, 184, 186
Peter, Patrick, 246
Peugeot, 15, 87-88
Model 201, 87
Piëch,
Anton, 16, 20, 130
Ferdinand "Bürly," 59, 79, 86, 96, 98-99, 102-104, 107-109, 112-113, 115, 122-123, 130, 132, 134-136, 138, 140-141, 146, 152, 169-170, 184, 207, 220, 289
Louise, 16, 96
Pilatus, 20
Pindar, Robert, 171-172
Pirelli tires, 171
Polak, Vasek, 184
Pontiac GTO, 179
Porsche active stability management system (PASM), 299, 325-327, 332, 345
Porsche Cars North America, 226, 264-265
Porsche composite brake system (PCCM), 345

Porsche *Exclusiv*, 149
Porsche Konstruktionen Ges. M.b.H, 11
Porsche Models and Engines
1300 series, 52
1500 engine
Super, 27
Normal, 27
GS, 43
RS, 39, 43
1600 engine
Normal, 48, 52, 56-58
Super, 48, 52, 55-56, 59
C, 59
GS, 48, 52
GT, 52
GTL
SC, 59, 88
2+2 model, 83
2000 engine
GS, 57, 69-70
GT, 65
America Roadster, 24-25, 27, 91
A-series, 92
B-series, 95
Boxster, 251, 254-260, 262, 264, 267, 269-270, 289, 293, 298, 338-345
Coupe, 337, 340
S, 266, 268-269
Bumblebee, 122
Carrera models, 26, 43, 48, 51-52, 57, 65-66, 68, 75, 87, 91, 132, 149, 154, 169, 171, 238, 242, 264, 276, 279, 292, 322, 328
Carrera 2, 56, 58, 69-70, 85, 224, 230-233, 249, 338
Carrera 2.7, 168, 227
Carrera 2.7 RS, 157
Carrera 3.2, 181, 202, 204-206, 219, 224, 233, 238, 329
Carrera 3.2 Speedster, 219-221
Carrera 4, 221-222, 224, 227-228, 230-232, 238, 242, 244, 249, 264, 327, 331, 333
Carrera 4S, 264, 327, 331, 333
Carrera 6, 88, 102, 104
Carrera 16, 66
Cup, 226, 244
de Luxe, 51
GT, 301-302, 305, 307-308, 310-311, 315
GTS, 67-68, 74
GTS6, 78-79
Panamericana, 36, 51
RS, 123, 145, 147, 155, 172
RS, 231-232, 245-246, 248
RSR, 165
S, 249, 321, 326-328, 335
Cayenne, 289, 290, 292-293, 295, 297-299, 308, 315
Cayenne S, 285, 289, 295, 297-298
GTS, 298-299
Hybrid, 299
Turbo, 288-290, 292, 295, 297-298
Turbo S, 285, 290, 293-295
Cayman, 338-340, 343-345
Cayman S, 341, 343-345
C-series, 95
D-series, 96
convertible, 26, 55
E-series, 99, 155
F-series, 99
GT, 51-52, 54-55, 62-63, 65, 74, 124, 127, 195, 322
GTP, 179, 195
GTR, 195
GTS, 195
Junior, 240, 252
N/GT, 232
Roadster, 52, 55, 62, 89, 92
RS, 157, 172, 231, 233, 245
America, 233
Club Sport, 245
RSH, 155, 158
RSK, 184, 254
RSR, 155, 158-159, 171, 246-247, 253
SC engine, 157
SC-RS, 158-159, 207
Super 75, 59

Super 90, 49-50, 55-56, 59
T-2 series, 51-52, 54, 62
T-5 series, 54-55, 57
T-6 series, 54, 56-58, 75
T-7 series, 82, 89
T-8 series, 83
TAG-P01 engine, 197
Targa, 91-92, 96, 99, 119, 120, 167, 206, 210, 248-249, 264, 322, 326, 328, 332-333
Targa 2, 331
Targa 2S, 331
Turbo, 209, 216, 231-232, 234, 246, 249, 264, 271, 328, 333, 338, 344
Turbo S, 231, 234-235, 248
Typ 7, 11
Typ 12, 11
Typ 60, 11-12, 14
Typ 60K10, 9-10, 12, 13, 14
Typ 64, 12-14, 18, 30
Typ 114, 12, 14, 18
Typ 356, 16, 18, 20, 24, 34, 36, 40, 41, 47, 51, 54, 55, 56, 57, 58, 59, 62, 66, 71, 77, 81, 82, 83, 87, 88, 89, 154, 179, 220, 325
356A, 37, 39, 42-43, 48, 55
356B, 48, 50, 52, 54-57, 59, 61-63, 65, 69, 82
356C, 56-59, 75, 88
356SC, 57-58, 88
356 Speedster 1500, 21, 27
356A Speedster1600, 22
356/1 roadster, 14-15
356/2 coupe, 16
356-001, 30
Typ 360, 16
Typ 369, 30
Typ 502, 30
Typ 527, 30
Typ 528, 30
Typ 530, 82
Typ 540, 23
Typ 547, 25, 32, 38-39, 51, 66, 132
Typ 550, 32-35, 37-38, 40-41, 51, 69
550/01, 339
550-01, 32, 34, 36
550-02, 33-34, 36
550-04, 36
550-06, 36
550A, 39, 40, 43, 45, 55, 69
550 Spyder, 18, 62, 254, 269
Typ 587/1, 85
Typ 587/3, 75
Typ 616, 85
616/16, 58
616/7, 50, 55
Typ 644, 83
Typ 692
692/3, 48, 66
692/3A, 63
Typ 695, 58
Typ 711, 107
Typ 718
718RS, 75
718RSK, 40-41, 43, 55, 67
718 W-RS *Grossmütter* Spyder, 75
718/2, 71
Typ 741, 55
Typ 745, 85, 89
Typ 753, 71-72, 85-86
Typ 754, 82
Typ 771, 70, 77-78, 104, 108
Typ 804, 68-69, 71, 74, 87-88
Typ 821, 86
Typ 901, 59, 70-71, 77-79, 81-87, 102, 170, 172, 203, 242, 252, 335
901/20, 79
901/36, 120
Typ 902, 86
Typ 904, 59, 67-70, 74-75, 77-79, 88, 95, 101-102, 108, 120
904/6, 78-79
904/8 Bergspyder *Kanguruh*, 77-79
904GTS, 78, 87, 102-103
904GTS6, 102, 132
Typ 906, 79, 88, 95, 104, 107-108, 124, 130, 132, 191
906 Carrera 6, 102, 104
906-001, 79

347

INDEX

906-8, 102
Typ 907, 107-109, 112, 115, 130, 134, 193
907/8, 107
907L, 113
Typ 908, 109-110, 112-115, 132, 134-136, 140, 193, 227, 231
908 Long Tail, 111, 115, 129
908 Spyder/2 Flounder, 112
908-001, 109
908-002, 109
908/02, 113, 115, 132, 136
908/03, 115, 134
908/2, 114
908/3, 112-113
Typ 909 Bergspyder, 112
Typ 910, 107-108, 130
910/8, 105, 108
Typ 911, 59, 86-90, 92, 94-99, 101, 102, 120-122, 132, 134, 146, 148, 152-154, 157, 159-160, 164, 167, 169, 170-171, 177, 179-181, 189, 199-201, 204, 207-212, 221-222, 228, 232, 238-242, 245, 248, 252-254, 258-260, 262, 264, 267, 270-271, 273-275, 280, 282-283, 290, 292-293, 298, 310, 322, 324-326, 329, 333-334, 343, 346
911 Carrera GT, 177
911 Carrera GTS Club Sport, 174, 176
911 Carrera RS, 145, 147-148
911 Carrera RSR, 150-152, 159
911E, 95, 97-98
911GT1, 273-275, 277, 279, 282, 307, 315, 335
911GT1/96, 276, 279, 281
911GT2, 274, 328, 334-335
911GT2 Evolution, 276
911GT3, 333, 335
911GT3RS, 335
911L, 93-95, 97
911 Panamericana Show Car, 289-290
911R, 107, 109, 152, 227
911RS, 227, 230
911RSR, 227
911S, 88, 91-95, 97, 99, 115, 121, 123, 127, 148, 152, 154-155, 157, 171
911SC, 156, 180-181, 199, 242, 329
911S-GT, 110
911S LM, 244, 274
911ST, 115
911T, 93-95, 97, 115, 121, 152, 167, 171
911 Turbo, 159, 206-207, 210, 212, 223, 265, 346
Typ 912, 88-90, 92, 94, 96, 98, 120, 126-127
912E, 126
Typ 914, 95, 117-122, 124, 126-127, 130, 172-173, 177, 207, 252
914 2.0 Special Edition, 122, 126
914/6, 120-125, 170
914/6GT, 124-125, 127
914/6R, 123
914/8, 122, 124
Typ 916, 121-122, 124
Typ 917, 113, 115, 130-132, 135-136, 138, 140-143, 152, 159, 161, 164, 170, 172, 191, 193, 228, 231
917K, 132, 135-136, 140
917 Long Tail, 129, 132, 134, 165
917 Short Tail, 135
917 Spyder, 136, 138
917 Turbo, 161, 170
917/10, 139-143, 152, 165, 170
Typ 924, 126, 172-174, 176-178, 181, 188-189, 195, 200, 203, 215, 226, 235, 240, 249
924 Carrera GT, 215
924 Carrera GTR, 188
924GTP, 204
924 Turbo, 175, 200
Typ 928, 170, 172, 176-179, 181, 189, 200, 203, 209-210, 213, 215, 224, 234, 238
928GT, 233
928GTS, 232-233

928S, 171, 212
928S2, 171
928S4, 214, 233, 242
Typ 930, 161, 171-172, 232, 333
930 Turbo, 171, 226
930S, 210, 226
Typ 934, 153, 159-161, 165
Typ 935, 154-155, 160-162, 164-165, 170, 184, 194-195, 210, 228
935/71, 162, 190-191
935/75, 183, 185
935/76, 191
935/77 2.0 "Baby," 155
935/78 "Moby Dick," 161, 190, 209-210, 213, 214, 226
Typ 936, 164-165, 170, 190, 200, 204
936/81, 165, 193
Typ 944, 178, 203, 213, 215-217, 233-235, 238
944GTP, 188
944S, 214, 234
944S2, 234
944 Turbo, 213-214, 217, 224, 234
944 Turbo Cup, 216-217
944 Turbo S, 214, 216, 234
Typ 951, 214, 216-217
951 Turbo S, 216
Typ 953, 207-209, 227-228, 231
Typ 956, 190-195, 208, 212
956-001, 189
Typ 959, 208-213, 220-222, 230, 247-248, 276, 286, 289, 308, 319, 326
959/50, 212
Typ 960, 209
Typ 961, 208-209
Typ 962, 194-195, 212, 276
962C, 194
962CK6, 195
962LM, 195
Typ 964, 221-224, 226, 228-229, 232, 238-239, 241-242, 244, 246, 249, 264, 289-290, 329
964C4S, 249
964 Carrera 4 Lightweight, 227, 230-231, 242, 244, 249, 332
964 Carrera Cup, 224, 226, 228, 230
964RS, 228
964RS America, 230
964RSR, 230
964-001, 230
Typ 965, 221, 223, 241
965 Turbo, 226, 241
Typ 968, 233-235, 241-242
968 Club Sport, 235
Typ 984, 240, 252-253
Typ 986, 254, 258-259, 286
986 Boxster, 264, 338
Typ 987 Cayman, 338
Typ 989, 226, 240-241, 338
Typ 991, 260
Typ 993, 232, 237-242, 244-245, 248-249, 252-253, 261, 264, 267, 274, 276, 280, 290, 325-326, 329, 331-332
993C2, 248
993C4, 238, 242
993C4S, 283
993 Carrera Cup, 244
993 Speedster, 248
993 Targa, 248
993 Turbo, 247-248
Typ 996, 241, 254, 258-262, 264, 270-271, 280-281, 286, 290, 321-329, 331, 333, 344
996C4S, 326
996GT1/98, 280-281
996GT2, 334
996GT3, 281-283, 326, 328
996GT3R, 282
996GT3RS, 282-283
996GT3RSR, 283
996 Targa, 267, 322, 332
996 Turbo, 266, 268-269, 271, 326-327, 340
996 Turbo S, 328
Typ 997, 290, 310, 321-332, 335
997C4 Targa, 326, 328, 333
997C4S, 333
997GT3RS, 332, 335

997GT3RSR, 328, 330
997 Turbo, 331, 335
Typ 1966, 118, 169
Typ 2708, 242
Typ 3512, 282, 302
Typ FA12, 302
Typ LMP1-98, 282-283, 311
Typ LMP2000, 282, 309
Typ M44/43, 235
Typ RS60, 43, 66
Typ RS61, 43, 62, 66, 69
Typ RS61LM, 43
Porsche Salzburg, 132-133, 140
Porsche stability management (PSM) system, 264, 267, 297, 345
Porsche,
  Dr. Ferdinand, 9-11, 13-16, 18, 20-22, 71, 84
  Ferdinand Alexander "Butzi," 65-69, 74, 76, 78-79, 82-91, 95-96, 119-120, 148, 177, 205, 262, 292, 294, 322, 328
  Ferdinand Anton Ernst "Ferry," 11, 13-16, 18, 23, 27, 30, 32, 38-39, 41, 49, 51, 66, 70-71, 74, 77-78, 81-85, 87-89, 91, 94, 96-97, 99, 103, 107, 120-122, 136, 168-170, 179, 181, 184, 189, 197, 200, 203-205, 210, 217, 242, 289-290, 292, 322, 331, 335
Porsche+Audi, 123, 141, 143, 184
Pre-A coupe, 18
Preston, Vic, 156
Preuninger, Andreas, 270, 334-335
Prinzing, Dr. Albert, 21, 27
Prost, Alain, 197
R Competition Option Group, 123
Rabe, Karl, 9, 14, 16, 18, 21, 23-24, 32, 39, 66, 82, 179
Raether, Wolfgang, 82, 88
Ramelow, Hermann, 29-31
Range Rover, 292
Ratel, Stéfane, 246
rear-wheel drive, 224, 226, 238, 246, 264, 332, 334-335
Recaro, 97
Redman, Brian, 136, 138, 140
Reimspiess, Franz Xaver, 12, 16, 20, 40, 66-67, 82, 85
Reitter, Horst, 274, 276, 280-281
Renault, 195
rennsport model, 39, 146, 154
Reutlingen, Germany, 38, 62
Reutter Karosserie, 12, 21, 24, 27, 54-55, 58, 63, 81, 84, 88-89, 104, 213
Richards, David, 160
Riverside, California, 139, 142, 151
Rodriguez, Pedro, 135-136
Röhrl, Walter, 174, 178, 305-306, 311
Rolls-Royce, 48
Rombold, Helmut, 37, 85
Rome, Italy, 9, 10, 12, 30, 154, 255, 338
Rosenberger, Alfred, 11
Rossfeld hillclimb, 77
Rossi, Count Luigi, 164
Rothmans International, 160, 192
Rouen, France, 72-73, 87
Russelsheim, Germany, 95
Safety package, 235
Salinas, California, 45
Samsung Group, 310
Sauter, Uli, 328
Scaglione, Franco, 62
Scarfiotti, Ludovico, 107
SCCA, 127, 186
Schäffer, Valentin, 141-142, 161, 170-172
Schmid, Leopold, 55, 82-83
Schmücker, Toni, 175, 176
Schnitzer, 146
Schröder, Gerhard, 65, 68-69, 74-75, 78-89, 120, 205
Schuppan, Vern, 195
Schurti, Manfred, 152, 154, 165
Schutz, Peter, 188, 190, 196-197, 200-201, 203-204, 207, 210, 213, 220-221, 224, 226, 238, 240, 274, 328, 335
Schwab, Fred, 256-257
Sebring, 40, 43, 66, 75, 77, 107-108, 113, 136
Segre, Luigi, 118
Segura, Fernando, 36
Sellar, Dawson, 173
semiautomatic gear-shifting system, 94
Shell, 200

Shin-Gijutsu, 242
Shinoda, Larry, 170
Siegert, Franz-Josef, 324, 328
Siffert, Jo, 104-105, 108-109, 111, 132, 136, 140-141
Silverstone, England, 190, 192, 273
Singer, Norbert, 146, 152, 154-155, 158-162, 164, 177, 189-190, 194-195, 200, 209-210, 226, 274, 276-277, 279-281, 283, 309, 314, 317
Snow White Coffin, 338
Society of Automotive Engineers (SAE), 87
Soderberg, Richard "Dick," 173, 209-210, 221-222, 226, 241, 276
Solex carburetor, 52, 58, 63, 85-86, 92-93, 97
  32PBIC carburetor, 48
  40 PII twin-choke downdraft carburetor, 38
  40 PII-4 carburetor, 51, 57, 59
Solitude circuit, 72, 74
Son-Auto, 23, 49, 124
Spa, 107, 279, 283
Spanish Grand Prix, 115
Speedster, 25-27, 45, 52, 91, 203, 219-220, 229, 231-233, 248, 257
Speer, Albert, 11
Spoerry, Dieter, 113
Sport package, 235
Sport Suspension, 327
Sport Techno wheels, 293
Sportkit option, 226
Sportomatic transmission, 94
Sports Car class, 103, 108-109, 115, 130
Sports Car Illustrated, 63
Springfield, Massachusetts, 48-49
Spyder, 38, 136, 138. 140
Stanek, Hans, 30
Steckkönig, Günther, 150, 153
steering,
  power, 217, 234-235, 286
  rack-and-pinion, 85
Steinemann, Rico, 113, 134, 136
Stommelen, Rolf, 108, 111, 113, 153, 154, 163, 165
Strähle, Paul Ernst, 48, 64- 66, 153
Stuck, Hans, 10, 279
Stuttgart, Germany, 10, 13, 21, 49, 63, 66, 69, 72, 74, 83, 98, 120, 136, 148-149, 187
Südschleife, 110
Supercup series, 232, 242, 244, 281, 283
suspension, 40, 55, 78, 83, 85, 87, 95, 102-103, 108, 123, 146, 151, 181, 190, 192, 221, 224, 248-249, 266, 276, 283, 295, 297, 310, 323-324, 326-327, 331
suspension, hydropneumatic front suspension system, 95, 98
suspension, swing-axle, 25, 27, 30, 90
Suzuka, Japan, 302
Tank Commission, 11, 13
Targa Florio, 40, 43, 45, 65-66, 69-70, 75, 77-79, 90-91, 102, 104, 107-108, 113, 115
Tatchun Centre, Canada, 262
Techniques Avant Garde (TAG), 192, 196-197, 274, 305
Teldix, 152
Teufenbach, Austria, 190
Thompson, John, 194
Thun, Switzerland, 55
Tiptronic S transmission, 261, 289, 295, 343, 345
Tiptronic transmission, 264, 297, 324-325
Tiptronic Turbo, 335
Tokyo Motor Show, 252-253
Tomala, Hans, 68, 74, 78-79, 85
Torrey Pines, 27
Tour de France, 246
Tour of Corsica, 48
Toyota Motor Company, 242, 259, 281, 299
transmission, 87, 93-94, 123, 213, 217, 232-233, 235, 241, 261, 264, 298, 345
Trenkel, Richard, 30, 32
Trento-Bondone hillclimb championship, 102, 107
Turbo look, 219-220, 229, 233, 249, 264
Turin auto show, 84
Turin, Italy, 23, 118
Tyrol, 13, 14
Ulm, Germany, 66, 120
Underwood, Lake, 77
United States Auto Club (USAC), 184-187, 189
Valhalla, 173
van Lennep, Gijs, 152, 159, 165
VarioCam induction system, 233, 241
VarioCam Plus, 264, 327
Varioram induction system, 241, 248

Veuillet, Auguste, 22-23
Vienna, Austria, 11
viscous clutch, 247, 265
Volks-Porsche (Vo-Po), 117, 121, 124, 173
Volkswagen, 9, 11-13, 16, 20, 29-30, 57, 87, 95, 117-118, 120-122, 124, 130, 132, 135, 140, 150, 168-169, 172-173, 175-176, 252, 281, 286, 289-290, 292
  Beetle, 10, 49, 118, 130, 140, 204, 252
  Eigenbau, 30
  Golf, 140, 169, 173, 175
  Golf Synchro, 286
  Kubelwagen, 16
  LT van, 176
  Passat, 175, 286
  Passat Combi, 290
  Scirocco, 175
  Toureg, 289-290, 295, 297
  Typ EA266, 152
  Typ EA425, 172, 175-176
  Typ 411E, 118, 121
  Typ EA266, 118, 169
  Variant, 118, 121
  EA425, 172, 175-176
Volkswagen of America, 121, 184
Volvo P1800ES, 338
von Frankenberg, Richard, 18, 20-22, 34, 36-37
von Hanstein, Huschke, 27, 32, 34, 36, 41, 49-51, 62, 66, 69, 71, 77, 87-88, 107
von Neumann, Johnny, 21, 23, 25, 27, 35, 45, 91-92
von Oertzen, Klaus-Detlov, 10
von Senger, Richard, 20
VW-Porsche Vertriebsgesellschaft GmbH (V-G), 121, 127
Wagner, Harald, 88, 91, 93
Wahl, Georg, 239-240, 252, 264
Waldegaard, Björn, 113, 115, 127, 153, 156
Wallek, Bob, 163
Wanderer, 11
water-cooled engine, 11, 127, 140, 146, 159, 162, 169-170, 172-173, 179, 184, 190-191, 194, 205, 212, 216, 226, 234-235, 241, 258-261, 275-276, 283, 285, 289, 328, 331
Watkins Glen, 162
Weber carburetor, 25, 40, 51, 63, 65, 70, 92-93
  40IDA3C, 92
  40IDS3C, 92
Weber, Friedrich, 16, 18, 20-21
Weinsberg Karosserie, 88, 104, 234
Weissach, Germany, 92, 113, 150, 168-169, 176, 181, 186, 189, 192, 197, 200-201, 203, 217, 220-222, 227-228, 231-232, 238, 240, 246, 248-249, 252, 257, 260, 264, 270, 274, 279, 283, 287, 302-303, 305-307, 309, 312, 315-316, 322, 324-325
Welti, Max, 244
Wendler Karosserie, 38, 41, 62, 75
Werke I, 82, 134, 149, 158, 203
Wiedeking, Wendelin, 224, 242, 244, 249, 256-257, 279-282, 284, 288-289, 292, 307-311, 314-315, 317, 319, 324, 342
Wilhelm, Anke, 324, 328
Williams, Frank, 197
Williams, Jonathan, 114
Wolfsburg, Germany, 173
Wolleck, Bob, 194, 279, 283
Wolpert, Klaus-Gerhard, 286-290, 292-293, 298
Wonder Bushing, 239
World Championship, 109, 112, 115, 130, 135-136, 140-141, 160, 162, 184, 197
World Fair, 11
Wütherich, Rolf, 45, 101
Yorke, David, 138
Zagato, Ugo, 61-63
Zandvoort, the Netherlands, 197
Zasada, Sobieslaw, 148
Zell am See, Austria, 15-16, 294
Zeltweg, Austria, 135-136, 141
Zenith 32 NDIX, 53, 59
Zenith carburetor, 97
Zetsche, Dieter, 288
ZF transaxle, 12, 52
Zuffenhausen, Germany, 13, 15, 18, 21, 25-26, 32, 37, 42-43, 47, 63, 65-66, 75, 89, 91, 95, 120, 122, 124, 155, 158, 168, 176, 203, 213, 220, 234, 242, 248-249, 280, 330
Zuhaï, China, 279
Zündapp, 11
Zurich, Switzerland, 20